Praise for JOURNEY

"The Church is starving from a lack of teaching that connects us to Christ and builds our foundation in Him. This is why I am so thrilled with JOURNEY TO FREEDOM. It is a marvelous discipleship tool that can inspire you in your walk with God and help you overcome every personal struggle. I hope you will make this part of your daily devotions. It is strong meat that boosts your spiritual diet!"

J. Lee Grady, director, The Mordecai Project;
former editor, *Charisma* magazine

"This comprehensive teaching about the ways, works and words of the living God invites us deeper into intimacy with Him. It is personal and practical, pastoral and prophetic, encouraging and educating, appealing and revealing. It is Christ-centered, Holy Spirit–empowered and inspired. I love it! I need it! I am going to use it! So should you!"

Stuart McAlpine, pastor, Christ Our Shepherd Church,
Capitol Hill, Washington, D.C.

"If you are serious about wanting to experience the deep truths of God in your life, then this is possibly the most relevant and pertinent tool of ministry I have discovered. It is insightful, challenging and informative. I heartily endorse this tool of transformation and challenge you to read it and prepare for change!"

Alistair P. Petrie, executive director, Partnership Ministries

"An amazing array of information that is at once biblical, practical and comprehensive. To find a guide like this, covering the simplest truths of the faith to the deepest and most profound, is like discovering buried treasure— simply outstanding!"

David Kyle Foster, director, Mastering Life Ministries, Franklin,
Tennessee; producer, *Pure Passion* TV program

"An incredible opportunity for the Body of Christ to help people grow into strong, mature Christians. Simple, understandable yet profound teaching that anyone interested in finding fullness in the Lord can easily access. The materials are presented in a practical way with opportunities for personal application."

Ruth Ruibal, president, Julio C. Ruibal Ministries, Colombia

Testimonies from some who applied the JOURNEY TO FREEDOM teaching in their lives when first published online

"It has changed my life forever. These past twelve months have been the most fulfilling and exciting experience I have had in my walk with the Lord."

"My relationship with God is going from strength to strength—I just love it."

"It has been a lifeline. It held me safe while Father God touched the broken places."

"I so long for everyone to experience what I'm now experiencing."

"The most important thing I've ever done—it's reality!"

"Truly life-transforming—and I still have a ways to go!"

"In faith, honesty and obedience, my heavy burden was lifted, and I was set free. What joy!"

"The relief from the hold of sin was wonderful—worth every pain and all the tears I've shed!"

"Now I know I have a Father in heaven. The lie of the enemy has been broken."

"The teaching is extraordinary and beautiful. It all makes perfect sense. I'm amazed at the things I am learning. I wish I'd had this when I first became a Christian."

"My formerly derailed destiny in life is being put back on the fast track!"

"Challenging and provoking. God is using it to wonderfully transform my life."

"Inspired and inspirational. The teaching is astounding and has opened up a whole new experience for me in my Christian journey."

"I now believe I have a destiny and a future that I didn't have before. Miracles *do* happen!"

"Excellent and brilliant foundational teaching for every Christian."

GOD, ME
AND THE
ENEMY

JOURNEY TO FREEDOM

GOD, ME AND THE ENEMY

What You Need *to* Know
to Live Victoriously

PETER HORROBIN

Chosen
a division of Baker Publishing Group
Minneapolis, Minnesota

© 2020 by Peter Horrobin

Published by Chosen Books
11400 Hampshire Avenue South
Bloomington, Minnesota 55438
www.chosenbooks.com

Chosen Books is a division of
Baker Publishing Group, Grand Rapids, Michigan

Printed in the United States of America

ISBN 978-0-8007-9946-5

Library of Congress Cataloging-in-Publication Control Number: 2019950236

Originally published under the title JOURNEY TO FREEDOM, Book 2, *God, Me & the Enemy* by Sovereign World Ltd, Ellel Ministries International, Ellel, Lancaster, Lancashire, LA2 0HN, United Kingdom.

Published digitally as *Ellel 365*.

Unless otherwise indicated, Scripture quotations are from the Holy Bible, New International Version®. NIV®. Copyright © 1973, 1978, 1984, 2011 by Biblica, Inc.™ Used by permission of Zondervan. All rights reserved worldwide. www.zondervan.com. The "NIV" and "New International Version" are trademarks registered in the United States Patent and Trademark Office by Biblica, Inc.™

Scripture quotations labeled AMP are from the Amplified® Bible (AMP), copyright © 2015 by The Lockman Foundation. Used by permission. www.Lockman.org

Scripture quotations labeled GNT are from the Good News Translation in Today's English Version-Second Edition. Copyright © 1992 by American Bible Society. Used by permission.

Scripture quotations labeled KJV are from the King James Version of the Bible.

Scripture quotations labeled NASB are from the New American Standard Bible® (NASB), copyright © 1960, 1962, 1963, 1968, 1971, 1972, 1973, 1975, 1977, 1995 by The Lockman Foundation. Used by permission. www.Lockman.org

Scripture quotations labeled NKJV are from the New King James Version®. Copyright © 1982 by Thomas Nelson. Used by permission. All rights reserved.

Scripture quotations labeled RSV are from the Revised Standard Version of the Bible, copyright © 1946, 1952 National Council of the Churches of Christ in the United States of America. Used by permission. All rights reserved worldwide.

Names and other identifying details of certain individuals have been changed to protect their privacy.

Cover design by Emily Weigel

20 21 22 23 24 25 26   7 6 5 4 3 2 1

CONTENTS

PREFACE

For God so loved the world that he gave his one and only Son, that whoever believes in him shall not perish but have eternal life . . . light has come into the world, but people loved darkness instead of light because their deeds were evil . . . but whoever lives by the truth comes into the light.

John 3:16–21

To all who did receive him, to those who believed in his name, he gave the right to become children of God.

John 1:12

In book two of JOURNEY TO FREEDOM, we are taking a detailed look at the nature of God, the nature of man and the works of Satan, the enemy of our souls.

If we are going to stand strong as believers, it is vital that we have a deep understanding of both the nature and character of God and of how He created us to be in relational fellowship with Him. I have heard many people testify to the fact that their knowledge of God had been so inadequate that they did not really know Him, even though they had been believers for many years. Little by little we will find answers to these fundamental questions, and my hope is that it will happen in such a way that the knowledge will not just be information that is gathered, but it will also create life-transforming revelation.

In his letters, Paul makes sure his readers are fully aware of who God is. He also does not want them to be unaware of who Satan is and how he operates, making it clear that he is not ignorant of Satan's attempts to undermine the faith of God's people (see 2 Corinthians 2:11). In Ephesians chapter 6 he gives Christians a detailed lesson in how to resist and overcome the enemy.

I believe that the introduction of book one is relevant to all of the books in this series. In case you are reading this book without having seen book one, I copied much of the introduction in the following paragraphs. But may I encourage you to also read book one to ensure that you have a solid Christian foundation in your life?

From the Introduction to Book One

In over thirty years of ministry, I have witnessed firsthand how the Lord has brought deep healing, restoration and freedom to even the most hurting and broken people. JOURNEY TO FREEDOM contains the life-transforming keys from God's Word that will enable you to enjoy personal transformation and freedom one step at a time.

The original edition of JOURNEY TO FREEDOM was published online under the title *Ellel 365*. It provided a whole year of teaching and training in 365 daily units. While thousands of people have enjoyed reading the lessons of *Ellel 365* online, there is still a large body of people who prefer being able to hold traditional books in their hands. These volumes, therefore, have been produced in response to popular demand.

This is a journey through which God can transform your life one step at a time as you understand and apply each chapter's scriptural teaching. I do not write these words lightly—I believe them with every part of my being. I *know* God changes people's lives. I have seen it happen. I *know* He brings healing and freedom to those who are struggling. I *know* God is interested in every detail of our lives. I *know* He wants to set us free from the hold of the enemy. And I *know* He wants to see you living in the destiny He has prepared for you.

We serve a truly awesome God who is as real and active today as He was in all the stories we read in the Bible (see Hebrews 13:8). Many have been set free from long-term physical and psychological conditions, addictions and generational curses. Deep wounds of abuse and rejection have been healed by our gentle Father God. Identities that have been crushed and sometimes burdened with guilt and shame have been restored, and relationships have been healed and repaired.

People have been healed from the consequences of deep trauma. Wounds have been touched by the Lord, and strongholds of the enemy have been broken. The fruits of bitterness have melted away through love and forgiveness. Debilitating fears have been discarded and replaced with courage and trust—many beautiful stories of life-transformation by a God who cares passionately for you and for me.

Strong and Lasting Foundations

All buildings need strong and lasting foundations. In a similar way your life needs to have strong and lasting spiritual foundations. When your life is built on solid foundations, you are able to enter into the calling and destiny that God has reserved for you. JOURNEY TO FREEDOM will help you establish strong foundations as a preparation for all that God has for you in the rest of your life.

I am excited about the faith journey we are embarking on together. A wealth of vital material has been made available to you. You will be able to make this journey at the pace that is right for you with the freedom to move on from one chapter to the next whenever you feel ready.

It may be tempting to flip through the book and dip into later chapters, especially on subjects in which you have a special interest. But as we have already established, you cannot construct a safe building without the foundations being in place. The foundations that will be built into your life through the early chapters of the book could be of critical importance to you. The most genuine and lasting works of personal transformation that I have witnessed have often come as part of an ongoing pilgrimage with the Lord. This is how the Holy Spirit works in our lives in order to establish godly order—one step at a time. For many of us the struggles in our lives are not going to be fixed in a day.

We may cry out, "Heal me, Lord," but for most of us, God does not heal us dramatically or through instant transformation. He heals us by working carefully and tenderly in our hearts in the hidden areas that we may have tried hard to ignore or discard. When our heavenly Father brings His truth into our innermost beings, He establishes strong and lasting foundations through which He brings stability, deep healing and wholeness.

Many of the people I meet and pray with come to our centers because of the unwelcome fruit they see in their lives, such as depression, relationship breakdowns, sicknesses, financial crisis or ruin, insomnia, addictions, pornography, obesity or many other problems with which people struggle.

This causes them to cry out to the Lord for healing of the symptoms. However, the roots of the problems can go much deeper. The pain they are experiencing often comes from issues such as despair, fear, anxiety or a sense of failure and unworthiness. They feel guilty and unfulfilled, angry, lonely, hopeless or have a lack of identity. They may even feel as though they have no reason to live.

You may be an expert at covering up your struggles, or you may try to function normally and ignore the inner limping that has become part of your everyday life. The Lord, however, longs to repair deep areas of your heart. He does not want to only deal with the fruit seen on the surface, He wants to free you.

Jesus said, "If the Son sets you free, you will be free indeed" (John 8:36). Unless He heals the foundation of our lives, we can never really become the people He created us to be.

Truth and Reality

On each stage of this journey as you read and take in one chapter at a time, I believe the Lord will begin to build new foundations of truth and revelation into your heart.

JOURNEY TO FREEDOM is not a Bible study aimed at making you more knowledgeable as a Christian. The heart of this journey is to learn how to apply both the truths of God's Word and His character deep into your being. Then He can transform the hidden depths of who you are into the beautiful creation He intended you to be. It is all for His glory and not for ours. My prayer is that by the enabling power of the Holy Spirit you will have the courage and the willingness to allow the Lord to shine His truth into every area of your being.

It is easy to hide the true motives of our hearts and to deceive ourselves, but it is only as we are real before the One who created us that we can allow

Him to make those essential differences in our lives. Psalm 51:6 says "You desire truth in the inward parts, and in the hidden part You will make me to know wisdom" (NKJV). Jesus said, "Then you will know the truth, and the truth will set you free" (John 8:32).

I encourage you to commit your life afresh to the Lord and give Him permission to shine His light of truth deep into your heart.

Father God, thank You so much for who You are, for Your love and for Your desire to restore my life so that I can walk in the destiny prepared for me from the very beginning. I pray that You will show me the areas in which I have been hurt and need healing. Help me to see the places where I have gotten it wrong and need forgiveness and restoration. Help me to give You first place in every area of my being as I learn how to apply the truth of Your Word in my life. I invite You to be Lord of every area of my being. In Jesus' name, Amen.

On a Practical Note

The original online *Ellel 365* program contained five teachings, one for each weekday. On the sixth day there was a review of what had been covered in the previous five days, and on the seventh day there was a devotional reading. The review and the devotional are omitted from this printed version of JOURNEY TO FREEDOM, but the structure of the original material has been retained. You can follow the same weekly pattern through a whole year.

You may prefer to work through the book at your own speed to suit your own personal situation, but whatever pattern you choose, I encourage you to persevere. Some of the most profound testimonies from *Ellel 365* were from people who did just that, and at the end of the journey they were amazed at all that God had done. I believe passionately in the God of miracles, but I also recognize that some miracles take place over a period of time. When I see the extraordinary transformation that God has wrought one step at a time, I stand amazed at the way the God of miracles has been at work.

I would love to hear what God does in your life on your own journey to freedom. You can share your testimony by writing to me at peter.horrobin@ ellel.org. I look forward to hearing from you.

THE **NATURE** OF **GOD**

If I fail to understand the nature of God,
I will never be equipped to live for God.

GOD IS ETERNAL

We are now going to take a closer look at the nature and character of God. We have already covered some of this ground as we looked at what it means for us to be in relationship with God, but now we need to go deeper.

You may be thinking, *I just want to know how to live on earth.* Or you may be wondering why this is necessary or asking how a closer knowledge of the nature of God is going to help with the daily issues of life. These are good and important questions.

The Answer Is Both Simple and Profound

God is our Father—*Abba* in Hebrew—and all children want to know as much as they can about who their dads are. That is part of both our spiritual and natural DNA.

My favorite stories as a child were the ones my dad told me about his own adventures when he was the same age as me. To me, Dad was my hero, and I was never tired of learning about him. I did not even mind how often he told me the same stories. I just wanted to know things about him. I recently read a letter for the first time that my dad had written over seventy years ago. Through this letter I found out something new and good about him. It moved me to tears.

A natural result of being in a restored relationship with Father God is wanting to get to know Him better. It is interesting that one of the things Jesus says about the reason He came to earth was to show us what the Father is like (see John 14:8–11).

If that was not important for us, too, then Jesus would not have drawn special attention to it. When we learn some wonderful truth about the God who loves us so much, it is not unusual to be stirred in our emotions and moved to tears. It is a natural and very precious response.

I usually have to fight back the tears when I hear stories of how people have come to know Jesus. Just this week, I was telling a friend something of great spiritual significance. She needed a tissue to wipe her eyes.

When Jesus saw the grief of Mary and Martha at the death of their brother Lazarus, He was deeply moved to the point of weeping (see John 11:33–35). Physical tears are a natural response to things that have a deep impact on us.

In answer to Philip's question about the Father, Jesus said, "Anyone who has seen me has seen the Father" (John 14:9). He continued in verse 10 saying, "The words I say to you I do not speak on my own authority. Rather, it is the Father, living in me, who is doing his work."

It was important to Jesus that His disciples understood that He was there to introduce them to the Father. He wanted to communicate that knowing the Father really matters. It is just as important for twenty-first century disciples. Some things do not change.

Scripture also tells us that we are all made in the image and likeness of God (see Genesis 1:26–27). By looking more closely at the nature of God, we will gain a closer understanding of how God intended us to be.

At school I studied two types of mathematics: pure math and applied math. Pure math had absolutely nothing to do with purity or morality in a Christian sense. It was a description of the branch of math that focused on the foundational principles of mathematical truth where there was no concern as to how the truth might be applied.

In applied math, however, we were studying how to use the foundational principles we had learned in pure math to solve real-life problems. We were no longer solving equations for the sake of knowing how to solve equations. The equations now had real-life applications that included designing bridges, flying airplanes and everything in between.

If someone tried to solve the problems posed in applied math without having learned the principles of pure math, they would find it impossible. The foundational knowledge of what pure math provided was essential for solving real-life problems.

In a very similar way, you could compare learning more about the nature of God as being equivalent to the study of pure math. Without that knowledge, you would not have the necessary understanding that would enable you to live an effective and fulfilled life.

If you give someone a set of beliefs to believe and obey without giving them understanding as to where those beliefs have come from or what they mean, you will find that people do not have much of an incentive to live by those beliefs. In discovering more about the nature of God, we are not only understanding more about Him and who He is, but we are also gaining important keys of how to live life as a citizen of the Kingdom of God more effectively.

God Is Eternal

There is a difference between the meaning of the words *eternal* and *everlasting*, although in some translations of the Bible they are used interchangeably. John 3:16, one of the most well-known verses in the Bible, is a good example. "For God so loved the world that he gave his one and only Son, that whoever believes in him shall not perish but have eternal life" (John 3:16).

The King James Version uses the words *everlasting life*, whereas the words *eternal life* are used in the NIV and the NASB. I believe the NIV and NASB translations have a more accurate translation of the meaning of the verse.

The difference between the two words *everlasting* and *eternal* is significant. Something that is everlasting will last forever through time. Something that is eternal has a totally different meaning. It is everlasting within time, but it is not limited by time.

My mom came from South Africa, and she was adept at producing everlasting flowers by drying certain varieties of flowers carefully so that they neither faded, lost their color nor dropped their petals. I marveled at these brilliantly colored flowers that seemed to last forever without any need of being watered.

They may have been everlasting as far as the earth is concerned, but there is no way that any such flowers could survive beyond the life of this planet. One might use a similar adjective to describe any of the world's natural features. The Grand Canyon, Ayers Rock in Australia or Mount Everest could all be described as everlasting.

One generation after another looks at these extraordinary features, and they do not change—at least not within the span of time that man is on the earth.

The Passage of Time

Whether or not we can actually see changes taking place, everything within our planet and the universe is subject to time. The seasons come and go and the years pass.

Our birth certificate tells us the day and year that we entered the world. We plan out our calendar by selecting the dates we will do activities. We go to the station to catch a train at the time when the train is due to leave. We look at the TV program guide and turn the TV on at a certain time to watch something we want to see. We go to church for the morning service at a specific time. I could go on and on.

Everything we do is controlled by time. We cannot escape it. We cannot slow it down or speed it up. The whole of the universe exists within a cocoon of time. The universe had a beginning (see Genesis 1:1) and according to the Word of God, it will also have an end (see Revelation 21:1). Ecclesiastes 3:2 tells us that there is "a time to be born and a time to die."

When Jesus was conceived by the Holy Spirit in the womb of Mary, He became subject to the same temporal limitations that we have. He was not exempt from the laws that govern time and space. Like every other human being, His birthdays marked the years of His earthly life.

When Jesus began His ministry at the age of thirty, His teachings, healings and deliverances took place within the framework of time. Like all of us, He got tired at the end of a long day.

I AM—the Eternal Name of God

It was in the midst of the normality of Jesus' life that He introduced a statement about time that was so shocking that the people started to pick up stones to stone Him to death. He had been talking about how Abraham rejoiced at the thought of seeing Jesus' day come to pass when He said casually, "Very truly I tell you . . . before Abraham was born, I am!" (John 8:58).

The two words *I am* were always understood by the Jews to mean God as He referred to Himself. In the dramatic encounter Moses had with the presence of the living God at the burning bush, God said to Moses, "I AM WHO I AM. This is what you are to say to the Israelites: 'I AM has sent me to you'" (Exodus 3:14). Everyone would have understood that *I am* means the God of their fathers, the God of Abraham, the God of Isaac, the God of Jacob.

Literally, the word translated as *I am* means "a state of being, an unchangeable state, unaffected by time, even beyond time, the same yesterday, today and tomorrow."

In Hebrew there are two primary names for God: *Elohim* and *Adonai*. *Adonai* comes from the same root as the word for *I am* and represents the essential and eternal being of God, the Messiah and the Holy Spirit. It means the "existing one" or "creator." Adonai is always faithful to His promises and is unchangeable. *Elohim* is the total majesty of all-powerful God. *Elohim* is the plural of *El* or "God Almighty."

When Jesus used the words *I am* to describe the fact that He knew life before time, He was saying that His nature was eternal. It is beyond time, and it is the very essence of God. He was saying "I am God."

For someone to make such extraordinary claims was blasphemy. Under the Law, the punishment for this was to be stoned to death. That is why the people wanted to stone Him then and there.

But what if the person making those claims was, indeed, God? That is probably why Jesus prefaced His words with the assurance that He was telling them the truth (see John 8:58). He needed to underline the significance and sincerity of what He was saying.

Yes, I am God. Yes, I was present before time began and will be after time has ceased. And yes, even though for the time being I have chosen to

21

be limited by the dictates of time in the universe that I created, I do know what I am talking about.

Time and Eternity

It is important for us to understand what the word *eternal* actually means and what its significance is for those of us who are made in the image and likeness of God.

A few years ago, I was quite ill with a severe bout of the flu. It was wintertime and I was lying in bed looking out of the window at the leafless branches of the trees.

As I stared at the trees (there was nothing else to see from that angle), the Lord gave me a vision. In that vision He took me through the seasons of winter, spring, summer and autumn. I was very aware that I was watching a cycle of change, a cycle of life and death and a cycle that was controlled by time.

As I wondered what the Lord was trying to say to me, I was suddenly conscious of the importance of seeing that this cycle of change only existed within the confines of time. I had a deep sense from the Lord of how important it is that we use the years of time wisely. For once we leave time and return to eternity, we are outside of time. In that realm, change is no longer possible. We are eternal beings, and whatever state we are in when we leave time becomes our destiny for timeless eternity.

In Ecclesiastes 3:11 the writer summarizes all I have been trying to say: "He has made everything beautiful in its time. He has also set eternity in the human heart." We are creatures who are living in time but who also have an eternal dimension that no one can take away from us.

For if God is eternal and unchangeable and we are made in the image and likeness of God, then when our spirits return to Him at death, we are also in an unchangeable state of timeless eternity (see Ecclesiastes 12:7). We are either in a state of eternal joy with God in heaven or of eternal remorse with Satan in hell.

The unchangeable nature of eternal God is one of the most wonderful truths we can ever come to know. It means that God is totally dependable, and His nature and character are always the same. But to me, this is also one of the most sobering thoughts we can ever have. Since we are made in His image and likeness, we are also eternal. Our destiny cannot change once we leave time.

Time is a gracious favor from God to give us the opportunity to enter eternity secure in Him. None of us knows when we will run out of our allotted time. Hence the urgency we must have to share the Gospel with those outside of Christ who, therefore, are outside of the possibility of spending eternity in heaven.

Because Jesus is *I am* (which means He is beyond time), when we come to know Him in time, we are also entering into life beyond time. The Bible refers to this as eternal life. Eternal life is not just life beyond the grave as a spiritual continuation of our earthly existence. That is the demonic deception of spiritualism. Eternal life is the timeless life that Jesus had when He walked this earth. He never lost it because He never submitted to Satan or came under the curse of death.

It is this eternal life that becomes a reality for us the moment we find faith in Jesus. We do not have to wait until we die to receive eternal life. We receive it here and now when we make Jesus the Lord of our lives.

That is why Paul could be so triumphant in the face of death and so disdainful of what death could do to him. He almost taunted the powers of darkness when he said, "Where, O death, is your victory? Where, O death, is your sting?" (1 Corinthians 15:55). He did not fear physical death for he already had eternal life. In Christ, we have already moved out of the limitations of death within the realm of time, and we are alive for evermore within the realm of timeless eternity.

In Christ, we take on the eternal nature of God. Through salvation our eternal God-nature is restored. What a wonderful reason for great thanksgiving. We can enter eternity in Jesus Christ and not have to endure eternity in hell separated from God. We know that God loved us so much that He sent His Son so that we may not perish but have eternal life (see John 3:16).

What Does Eternity Look and Feel Like?

We see only glimpses of an answer to this question in Scripture. I believe one of the reasons why little is described in Scripture may be that God wants us to have the opportunity of loving Him for who He is instead of for what benefits there might be in eternity.

For now, I am content to trust the God who created such an incredible universe within time with my eternal destiny. No wonder Paul could smile in the face of death. He had seen a glimpse of heaven and could look forward to it with eager anticipation (see 2 Corinthians 12:1–6). So can we!

SUMMARY

God is not confined to the limitations of time, and we are made in His image and likeness. That means He has placed eternity in our hearts. How and where we spend eternity is related to how we respond to the love of God for us. For those of us who are in Christ, a thrilling prospect awaits us beyond the grave.

PRAYER

Help me, Lord, to always be aware of the eternity that You have placed in my heart. Help me to live my days within time, knowing that my experience of eternity will be related to how I spend the hours of my life here on earth. In Jesus' name, Amen.

GOD IS CREATOR

When we looked at the eternal nature of God, we saw how there is also an eternal dimension to every human being. This is because we are created by God in His image and likeness. God is incredibly creative. It is exciting to discover how His creativity is reflected in the hearts of every human.

In the Beginning God Created . . .

The opening words of the Bible declare this simple fact that is also a statement of faith. It is a statement of faith because none of us were around to witness the Creation taking place. Jesus had no doubts about the veracity of the Old Testament Scripture or who was the creator of the world. On the strength of His personal testimony, I am happy to declare this statement of faith as a fact, despite the efforts of some misguided scientists who would wish to disprove what they would call the "theory of God."

Jesus gave an eyewitness account of the fall of Satan from heaven. He said, "I saw Satan fall like lightning from heaven" (Luke 10:18). In just the same way, His statement "God created the world" (Mark 13:19) was that of a reliable eyewitness who saw the Creation taking place.

Throughout Scripture there is an explicit assumption that God is the creator of all things. This assumption is expressed forcefully on many occasions, particularly by the apostle Paul when he said:

> The Son is the image of the invisible God, the firstborn over all creation.
> For in him all things were created: things in heaven and on earth, visible and
> invisible, whether thrones or powers or rulers or authorities; all things have
> been created through him and for him.
>
> Colossians 1:15–16

In fact, without a belief in God as the creator of all things, most of
Scripture would make no sense whatsoever. If we cannot trust the Word of
God as to what it says about Creation, we would have to ask if we could
trust it about anything.

Out of Nothing

Common sense says that this amazing world in which you live, move and
fulfill your destiny could not have been created accidentally out of nothing.
The extraordinary scale and mass of all the billions of heavenly bodies in
the universe is beyond the capacity of man to even record, let alone measure. It must have had a designer and a creator.

If I came home from work one day and found there was a meal ready
for me on the table, I would not assume that the ingredients had jumped
accidentally out of the refrigerator, cooked themselves on the stove, ar-
ranged themselves on the plate and jumped on the table in readiness for
my return.

If I went around telling everyone such rubbish, I would very quickly
find myself in an institution for the insane. Everyone, without exception,
would tell me the obvious truth—this was no accidental miracle. Someone
had prepared the meal for me.

Yet the likelihood of a meal having prepared itself in this way is hundreds
of millions of times more likely than the untold billions of tons of matter
in the whole of the physical realm creating themselves accidentally in a
place that did not exist previously.

To believe that everything we know in both the world and the unmeasur-
able vast universe appeared accidentally and then evolved requires a measure of faith that far exceeds the faith required to believe and trust in God.

Common sense, therefore, says that there must be a creator who has the
power and the authority to create matter and set the universe in motion

within a capsule of time that is embraced by eternity. This one creator of the universe must be God. There is only one God.

The Source of Life

Everything we have and everything we are has come from God. He is not only the creator of the physical universe in which "we live and move and have our being" (Acts 17:28), but He is also the source of life itself (see John 1:3–4). When we look around the created realm we see such an extraordinary variety of living creatures. All of them owe their lives to Creator God.

One day when I took our dog for a walk, I watched rabbits playing in a field. I also admired the energy and sound of a pair of oystercatchers, two beautiful birds who were defending their young in their nest from an invading predator. I marveled at the incandescent blue of a dragonfly hovering by the edge of the canal.

I saw the movement of fish beneath the surface of the water and the heron that was standing there, motionless, waiting to pounce on one for its lunch. I looked at the flowers in the hedgerow and anticipated the blackberries that would soon be ripening. I stood in awe at the extraordinary and beautiful patterns on the upper wings of a butterfly. I worshiped the Lord as I admired His amazing creation and the incredible provision for humankind provided by His created realm.

It is beyond understanding to me that anyone could see all this and think that there could be a world without a creator. In reality, we are totally dependent on Him for every breath that we take. The psalmist expressed it so well when he said, "For you created my inmost being; you knit me together in my mother's womb. I praise you because I am fearfully and wonderfully made; your works are wonderful, I know that full well" (Psalm 139:13–14).

As I watch natural history programs on television that show the wonders and intricacies of the natural world, I love worshiping God. I only wish the commentators who put them together so brilliantly would also stand in awe of the Creator. They marvel at the wonders they are seeing, but to them, the wonders are nothing but an accident of evolution without any creative intervention in the design.

C. S. Lewis, the distinguished Oxford professor responsible for so many remarkable books, including the CHRONICLES OF NARNIA series, said, "No philosophical theory which I have yet come across is a radical improvement on the words of Genesis that, 'In the beginning God made Heaven and Earth.'"[1]

Ultimately, there should be no conflict between science and theology. Scientists desire to discover the truth about every single aspect of the universe, and the faith community wants to discover all of the intricate truths about God.

Astronomers study the extent of the universe, chemists study what the universe is made of, doctors study how our bodies work and theologians study the God who made all things. There is one objective that unites them all: the discovery of truth. But the scientific search for truth about the origin of the universe will always be compromised if the scientists remain in ignorance of the Creator.

Human Evidence for Creator God

If it is true that we are made in the image and likeness of God (see Genesis 1:26–27), then we should be able to see further evidence of the existence of a Creator God in the creative ability of human beings. We see that evidence in abundance.

As my wife and I sat and listened to the music and songs of *The Messiah* in London's Royal Albert Hall, we were lost in worship of the God who gave the composer Handel the extraordinary gifting that enabled him to create such exquisite musical beauty.

At one time in my life, I was privileged to be responsible for a library in which there were original drawings by many famous artists, including some by Leonardo da Vinci. I stared in amazement at his work and admired his stunningly creative genius.

I looked at the paintings of a young girl who was creating characters from her imagination on a blank piece of paper. There was only one source from whom her natural ability could have come.

I read *A Christmas Carol*, Charles Dickens's famous Christmas novel, and I marveled at his ability to create pictures out of words that fired the imagination and motivated the heart.

I read a history of medical science and was stunned at the creative genius of those who were researching diseases so that they could develop treatments and cures. Their creative genius may not have been considered to be a work of art that could be sold for a great price, but it was, nevertheless, an expression of creativity that has saved countless lives.

I looked at the beautiful gardens at Ellel Grange that were created over a century ago by a man with great vision. Even today they reflect the designer's creative genius. While he did not live to see the beauty that he created for future generations, the saplings he planted have now matured into full-grown trees.

I sat in an airplane and returned to the United Kingdom from Israel in a matter of a few hours. The creative genius behind the design of such an aircraft bears extraordinary testimony to the Creator who gave the designers and builders their skills.

I watched as a young man used his iPhone to connect with the whole world via the internet, to download his emails, to play games and to find out where he was going with a satellite navigation system. Think about the creative genius that was behind such a staggering electronic device.

There is no doubt that the world recognizes and values the creative genius of humankind. Human creativity is simply a reflection of our Creator. In retrospect, perhaps the greatest single piece of evidence for the fact that God is the creator of all things is that mankind who is made in the image and likeness of God has created so much out of the raw materials that God gave him. Creativity in humans is the hallmark of God's creative genius.

Healing through Creativity

In recent years we have developed some special courses within Ellel Ministries to help people take their healing journeys to a new level. Many men and women have grown up believing that they are not creative at all, which is a lie.

Sometimes they have believed such things because people have said negative and even cruel things to them about their abilities when they were young. As a result, they have gone into their shells, never daring to even try anything creative. Some, due to family circumstances or poverty, have never had the opportunity to find ways of expressing their individual creative abilities.

But the fact is that if we are made in the image and likeness of God, then all of us have creative abilities. We are all a reflection of our Creator. It is also a fact, however, that if we never learn to express any of that creative ability, we can suffer and be in need of healing.

Using our creative gifts is one of the essential primary activities that equips people for living. If that is missing from any child's development, there will be a consequence. It will be as noticeable as an absence of certain vitamins in the diet or a lack of education in the basics of reading, writing and arithmetic. All such absences in the development of a human being produce a form of disability.

It has surprised the teams at our centers to discover how disabled many people are in the realm of creative expression. It has stunned us all to see what extraordinary healing can take place when a person is given the opportunity to express this aspect of themselves.

I watched in amazement as a man who normally never got excited about anything spent time in our woodworking shop making a model train for his grandson. His face was radiant with joy as the different components of the engine were brought together and as he painted the finished product.

The engine had been really well made and would be a very special gift for his grandson. He had never built anything before, let alone something that was to be given as a gift to someone else. As a child he had never been allowed to do anything like that. In that creative moment, it was as if the simple process of making a model train had allowed God to build a life-time of healing into the man. While he had been a child who had grown up without any creative opportunities, his personality had been remade as a result of this creative effort.

What a difference that model train made in his life. He was discovering aspects of who he was as a human being, and God was restoring a very precious part of his God-given nature. Two things were happening that were a direct reflection of the nature of God as Creator.

First, there was the joy of being creative. I have no doubt that God enjoyed creating the universe. The first chapter of Genesis ends with these words, "God saw all that he had made, and it was very good" (Genesis 1:31).

It is very satisfying to enjoy looking at what you have made. Every child who comes home from school with his or her first painting considers it to be a masterpiece—and rightly so. What normal mom or dad would do anything less than tell them how wonderful it is? When children are pleased with what they have done, they are simply reflecting the God-nature that is within them.

Second, there was the joy of creating something for someone else—the joy of giving. The whole of the universe was created for humankind to enjoy and be in charge of. It was God's gift to the human race (Genesis 1:26–30). There is something deep inside every one of us that wants to make or buy gifts for others. This selfless enjoyment comes directly from the heart of God. The man who made the train experienced some very deep healing, both as he made the train and as he gave it away. It was a double blessing to him.

It is no surprise, therefore, that during these creativity courses we have witnessed some wonderful healing moments as a result of people rediscovering who they are and allowing those hidden creative abilities to be expressed. When people are being creative, God, the Creator, rejoices to bless them in their creative explorations, and we get to see miracles take place. You can find out about these and all other Ellel courses by going on the Ellel Ministries website at www.ellel.org.

A Life Restored

God first led us into this very special part of the work of healing by allowing us to minister deeply to individuals who had come from very damaged and broken backgrounds. Initially, it was hard for the people to believe that they could do anything, often because they did not believe they were valuable. A deep inner sense of worthlessness is a terrible curse on a human life.

God values every single human being, and little by little people's eyes were opened to this life-changing truth. Through many different forms of creative expression, God began to rebuild their lives. Without knowing the damaged background of the participants, someone would consider them to be normal folks with a highly developed creative ability. But for those who knew them before they came for help, they know that a miracle has taken place.

God the Creator is not only the creator of all things, but He is also the re-creator of the treasure that He considers every human being to be. What a miracle-working God we have!

SUMMARY

God is the creator of all things, and every human being carries within his or her nature something of that creative gifting that comes from God. If that creative gifting is not given rightful expression when people are young, it can have a long-term disabling effect on their characters and personalities. But God is in the business of healing, and He rejoices to put back what the enemy has stolen in order to see people's lives restored.

PRAYER

Thank You, Lord, that You made us in Your image and likeness and that You want us to express our creativity through the way we live our lives. Help me to recognize the gifts You have given me and to enjoy using and developing them. In Jesus' name, Amen.

GOD IS HOLY

In the past two chapters, we have seen how the eternal and creative natures of God are reflected in the nature of man. They are reflected in both the eternal dimensions of our existence and the creative giftings that we have. We are now going to shift to take a look at how the holiness of God is reflected in the nature of humankind.

What Does Holiness Mean?

The anointed words of many hymns have been influential in my life. "O Worship the Lord in the Beauty of Holiness," written by John Monsell, who wrote over 300 hymns, had a large impact on me in my youth. This hymn urges us to worship the Lord in the beauty of holiness. While I recognized that holiness was at the heart of true worship, I wrestled with what I understood as the seeming impossibility of me being holy. I was not quite sure whether or not I was entitled to sing the hymn.

Revelation 4:8 tells us that the living creatures around the throne of God never stop saying "Holy, holy, holy is the Lord God Almighty, who was, and is, and is to come." It is clear from this and other similar references in Scripture that holiness is not defined by the behavior of people who wear religious clothing or who happen to keep all of their self-imposed rules. It is defined by the nature and character of God.

There is only one God, so there cannot be degrees of holiness based upon which god you are worshiping. Things are much simpler when you realize that God is God and that every other spiritual being that is declared by man to be a god is a deception.

All of the so-called gods that lie behind the false worship that is offered through thousands of deceptive religions are not an array of alternative gods as the Greeks believed. These gods are simply deceptive spiritual beings who direct all of the worship they receive to Satan.

Paul took advantage of this situation when he preached to the Areopagus in Athens (see Acts 17:16–34) and drew the people's attention to one of their altars that was inscribed with the words "to an unknown god" (Acts 17:23). He told them:

> "You are ignorant of the very thing you worship—and this is what I am going to proclaim to you. The God who made the world and everything in it is the Lord of heaven and earth and does not live in temples built by human hands."
>
> Acts 17:23–24

The God who made the world is the one true God. There can be only one Creator, and holiness can only be defined as being everything that our Creator is. If God thinks something, then that is a holy thought. If God does something, then that is a holy act. There is nothing that God is or does that is not holy. Who God is defines holiness. His presence speaks of holiness. Holiness is not just an attribute of God, but it is part of the essential nature of God.

When applied to objects, the word *holy* means "something that is consecrated or sanctified and set apart for sacred use." When applied to God, the word can also mean "to be perfect in a moral sense or pure in heart." It means that there is an absence of the common or the profane.

The holiness of God refers not only to the absence of evil and sin, but also to an abhorrence and hostility toward them. When we sing the lyrics in the above-referenced hymn "O Worship the Lord in the Beauty of Holiness," we are able to sing those words with a clear conscience because His holiness makes it possible.

Closely allied to holiness is truthfulness. God is the source of all truth, and Jesus said, "I am the way and the truth and the life" (John 14:6). God has nothing to fear from anyone, for He is also the source of all power and authority. There would never be any reason for God to be anything but truthful. Holiness and truthfulness are unchangeable characteristics of the God who made us.

But What about the Holiness of Man?

When we look at the way humankind behaves, however, we see little evidence that human beings have any desire to be holy. You might say that it is the unholiness of humans that creates the news that sells newspapers.

Is there any evidence of the holiness of God in the nature of man? Do we in any way reflect the fact that we are made in the image and the likeness of a holy God? For if we truly are made in His image and likeness, then surely holiness, like eternity and creativity, should be evident somewhere. If we look carefully, we find that it is.

The Straight Edge in the Heart

On the day I wrote this chapter of JOURNEY TO FREEDOM, I saw a newspaper article that commented that while biologists believe that doing good deeds is part of human nature, they have no idea why humans do them. After all, the biologists thought, what value is there in helping others if there is no guarantee of the favor being returned? They have reckoned without the selfless love of God being reflected in the heart of man.

Ezekiel Hopkins, a seventeenth-century bishop of Derry in Northern Ireland, made his personal deduction about the existence of God from the fact that there is a conscience in man. He simply said, "There is a conscience in man; therefore there is a God in Heaven."[1] Hopkins recognized that we are made in the image and likeness of God and that our conscience is ample evidence that God made us.

The conscience is the straight edge of God's holiness in the heart of man. When God created human beings, He created man's heart to be an exact reflection of His heart. Because of this, it was holy. Our nature was also holy, like the God who had made us. Paul said, "You yourselves are God's temple" (1 Corinthians 3:16).

35

The immediate consequence of the Fall was that man acquired an alternative and carnal nature. The heart of man then contained not only a true reflection of the heart of God, but also a reflection of the heart of Satan, whose every thought, motive and action is fundamentally opposed to God. Humankind acquired an alternative father who gained access to their hearts as a result of their choice to obey Satan rather than God.

When Paul wrote about his problem of wanting to make ungodly choices at times, he was not just describing a problem that was unique to him, he was also describing the condition of the whole human race (see Romans 7:14–20). There is a battle in our hearts between sin and righteousness, between obeying Satan and obeying God, and between obeying our carnal natures and listening to our consciences.

When we think of doing something that is untruthful or contrary to the will and purpose of God for us, the part of our heart that still reflects the nature of God tells us that something is wrong. Our conscience has spoken, and we then have the opportunity to change our thinking, make a new decision, change our subsequent actions and put things right.

In this fallen world our consciences have plenty of opportunities to work overtime. We need to be on our guard constantly about polluting our minds with things that we might see, read, hear or be tempted to do that are distinctly ungodly, often pornographic and sometimes downright evil.

Paul gave us the positive side of the things that we should focus our attention on when he told the church in Philippi

> Finally, brothers and sisters, whatever is true, whatever is noble, whatever is right, whatever is pure, whatever is lovely, whatever is admirable—if anything is excellent or praiseworthy—think about such things.
>
> Philippians 4:8

And when he was writing to the Ephesians he encouraged them to

> Live as children of light (for the fruit of the light consists in all goodness, righteousness and truth) and find out what pleases the Lord. Have nothing to do with the fruitless deeds of darkness, but rather expose them. It is shameful even to mention what the disobedient do in secret.
>
> Ephesians 5:8–12

In both of these passages of Scripture, Paul gives practical advice about how to keep yourself from evil by listening and responding to your conscience. Billy Graham said, "Conscience tells us in our innermost being of the presence of God and of the moral difference between good and evil."[2] A tender conscience is one that is very sensitive to right and wrong. It is the most precious attribute that any human being can have. If you listen to your conscience, it will keep you from sinning and save you from much grief.

One of the greatest scientists there has ever been, Albert Einstein, advised people to "Never do anything against conscience, even if the state demands it."[3] For him, obedience to God (within) was more important than obedience to the government (without).

The man who tried to assassinate Hitler during the second world war, Lt. Col. Claus Von Stauffenberg, is reported to have said, "Better to be a traitor to my country than a traitor to my conscience."[4] His conscience could not live with the evil fact of Hitler's rule in Germany and him choosing to do nothing about it. His conscience made him act.

A Seared Conscience

The conscience begins its life in every human being as a very tender and sensitive instrument. Charles Spurgeon, the great Victorian preacher, referred to the conscience as both a candle and an alarm bell. As a candle, it shines light on the issues of life to show people what is right and what is wrong. As an alarm bell, it warns people when they are about to make a decision or take a course of action that will be contrary to the heart of God or that will put them in danger.

When the light goes on or the alarm bell rings, the conscience does not make a decision for us, it only informs us of the situation. Any decision that has to be made is then left to the will. At that point there is often a conflict between the desires of the flesh (the carnal nature) and the will of the spirit of man. The spirit responds to the voice of God, and the carnal nature responds to the voice of the enemy of God.

Thomas à Kempis, the fifteenth-century author of *The Imitation of Christ*, one of the greatest and best personal devotionals that has ever been written, said, "The devil does not sleep, nor is the flesh yet dead; therefore, you must never cease your preparation for battle, because on the right and on the left are enemies who never rest."[5] The power of temptation to hold us in its grip is very great, but a well-trained conscience will always steer us away from trouble.

But what happens if we override our conscience with our will? The effect is serious, especially if we keep on overriding it. Little by little the voice of the conscience ceases to be heard, and we lose the means that God gave us to be alert to sin's danger. It is as if the conscience becomes covered over with a tough, impenetrable callus or, to use a scriptural picture, the conscience becomes so seared that all of its sensitivity is lost.

Paul used this term to describe people who formerly had faith in God but who allowed deception a place in their lives. They ended up believing things that were a long way from the truth. He said their "consciences have been seared as with a hot iron" (1 Timothy 4:2).

Peter wrote about a similar group of people who had once known freedom in Christ but had fallen back into sin and had become slaves to their sinful natures (see 2 Peter 2:10–22).

In this state, the conscience is no longer a sensitive spiritual instrument that is able to measure the holiness (or otherwise) of what a person wants to do. This is a very dangerous state to be in, for without a sensitive conscience there is little to stop a person from indulging in the most depraved of behaviors.

Does that mean that there is no forgiveness for such sins? No, but it means the likelihood of a person wanting to be in a place where the Holy Spirit of God can bring conviction of sin will diminish rapidly.

Renewing the Conscience

When a conscience has become seared, or even just less sensitive than it should be, it is vital to get back on track with God quickly. Otherwise, even in the most serious situations there will be no warning of danger.

On our Healing Retreats, we encounter people who have allowed their consciences to grow less sensitive or seared. As a result, their lives reflect the consequences of very bad choices. In 1 Timothy, Paul talked about the blessing of holding on to faith and a good conscience, but then he warned, "some have rejected [these] and so have suffered shipwreck with regard to the faith" (1 Timothy 1:19). What a terrible summary of a person's life—shipwrecked because he ignored his conscience.

But praise God, there is always a way back to God if we are willing to yield to His way for our lives. It is our privilege to stand with the people whose consciences are damaged as they walk through the process of repentance during our Healing Retreats. When they ask God to renew their consciences, they can get their lives back on track.

Because King Jehoshaphat ignored his conscience when he disobeyed God and entered into a trade alliance with an ungodly king, he literally ignited a shipwreck. The wreck was not just seen in his own life, but also in a whole fleet of ships. Because of his disobedience to the voice of God (his conscience) he had lost the protection of God in his affairs (see 2 Chronicles 20:35–37).

To renew your conscience and get back on track with God, there are three things you must do:

- Repent of not respecting the holiness of God (in your conscience) and of closing your ears to the voice of God.
- Ask God for forgiveness, healing and restoration, both in your relationship with Him and in the sensitivity of your conscience.
- Drink deeply of the Word of God and ask the Holy Spirit to restore your conscience to a correct understanding of what is right and wrong.

The Holy Presence of God

The holiness of God is like a light that shines in the darkest of dark places, exposing all that is hidden. Everything that is unholy is exposed by His presence. That is how the conscience works.

It is the presence of a holy God in the heart of man—remember what it says in Ecclesiastes 3:11 about God having put eternity in our hearts—that is the operating force in our conscience. But not even God operating in our conscience will override our free will. We must use our will to cooperate with our conscience to make right choices and to enjoy the constant presence of God.

There are two ways the presence of God can be experienced: internally within the heart of man, or externally when He makes His manifest presence known. There are many references in Scripture to the presence of God being made manifest.

In Exodus 3, Moses heard the voice of God coming out of a burning bush. The presence of God made the whole area that was around the bush holy. He told Moses to remove his shoes, for he was now standing on holy ground. It was during this experience that God shared with Moses what his calling was, and it was this experience that launched him into the journey toward his destiny. The impact that this encounter had on Moses never left him.

In Isaiah 6, Isaiah describes his experience of being ushered into the holy presence of the Lord. As a result, Isaiah saw everything in a new light, both his own life and the lives of the people around him. He cried out, "I am ruined! For I am a man of unclean lips, and I live among a people of unclean lips, and my eyes have seen the King, the LORD Almighty" (verse 5). The holiness of God exposed the sinfulness of humankind.

During times of revival, the greatest single hallmark of the genuineness of such experiences is an overwhelming sense of the holiness of God. As with Isaiah, this is followed by the conviction of sin. The holy presence of God will always expose darkness for what it is.

In the early days of Ellel Grange, we had an extraordinary experience of the movement of the Holy Spirit. God moved in such power that His presence was almost tangible. All over the building people were in deep repentance as they saw their lives in the light of God's glory. That experience still has an impact on the lives of the team members who were present.

In our personal walk with God, there is a temptation to long for such experiences. They are very precious, and they have a radical impact on our lives for the rest of our days on earth—but they are rare events. What we all need every moment of every day is the constant, sweet presence of God. This is how He will guide us safely through all of the adventures of life until we arrive safely at our destination (heaven) having fulfilled our purposes here on earth.

It is that constant, sweet presence of a holy God that we should crave. We should keep our consciences pure and holy and able to provide unerring direction and encouragement for the lives He has asked us to live. That is the only way that we can follow the advice and direction of Peter when he said, "Just as he who called you is holy, so be holy in all you do; for it is written: 'Be holy, because I am holy'" (1 Peter 1:15–16).

What a privilege it is to know and love such a wonderful God who enables us to walk in His ways and blesses us with His blessings along the way.

SUMMARY

Only the one true God is holy. Everything that is not of God or is ungodly in nature is unholy. The holiness of God is made known to us through our conscience, and if we listen carefully to its voice, it will be the very best defense we can have against the traps of the enemy.

PRAYER

Lord, I ask You to restore my conscience so that now and always I will be sensitive to the gentle leading of Your Holy Spirit directing my life and warning me of danger. I do not want to stray into pathways that are an offense to You. Keep me close to You, I ask, all my days. In Jesus' name, Amen.

GOD IS FATHER, SON AND **HOLY SPIRIT**

When I was planning the structure of JOURNEY TO FREEDOM, I felt it was very important to spend quite a lot of time focusing on who God is. If we learn who God is, we also learn about who we are. The more we know about God, the more we love Him and the more we will want to serve Him.

So far we have seen how the eternal and creative nature of God is evident in the nature of man. We have seen how the holiness of God fuels our conscience with truth and provides a straight edge we can use to measure all of the decisions we are faced with in life.

Now we will focus on the nature of the Godhead—God the Father, God the Son and God the Holy Spirit. Then we will look at the corresponding nature of man.

The Trinity of God

After the description of the creation of the universe in the book of Genesis, we come to the creation of man. Genesis 1:26 is full of profound significance, for in it we have the statement in which God says, "Let us make mankind in our image, in our likeness."

The word *us* is plural. You do not use the word *us* when only one person is being represented. This is a clear indication that even though

God is one, He sees Himself as being a unity of more than one being. Genesis 1:26 does not tell us whether God is talking about two or three "of us," but there are clues provided in later passages in the Bible. One of the wonderful things about Scripture is that it constantly provides more insight into itself.

The writers of all the different books of the Bible were inspired by the Holy Spirit to provide for us a comprehensive foundation of truth (see 2 Timothy 3:16). We can look through the whole Bible to find out more about what the word *us* in Genesis 1:26 actually means. But even in just the first three chapters of Genesis we see an outline of the answer.

At the beginning of the creation story when the earth is described as having been formless and empty, we read that "the Spirit of God was hovering over the waters" (Genesis 1:2). Not God Himself, but the Spirit of God. The Spirit is the giver of life. We see in succeeding verses that conditions were created so that every possible form of life could and would thrive on planet earth.

Already we have two parts of the Godhead referred to in Genesis 1— God and the Spirit of God.

In Genesis 3 we then read what happened at the Fall. Humankind listened to the voice of Satan, and both the earth (over which God had given humans authority) and humanity came under Satan's control.

At this point God spoke a prophetic word to Satan. He said that the offspring of woman would crush the serpent's head (see Genesis 3:15). This passage is understood to mean that one day a woman would deliver a special child who would have greater authority than Satan, who would crush the head of the serpent (Satan) and who would overrule his authority.

This is the first Messianic prophecy in the Word of God. It prophesies the coming of the Son of God as the Redeemer of the world and the Savior of humankind. It also gives us another being that makes up the us. In the first three chapters of Genesis, we have reference to God the Father, God the Son (Messiah) and God the Holy Spirit.

Throughout the writings of the Old Testament, there are many such prophecies. All of them culminate in the message of the archangel Gabriel to Mary. He said that the Holy Spirit would cover Mary, and she would conceive a child who would be called Jesus. He would be the Son of the Most High (see Luke 1:26–35).

Mary asked the angel the sixty-four-thousand-dollar question: "How will this be . . . since I am a virgin?" (Luke 1:34). In Gabriel's reply, we have one of the fullest descriptions in the whole of Scripture of the different persons of the Godhead working together in their respective roles. Gabriel said, "The Holy Spirit will come on you, and the power of the Most High will overshadow you. So the holy one to be born will be called the Son of God" (Luke 1:35). It follows that if Jesus is the Son of the Most High, then the Most High is God the Father.

Here we have the Trinity of God fully expressed—Father God, God the Son and God the Holy Spirit. The word *trinity* is not actually used anywhere in Scripture, even though there are dozens of places that refer to the three members of the Godhead by name. The word *trinity* was first used as an accurate description of the Godhead by Theophilus of Antioch in AD 180, and it has been used since by every generation of believers. God the Father, God the Son and God the Holy Spirit are all fully God. They are all unique within the Godhead, but together they are also one God.

This trinitarian understanding of the Godhead is found clearly in Jesus' final instruction to His disciples.

> Jesus came to them and said, "All authority in heaven and on earth has been given to me. Therefore go and make disciples of all nations, baptizing them in the name of the Father and of the Son and of the Holy Spirit, and teaching them to obey everything I have commanded you. And surely I am with you always, to the very end of the age."
>
> Matthew 28:18–20

The Unity of the Godhead

When talking about His relationship with the Father, Jesus expressed His unity by saying, "I and the Father are one" (John 10:30). Jesus said to Philip, "Anyone who has seen me has seen the Father" (John 14:9).

He goes on to say, "If you love me, keep my commands. And I will ask the Father, and he will give you another advocate to help you and be with you forever—the Spirit of truth" (John 14:15–17).

In the same chapter, Jesus told the disciples that "the Holy Spirit, whom the Father will send in my name, will teach you all things" (verse 26).

There is constant unity being expressed between the three persons of the Godhead in these and many other Scripture verses. They are one with each other. In Peter's great Pentecost sermon, he said, "God has raised this Jesus to life. . . . Exalted to the right hand of God, he has received from the Father the promised Holy Spirit and has poured out what you now see and hear" (Acts 2:32–33).

All three persons of the Godhead are working together in total harmony acting as one. Are there three gods? Of course not. But some critics of Christianity use the facts of the Trinity to try to discredit Christianity. They correctly say that there can only be one God, but incorrectly add that Christianity teaches there are three gods.

This is a superficial criticism by people who have rejected the triune nature of the one true God. Sadly, it is used to keep millions of people away from Jesus and to prevent them from responding to His love and salvation. Many of them have been influenced by the unyielding monotheism of Islamic teaching and false cults.

Fallen man has difficulty understanding the concept of a triune God who acts in perfect harmony. Throughout history there have been various individuals and groups that have tried to interpret Scripture in a non-Trinitarian way. This has invariably opened the door to deception and error.

In trying to rationalize their arguments, they describe the Holy Spirit as merely some sort of force, despite the fact that many Scripture verses accord personality and will to the third Person of the Trinity. Jesus is reduced to either being simply a good teacher, a manifestation of an angel or blasphemously as the brother of Lucifer, despite many Bible verses that speak about His deity. Christianity without a Trinitarian view of God becomes a man-made religion or cult that leads many astray and away from their only Savior.

The Trinity of Man

Throughout this stage of our journey, we have established a very important principle: The nature of God is reflected in humankind, God's special creation. When we read in Genesis 1:26 that man is made in the image and likeness of God, we have to ask if the Trinity of God is also a picture of the nature of man.

The answer may seem to be obvious, but we do need to be clear in our understanding of the triune nature of man. For in this understanding, we will also have an answer to those who condemn Christianity because of their belief that Christians have three gods.

When the egg and the sperm came together at the moment you were conceived, the living sperm fused with the living egg. An embryonic human being began its journey through life. Not only did you then have a body in the making, but you were also given your own spirit and soul. You inherited a huge amount of genetic coding from both of your parents that would have a powerful influence on your physical development, your look and your nature.

While we all remember and celebrate the dates of our birthdays, in reality, we were already nine months old when that momentous day arrived. Sometimes people make the mistake of thinking that those first nine months were just a period of physical growth; however, every part of our being had also been developing during this vital time of our lives. Not all of the influences we were under were necessarily good.

From conception, you were influenced by your generational inheritance. Just as there can be a strong genetic influence on the physical characteristics of a child, there can also be strong spiritual influences on the personality and character of the growing child.

Isn't he just like his mom (or dad)? is probably the question that is heard most frequently about a new arrival in the family. As the years go by, it is not just the physical looks that are reminders of previous generations, but also behavioral and spiritual influences that are conveyed down the generational lines. There must, therefore, be a part of our creation that is fundamentally different from the physical body in which we live. To be more accurate, there are two other parts.

The Spirit of Man

Although human beings are very body conscious, Scripture is clear that humankind has more than a body. In his letter to the Thessalonians, Paul prayed, "May your whole spirit, soul and body be kept blameless" (1 Thessalonians 5:23). David said, "Praise the LORD, my soul" (Psalm 103:1). His spirit is taking authority and speaking to his soul. He is telling it to worship God.

When Jesus was talking to the woman at the well, He said that those who worship God "must worship in the Spirit and in truth" (John 4:24). *In spirit* implies that man must have a spirit with which to worship God. *In truth* refers to the part of man that can make godly or ungodly (truthful or untruthful) choices.

At the beginning of Jeremiah, we read these awesome words: "Before I formed you in the womb I knew you" (Jeremiah 1:5). This verse states that God knew us even before we were conceived. It certainly was not our physical beings that He could have known. Ephesians 1:4 says, "For he chose us in him before the creation of the world." These Scripture verses are talking about the spirit—the very essence of your nature given by God to be the head over your soul and body.

Steadily, we are creating a picture of the nature of man. He is a spiritual being—where the core of his identity is. It is what makes me, me and you, you.

In the spirit we can enjoy fellowship with God, we can communicate with Him in prayer and we can know the unparalleled joy that flows from being in harmony with Him. Through our spirit, we can take up godly order and authority to establish godliness in every area of our being.

We can have spiritual emotions as we respond with joy or sadness to things we see happening around us. We can feel God's point of view. We have spiritual senses, too, as the psalmist implies when he says, "Taste and see that the LORD is good" (Psalm 34:8). We can see the beauty of God's creation, and our spirit can respond by soaring in thanksgiving and worship as we are overwhelmed with the love, provision and mercy of God.

In our spirit we can have God-inspired experiences. We can conceive visions, hear the voice of God and dream about fulfilling our destiny. It is in our spirit that we experience eternity in our heart, where we express our creativity and where our conscience is at peace.

The Soul of Man

But humankind is more than just spirit, for we are tied into physical reality by our flesh. The flesh in Scripture does not refer to just the body. The flesh is the soul and the body together. We read of the sins of the flesh. This does not mean that the body can sin independently of the soul. The body cannot go off on its own and do something wrong without our agreement and instruction.

The soul within us is in charge of the body. When the body is involved in something sinful, it is only doing so because the soul has made a choice to use the body for this particular purpose. Our soul is like the driver of a machine, while our body is the machine. The two together form the flesh. Within our soul is our mind, our emotions and our will.

These three are the primary contributors to our behavior and what others may describe as our personality. With our mind we think. Everything we choose to do begins as thoughts in our mind. With our emotions we react to these things, and with our will we make decisions. All three will motivate our soul to use our body to carry forward our thoughts and intentions into physical activity—both the good and the bad.

Just as God is able to exercise His will in a free way, we also have free will. It is one of the gifts that God gave to humanity. It derives from the nature of God. Free will is the most precious and yet the most dangerous thing that God could ever have given us.

It is precious because it is such an incredible privilege to use our will to make right choices and to be creative with all of the resources we have at hand. It is dangerous because men and women have learned how to use their free will to make ungodly decisions and to break the covenant relationship with God.

And yet, if God had not given you a free will, He could never have enjoyed relationship with you. Free will and the capacity to enjoy relationships go hand in hand with each other.

The Body of Man

Finally, there is the body, the part of your being that generally receives the most attention. In the overall scheme of eternity, however, it seems to be the least important. You only have a physical existence for a limited period of time, and then you wait for resurrection, when you will receive a spiritual body for eternity. Yet it is through your body, from your first cry to your last breath, that your humanity is expressed.

Our bodies are the most amazing of machines—a billion times more complex than any computer or machine humans could construct. They are chemical processing plants extracting the necessary goodness from food and eliminating the waste. They supply oxygen via an incredibly efficient breathing machine. The oxygenated blood is pumped around the body by a heart that beats faithfully about two billion times in an average lifetime.

Our brain and our sensory organs manage and control the machine, giving constant instructions to all of the muscles and bones. A thermostat controls our bodily temperature within a very narrow band of efficient operation. Our sexuality makes reproduction and the continuation of the human race possible. What an incredible machine God has given us.

When this wonderful body is working according to the maker's instructions, we say that we are well. When it experiences malfunction, we say that we are sick. For many conditions the body acts as its own healer, fighting off infection and self-repairing such physical damage as cuts and bruises. When the conditions appear to be beyond the normal capacity of self-repair, a sick body is referred to a medical professional for treatment.

Spirit, Soul and Body—but One Person

We will be returning again to look in much more depth at the nature and function of our spirit, soul and body. For now, we are establishing the fact that humanity is a true reflection of the nature of God, who is three in one. Humans are also three in one. We are made in His image and likeness.

If you have three parts to your created order, does that mean that you are three people? Not at all. It means simply that the three parts of who you are working together to fulfill their different functions and relate with others as one human being. It would be foolish to think in terms of any other interpretation of the facts of our humanity.

I am one person. I have a body, I have a spirit and I have a soul. In just the same way, God is one. In God there is the Most High (or Father God), there is Jesus (the Son of God) and there is God the Holy Spirit. The threefold nature of man not only tells us that we are made in the image and likeness of God, but it also tells us how God must be. The trinity of God and the trinity of man are exact reflections of each other. There is one God, and each human being is one person.

In just the same way that understanding the three persons of the Godhead is important to us, understanding how God has put us together is also of critical importance. When we pray for people, we need to know where the roots of their problems are. But that is a topic for a later chapter.

SUMMARY

Both God and man are three in one. God is Father, Son and Holy Spirit, and all human beings have spirits, souls and bodies. You have a spirit that allows you to be able to relate to God and to discern and enjoy spiritual things. You have a soul through which you express your personality. And you live in a body. Your whole being is made in the image and likeness of God.

PRAYER

Thank You, Lord, for each part of my created being. Help me to understand how You want me to live with my spirit relating first and foremost to You. Help me to choose to live under Your authority all of my days with my soul and body. In Jesus' name, Amen.

GOD IS LOVE

Throughout this stage of our journey we have been exploring a very important principle: Man is made in the image and likeness of God; therefore, we can expect the nature of God to be reflected in the nature of man.

We have seen that God is eternal, He is Creator, He is holy and His presence includes the Father, Son and Holy Spirit. We are now going to look at the very essence of the heart of God. If we could take hold of the heart of God and squeeze it, the only thing that would come out would be love.

Created by a God Who Is Love

None of the other attributes of God would be of any benefit to humankind if love was not at the very core of who God is. In his great teaching on love, John made some extraordinarily powerful statements about God and about love:

> Whoever does not love does not know God, because God is love.
>
> 1 John 4:8

> This is love: not that we loved God, but that he loved us and sent his Son as an atoning sacrifice for our sins.
>
> 1 John 4:10

And so we know and rely on the love God has for us. God is love. Whoever lives in love lives in God, and God in them.

1 John 4:16

There are many other Bible verses that highlight the loving nature of God and the fact that God is love. Perhaps the most famous Scripture of them all, John 3:16, sums up God's heart of love for all humankind, including those who have turned away from Him: "For God so loved the world that he gave his one and only Son, that whoever believes in him shall not perish but have eternal life."

The statement John made in his epistle that God is love is one of the most significant and wonderful truths you could ever understand about our amazing Creator God. It would have been horrible to have been created by a God who did not love His creation, who did not care for those He had made or who played abusively with us like toys.

But it would also have been terrible for us if we had been created by a God who looked at the people He had made and only then decided to love them. For if He had decided to love us today, how could we possibly know whether or not He would still want to love us tomorrow? That insecurity would cause our hearts to go from summer to winter in an instant.

Mercifully, Scripture tells us the glorious, the wonderful, the amazing fact that God is love. And because He is love, He cannot be anything else. This means that if we get some things very wrong or mess up completely, God still loves us. He loves us not because of who we are or how we behave, but because of who He is and the fact that we are made in His image and likeness.

You may ask, "How do you know that?" I will tell you how I know.

Jesus told the story of the prodigal son (see Luke 15:11–32). He was the son who wanted his share of his inheritance in advance so that he could live it up away from home, doing everything that a reckless young man about town might think to be exciting. He spent it on the typical wine, women and song that a young man with money and false friends would spend it on.

This young man betrayed his father (who represents Father God in the story). Jesus portrayed the father as being desperate for the return of his son. And when he saw him coming in the distance, he ran to greet, to welcome and to love him.

The father threw a huge party, killed the fatted calf to celebrate and concluded with thanksgiving for the son who "was dead and is alive again," who "was lost and is found" (Luke 15:32). These are not the words of a cruel despot who created humankind as a plaything. These are the words that can only come from the heart of a God who is love.

Charles Spurgeon said, "Divine love can rake a dunghill and find a diamond."[1] There are many such diamonds that have been rescued by the love of God from the dunghills of life. Author Glynn Harrison wrote, "God doesn't love us because we are worthy; he loves us and so we are counted as worthy."[2]

The fact is, God will stop at nothing to love you back from the grip of the enemy. At the end of the day, He will not override your free will to maintain your independence from Him or to go your own way; however, because He loves you so much, He will pursue you down the avenues of life to try to get your attention in the hope that you will turn again and find Him.

It is when this extraordinary message of unconditional love is truly understood by those who come on Healing Retreats, many cross a bridge from despair to hope. Pursued and caught by the God of love, they realize that love gives birth to faith, and faith opens a door of hope that brings healing and restoration.

If we really are made in the image and likeness of God, then we should expect to see something of the behavior of the prodigal son's father reflected in the way human beings relate to their own children. And that is exactly what we do see.

All children get it wrong at times, especially when they are young. But most parents do not respond to their child's naughtiness by wanting to exchange their precious child for a different model. They persist in loving their child.

What I have seen time after time is parents doing everything they possibly can, often at great expense, to help their kids when they have gotten into trouble. Their children are flesh of their flesh. It is only their children who carry their generational hallmarks. And it is only their children for whom the deepest chord of love is played in the hearts of the mother and father.

The love of most parents for their children knows no limits. There is only one place where they could have received such sacrificial love. It is from Father God. They are behaving just like their Father.

What Is Love?

When we look at the word *love* in Scripture we find that two primary Greek words are used to describe the nature of love. Each one gives us a different insight into what love means.

The word used to describe the love of God is always *agape* (from the verb *agapeo*), which means "sacrificial, selfless love that considers primarily the welfare of others before one's own considerations."

Agape love always wants the very best for another person, regardless of what that person may have done. This is the heart of God for His children.

This does not mean that God condones sinful behavior or that He is not angry about the consequences of sin that bring pain and damage to others. He wants the best for that sinner, and His best only comes about through that person repenting and choosing to come into a right relationship with God through Jesus.

The other word, *philanthropia* (from the verb *phileo*), describes the love of affection and friendship in relationships between human beings. It is not a sexual word, and it is only used to describe the deep affection that can exist between two people regardless of what gender they are.

Interestingly, the word for sexual love, *eros*, from which we get the word *erotic*, does not appear in the New Testament even though right and wrong sexual relationships are discussed. It is implied clearly that there is only one right place for the erotic expression of love, and that is within the covenantal relationship of marriage.

Sadly, today's society has brought sexual activity into the public and entertainment domains with terrible consequences to the morality and sexual behavior of a generation. The average age of today's young person's first sexual relationship has plummeted tragically to the early teens.

Open eroticism has robbed a generation of experiencing real love. Girls as young as five, six or seven are being prepared for early sexual encounters by being sold sexually provocative clothing. We will look at the consequences of right and wrong sexual relationships at a later stage.

Agape

In 1 Corinthians 13, that famous Scripture passage that is read at countless weddings every year, the selfless and sacrificial love of God is described as the standard God intended for humankind in their relationships.

In this glorious passage of Scripture, Paul begins by saying that whatever we do—including the sacrificial things carried out in supposed obedience to God or the practice of the gifts of the Spirit—if they are not motivated by agape love, then they have no eternal value (see 1 Corinthians 13:1–3). He is echoing some of the words that Jesus spoke to the Pharisees when He condemned the externals of their Jewish traditions because their hearts were far from God (see John 8:47).

In the second part of the passage, Paul defines some of the qualities of agape love. In so doing he is both describing the love of God and setting before us a way of life for the disciples of Jesus who are motivated by agape love.

> Love is patient, love is kind. It does not envy, it does not boast, it is not proud. It does not dishonor others, it is not self-seeking, it is not easily angered, it keeps no record of wrongs. Love does not delight in evil but rejoices with the truth. It always protects, always trusts, always hopes, always perseveres.
>
> 1 Corinthians 13:4–7

In the final part of this chapter, Paul paints a picture of how temporal things, even prophecies and the need to have the gifts of the Spirit practiced, will cease. He explains how our spiritual understanding of the majesty of God's love, which is now limited severely by the fallenness of humanity, will one day be very clear. The shades on our eyes will fall away as we enter into the reality of eternity without the limitations of polluted time.

He concludes with a summary of the things that will remain in eternity after we have shaken off the shackles of time. He says "And now these three remain: faith, hope and love. But the greatest of these is love" (1 Corinthians 13:13).

Why is love the greatest? Because God is love—everything else is a consequence of the nature of God. We have faith because God is love, and love will never cease because God will never cease. The love of God is not like a battery that will one day run out.

We have hope because God is love. When we read Paul's description of the nature of agape love, we have every reason to hope in God. His love goes against the grain of fallen humanity and stands alone in time and eternity.

But if God was not love through and through, then having faith or hope in Him would be misplaced. God could not be depended upon. It is His love that is at the core of the unchangeable nature of the heart of God that gives us our confidence. We can always trust someone who loves us with agape love, for we know that their love is not a selfish or grasping sort of love. Agape love is interested in caring selflessly for the object of love.

This is the love that is truly in the spiritual core of every human being. It is contained within the seed of eternity that God planted in the hearts of every man and woman. We have seen across the world and down the centuries how countless thousands and even millions of people have chosen to encourage that seed of agape love to grow in their lives. Many have done so without ever having heard the Gospel or without having known how to respond to it. As a result, some have even laid down their own lives for others.

This is what Paul was hinting at in his letter to the Romans. In chapter 1 he talks about those who were living in wickedness. He said that, even though they may not have heard the Gospel, they were still without excuse. "Since the creation of the world God's invisible qualities—his eternal power and divine nature—have been clearly seen, being understood from what has been made, so that people are without excuse" (Romans 1:20).

Conversely, it must also be the case that there are many who have listened and responded to the voice of eternity in their hearts and have been motivated by God's agape love. They have lived lives that have reflected their selfless love. These lives are indeed pleasing to God. It may be that one day in heaven there will be some surprise inclusions in the ranks of heaven, people who were not known to the believing community here on earth.

There could even be some other surprises on that day. There might be people who did amazing things in Jesus' name but who are missing from heaven because their lives were not motivated by love. Jesus said there would be some to whom He would even have to say, "I never knew you. Away from me, you evildoers!" (Matthew 7:23).

It is so important that we weigh carefully the motives of the heart, for these motives will determine both the fruitfulness of our earthly lives and our eternal destinies. The writer to the Hebrews summed it all up for us when he said,

> For the word of God is alive and active. Sharper than any double-edged sword, it penetrates even to dividing soul and spirit, joints and marrow; it judges the thoughts and attitudes [intentions] of the heart. Nothing in all creation is hidden from God's sight. Everything is uncovered and laid bare before the eyes of him to whom we must give account.
>
> Hebrews 4:12–13

Even if you are involved in the healing ministry and want to see people's lives restored by Jesus, if your reason for helping people is so that others will think well of you, your motive is not agape love but selfishness. You could even want to be an evangelist, but only because of the affirmation and fame your success may bring. You could see people come to faith in Jesus Christ, but it is your heart's motive that will be judged at the end of time.

I realize that these are very challenging words, but how can I write all that God has put before us in JOURNEY TO FREEDOM without being willing to declare what I believe to be the whole counsel of God? Even as I write these words, I am being challenged to examine the motives of my own heart as Paul encouraged us to do in 1 Corinthians 11:28.

It is so important that you keep your relationship with the Lord sweet. At all times you must trust in His grace and mercy. And whenever you sense that anything is out of line with His agape love, you should confess it, repent and move on knowing that you are forgiven and restored.

Philanthropia

The philanthropia love we can have one for another is totally different from the unchanging agape love of God. Agape is love that is not dependent in any way on the relationship we have with anyone. It is the selfless expression of God-motivated love to all.

Philanthropia, however, is the love within a friendship that we may have with particular individuals. I may have agape love that God placed in my

57

heart for all human beings, but there is only enough time and space in my life to have the philanthropia kind of love with very few individuals. The relationship that David and Jonathan had with each other is a wonderful example of philanthropia love in action (see 1 Samuel 18).

The difference between philanthropia and agape love is no more clearly portrayed than in the way the Holy Spirit inspired the conversation between Jesus and Peter recorded in the New Testament.

After Simon Peter had betrayed Jesus during His trial in Jerusalem, Jesus sought to restore Peter by the lakeside at Galilee. He asked Peter "Do you love [agapeo] me more than these?" (John 21:15). Peter, who had just betrayed Jesus and failed the agape test, was humbled and broken. He was not up to giving Jesus the reply that Jesus wanted. He only replied, "Yes, Lord, you know that I love [phileo] you."

Jesus repeated the question in the same way and got a similar answer from Simon Peter. The third time Jesus asked the question, He asked an easier question for Simon Peter to answer. "Simon son of John, do you love [phileo] me?" (John 21:16).

For each betrayal, Jesus gave Simon Peter the opportunity to express his love. Peter was a hurting, broken man who was being honest in his replies. He could only respond with the love of friendship and not the love of sacrifice. That would come later. But Peter needed to know at that moment that Jesus loved him as he was. It was a powerful and healing experience, and one that I have seen repeated more than a thousand times over in my years of ministry.

The most positive confirmation to Simon Peter was that Jesus still commissioned him to care for His sheep. Jesus did not reject Simon when it was obvious that he was going through a tough time. He met Simon at his point of need—just as He does with you and with me. But He loves us too much not to urge us to live our lives in His grace, mercy and healing.

We all need to have and enjoy the friendships that meet the needs of our souls for genuine philanthropia love. But we also need to be on guard constantly against three things:

First, the needs of friendships should not take the place of agape love in our hearts.

Second, we should guard our hearts against developing philanthropia friendships simply to meet unhealed needs in our hearts. Such friendships should be selfless relationships that also have agape love at their cores.

Third, we must watch out for the traps of the enemy. He might tempt us to turn a philanthropia friendship into a sexually motivated friendship—either with men or women.

And There Is So Much More

This is a topic on which we could spend many days. There is so much more in the Scriptures that we could study, but we must move on. In the future we will cover more of this ground.

There was a day when a teacher of the Law asked Jesus what the most important commandment was. This was Jesus' reply:

> "'Love the Lord your God with all your heart and with all your soul and with all your mind and with all your strength.' The second is this: 'Love your neighbor as yourself.' There is no commandment greater than these."
>
> Mark 12:30–31

In this very significant passage, the only word Jesus uses for love is *agape*. It is agape love with which we should love God and learn how to walk in His ways, and it is the selfless agape love with which we should love our neighbors.

It is this love that also finds a reflection in our own hearts, because we are made in His image and likeness. I would encourage you to spend some private time with the Lord over the next few days to examine the motives of your heart, to discover afresh the depths of His love for you and to renew your agape love relationship with Him.

SUMMARY

When the Bible says that God is love, it is referring to selfless agape love. This is the heart of God and the nature of God. It is only because of His total selflessness that He can be trusted completely. And this is the love that He has put in our hearts that we can choose to express in all our relationships—with God and with man.

PRAYER

Help me, Lord, to examine my heart in the light of Your agape love so that I can walk in Your ways and have God-inspired motives in all that I do. In Jesus' name, Amen.

THE **CHARACTER** OF **GOD**

When Christians know little about the character of God, they are unable to be His faithful representatives.

GOD'S LOVE IN ACTION

It may have been a surprise for you to discover how the nature of God has such an important impact on who we are and on our daily lives. The nature of the Godhead is reflected in the nature of man in so many different ways.

There has been a heavy distortion in the human heart because of the work of the enemy, and as a result we have a carnal nature. But Satan cannot destroy what God has made—he can only distort it. The intrinsic, God-given nature can still be evident even in fallen and unredeemed men and women.

The carnal nature is an offense for those who have been redeemed out of the hand of the enemy. We must learn to recognize and hate the carnality of our lives in the flesh. Paul urged all believers to "put to death the misdeeds of the body" in the power of the Spirit of God (Romans 8:13). In this way the redeemed nature can take on more of the character of God.

God's love in action means that we can dare to be honest about ourselves without risking the loss of His love. Recognizing that God's love for us is an agape love means that we can be totally honest with both God and ourselves and not fear the consequences.

Being honest means owning what is true regardless of the circumstances. In God, truth and honesty have never been separated. But the deceived human heart wants to use dishonesty as a means of covering up the truth. Dishonesty is simply lying—first to oneself and then to others, and in both cases to God.

Agape Love or Codependency?

We saw how the Greek word most often used for God's love in the New Testament is *agape*. That is a good word to describe the nature of God's love. It is the selfless desire of His heart to be a source of unconditional blessing to others. Agape love, as described beautifully in 1 Corinthians 13, never manipulates others to gain an advantage and is always truthful and honest.

When motivated by agape love in relationships, we do not require a complementary response before making a decision to bless someone. It is not a "you love me and I will love you" sort of negotiated deal. Often the love that is offered is conditional upon getting something back, or it is offered only if we have already received something we consider to be at least as valuable. That kind of arrangement is common in relationships and is sometimes referred to as codependency.

Depending on others in a codependent relationship is not love. It is a transactional form of relationship where we pay for having our needs met by providing something similar for someone else.

Even a minor form of codependency can be a real obstacle to healing. It can provide people with an excuse not to face the deeper issues in their lives.

It is a bit like providing a walking stick for someone who has an infected wound on his foot without offering him any treatment. It would be much more sensible for the person to have the foot treated, no matter how painful the short-term experience might be. The person would not need the stick after the infection was removed. But without essential healing, the wound and the stick would become permanent features in the person's life. Limping would become his normal way of getting around.

In a similar way, many people choose to work around the issues associated with wounds from their pasts rather than face the truth about themselves. Past wounds can cause symptoms such as fear, pain, anger, shame or need for attention.

It is not unusual for people with very real, personal needs to attend one of our Healing Retreats. Oftentimes when they ask for prayer, however, they ask only for healing of the symptoms they are experiencing. These symptoms might be physical illness, exhaustion, depression or explosive anger. In reality, they do not want to rock the boat of their inner lives by having to deal with what the real causes are.

Often codependent human relationships become the crutches (or walking sticks) that keep people from the real healing that they need. The very real feelings, for example, that come from the hidden inner wounds of Lucy are projected toward her friend Jane. Lucy gets some inner release through having let off steam at someone safe, but Jane, who has little self-worth of her own, now finds her worth and value in pacifying and comforting Lucy.

This sort of behavior, which goes usually in repetitive cycles throughout a relationship, keeps both parties from receiving the real healing that they both need. They cope fairly well with life by using one another to meet their needs. Why ask them to look any deeper than the superficial problems of headaches or exhaustion if looking deeper might mean upsetting the existing codependent relationship that they have become familiar with and that gives them a measure of personal security? The answer is that what they are doing is depending on each other and not on God.

A sad thing about such codependent relationships is that if one person makes the decision to face the roots of their real issues with God, the other person can sink into despair. It forces the other person to turn to God to face their own real issues. It is often the fear of how the other party will respond that prevents a person from taking the step of faith to begin the journey to achieving permanent freedom.

When people choose to stay in such codependent relationships they can never receive God's love and comfort. His is the true love and comfort they need to bring healing into those inner places of hurt, loss and wounding. Isaiah realized that receiving God's love is the only path of hope. He said, "In his love and mercy he redeemed them; he lifted them up and carried them" (Isaiah 63:9).

Even marriages can be dysfunctional as love relationships. Often agape love, which should be the real strength of a good marriage, is replaced by a form of codependency.

Being Honest with God

Sadly, however, some people are deceived into thinking that they can have a codependent relationship with God. They offer God a sort of reluctant obedience in the form of religious activity because they think that is what He wants. They believe that what they get back in return is His protection for now and a guarantee of a place in heaven for later. They have misunderstood completely the free grace that Jesus provided for them on the cross. They are trying to earn their salvation without even realizing it.

They think God needs their religious acts of devotion. They do a sort of trade-off with the Almighty, thinking that the cost of what they do for God here on earth is a fair price to pay for what they are expecting to get from God in heaven. They forget that God hates religion because it separates people from the truth of experiencing His love. Agape love is always at the heart of a real relationship with Him (see Isaiah 1).

In their selfishness, they offer Him the bare minimum they think they can get away with as the price of an admission ticket to heaven. But they miss the point. God can exist without us. He does not need our religious routines. There cannot be any possible trade-off with Him. Even if we could offer Him the whole world, it would still be an inadequate offering for His agape love. As Isaac Watts put it in the last verse of his amazing hymn, "When I Survey the Wondrous Cross":

> Were the whole Realm of Nature mine,
> That were a Present far too small;
> Love so amazing, so divine,
> Demands my Soul, my Life, my All.[1]

You may be nodding your head in agreement and thinking of people you know whose relationship with God resembles this sort of super-spiritual codependence. But before we move on, we need to ask ourselves to what extent we might be guilty of treating God this way.

Please ask yourself, "Is it possible that I have chosen not to face some of the deep issues that I know are in my life? Have I chosen to live with unhealed areas of my being? Can it be that I use God, or what I see as my service for God, as a sort of prop to support me through difficulties rather than own the fact that I am actually trying to keep God out of the area of my life where the difficulties are?" It can be painful to turn the spotlight on yourself, but it is an essential step in personal growth.

I realize these are hard questions, but I am not writing this material speculatively. I am not wondering if there is anyone out there for whom this could be true. I have prayed for many, many people over the last thirty years for whom this has been the reality of their lives.

I have even known people who traveled to faraway places on the mission field to avoid bringing their hidden sins and wounds to God. Mistakenly, they thought that by serving God overseas the problems would go away. Many return damaged and broken, sometimes even having turned their backs on the God who they believed did not solve their problems for them.

It would have been so much better if they had learned to trust God's love enough to let Him into that private inner space where ungodly thoughts, attitudes and memories are treasured and nurtured. He will not invade our spaces uninvited even though He knows exactly what is in them. It would be easier if we allowed Him to help us with the real issues.

God's agape love will not allow Him to reject you because of what you have hidden from Him. What sort of love would God have if He were to love and support you before you confessed your hidden sins, but the moment you confessed it all He were to leave?

The enemy can also deceive us into thinking that without our inner, and often sinful props, we will have nothing to lean on, especially when it seems that God is not there for us.

"How will you cope," Satan might ask, "if you need to escape into the comfortable room of your private ungodly thinking but find that the room no longer exists?"

Even more subtly, the enemy makes us fear that God will not be able to cope with us being honest with Him. We fear that if we tell God everything, He will not love us anymore.

God wants us to give Him permission to show us what messes there have been in our lives so that we can be healed and restored. There is nothing God does not already know about, so we have nothing to fear in bringing absolutely everything to Him. We can trust Him to take us by the hand and lead us out of the circumstances. Then we can start to run the race that He has set before us (see Hebrews 12:1–2).

If Satan cannot keep us from following Jesus, he will try to deceive us into being content with our inner limitations so that we will never know the true freedom that Jesus wants us to enjoy.

Sadly, many people opt for the safety of what they are familiar with or what they can control instead of choosing the One who loves them unconditionally and who does not require anything back in return.

Satan tries to make us think that a well-worn path, even a sinful one, can seem safer and less threatening than standing with our hands in His, facing the wide-open space where He is leading us. In reality, the most secure place in which any of us can be is facing the unknown with God holding our hands. This is truly God's love in action.

God of Love, God of Justice

People sometimes get confused about the justice of God and, therefore, the judgment of God. They seem incapable of recognizing that the character of a God of love is not incompatible with a God of justice.

Love cannot tolerate sin or sweep it under the carpet as if it is of little consequence. For God to do this would mean He would have to be dishonest and pretend the sin is not there.

Justice demands that the consequences of sin (rebellion against God) must be faced. As we saw earlier, eternal justice was fulfilled at the cross when Jesus became the victim of God's judgment on behalf of humankind.

Just as the eternal consequence of sin was separation from God, there is also a consequence of sin in this life. Paul referred to it as a law of sowing and reaping (see Galatians 6:7–8). The forgiveness of God is possible only because the price for sin was paid at the cross. Justice was done. But the forgiveness of God, which leads to a restoration of relationship, does not mean that humanity can escape the consequences of justice in this life.

I may be forgiven by God for driving too fast and breaking the law of the land, but when I am caught in the police speed trap, I still have to pay the fine. God's agape love, through which I can receive forgiveness, does not excuse me from the requirements of justice. A person who steals money may confess the sin to God and be forgiven, but that does not mean they do not have to make restitution (repay what they have stolen) or accept whatever punishment the law of the land requires.

When my children were young and disobeyed deliberately, my love for them would want to see them forgiven and restored to me in relationship. But I would not have been a loving father if I had not used such opportunities to exercise fair discipline. Without fair discipline, children learn to abuse love.

"If you are not disciplined . . . then you are not legitimate, not true sons and daughters at all" (Hebrews 12:8). Discipline (justice) is simply an outworking of love.

Agape Love and Kingdom Blessing

There are many Scripture passages that talk about the rewards there will be in heaven for God's people. God is motivated by agape love, which means He wants blessings for you. God loves you enough to bring both order and discipline into your life because He wants to heal you at the very deepest level. He wants you to enjoy the greatest blessings in the heavenly realm.

In this way, your earthly life will become more fruitful. In that wonderful passage in John 15, Jesus teaches His disciples by drawing lessons from the life of a vine. He explains how pruning (discipline) and fruitfulness go hand in hand. He says that it "is to my Father's glory, that you bear much fruit" (verse 8).

As we respond to the agape love of Father God, we will then become a true reflection of who He is in this fallen world. The fruit we bear will be an eternal blessing to Him. One day we will discover how much fruit there is in eternity as a result of how we respond to His love now.

SUMMARY

God's love for us is so wonderful that we should never fear being honest with Him. His love in action longs to see us healed, restored and living in His ways so that we can serve Him. We do not need the props of a codependent relationship, but rather the freedom and liberty that comes through being transparent before Him.

PRAYER

Thank You, Lord, for Your wonderful love. I am sorry for trying to hide things from You and for not fully trusting You. I choose to be open before You. I do not want to live a restricted life. I want to throw away the ungodly props and risk trusting You unconditionally—for ever and ever. In Jesus' name, Amen.

GOD IS ALL-POWERFUL (OMNIPOTENT)

I stood at the base of a huge tree. It towered above my head for over eighty feet, and it must have weighed forty tons. It was magnificent. Clearly, no one could lift such an enormous object high into the sky and simultaneously anchor it safely to the ground.

Alongside this mighty tree was a seedling. It was just a few inches high and totally insignificant. If I could go away and come back in a hundred years, I would see that this seedling would have also become a magnificent tree that was lifted high into the sky. God has orchestrated this growth by the creation of new cells throughout the growing season year after year.

At the same time, I looked up into the sky. The morning sun was breaking through the clouds, and its rays were beginning to stir the natural world with light and heat. Only eight minutes earlier, these rays had begun their journey from the sun where an endless series of nuclear reactions created phenomenal amounts of intense heat and light. The rays that filtered through the trees brought the sun's power to earth. The sun is sufficiently far enough away for the rays not to consume everything on earth in an uncontrollable fire and near enough to give humankind exactly the right living environment.

It had rained overnight, and the ground was still wet. Gravity was drawing the water downward into a small brook that joined a stream that was flowing into a river that would finally reach the sea. I remembered standing by the Niagara Falls on the border between the United States and Canada. I was awed at the extraordinary power of flowing water that was being drawn downward by the force of gravity. It crashed over the edge, falling hundreds of feet into the watery abyss below.

I looked again at the resplendent tree. I felt the warmth of the sun on my face, and I heard the sound of the water in the stream as it began its journey toward the sea. I worshiped the God who made all of this and whose power sustains the physical universe.

Paul expressed the wonder of God's creation, which is a witness to the unbelieving world, in this way: "For since the creation of the world God's invisible qualities—his eternal power and divine nature—have been clearly seen, being understood from what has been made, so that people are without excuse" (Romans 1:20).

There is no excuse for anyone who fails to see the evidence of God in the incredible world He has made.

Our Omnipotent God

The word *omnipotent* appears occasionally in some of the older hymns. It is a very expressive word and sums up so much about the nature of God. By breaking the word down so that we can better define it, we get *omni*, meaning "all," and *potent*, meaning "power." Only God is ever referred to accurately as being omnipotent—all powerful.

Down the centuries kings and emperors have referred to themselves as omnipotent, but no king or emperor has ever been able to sustain himself even for a short period of time without an army to defend his territory and possessions. Without military might, the attempts of emperors to achieve omnipotence would have foundered on the rock of impotence. Even with military might, their power lasted only for limited seasons. History has proven their fallibility and ultimate powerlessness.

God is the source of all power. Everything has its origin in Him. He needs no army to defend His territory. He has no fear of invading armies. It is in Him only that all power resides and from Him only that all power originates. And whatever powers any human being, organization, nation or group of nations might have and exercise for whatever purpose, good or bad, they are using power that ultimately has its origin in God.

Some people struggle with understanding that all people who exercise power are using God's power. To understand this, think for a moment about a mighty hydroelectric power scheme. In this model the power of gravity is harnessed by collecting rainfall in huge reservoirs and then releasing it in a controlled way through turbines that generate electricity.

No one who believes in God would even begin to question the fact that the power generated by harnessing the force of gravity is God's power. He created the universe and everything in it, so the electricity that flows down the cables to empower the world of business and to be used in people's homes is clearly God's power. But how is it used?

The electricity could be used by a family to cook food in their home to feed the hungry, it could go to a hospital to provide life-giving warmth and care for the sick and dying, or it could be used to give light and power to a school to educate the next generation. It could even enable the use of a computer to write Journey to Freedom.

But electricity from that same hydroelectric power station, which we have identified had its origin in God, could be used as easily to process illegal drugs, to seduce young people into watching pornography on television or their computers, or to rob vulnerable people of all of their available funds as they feed electric gambling machines. God is the source of the power in all of these situations—both the good and the bad.

For a season in history, the Roman Empire ruled the known world. It was during that season that Jesus lived and died as a citizen of a remote Roman colony. Pilate, the governor of the province, had ultimate control in the territory, and his authority as governor was backed up by the presence and power of the most fearsome and ruthless army the world had ever seen. Pilate was all-powerful in first-century Judaea.

It was Pilate who said to Jesus, "Don't you realize I have power either to free you or to crucify you?" (John 19:10). But Jesus replied, "You would have no power over me if it were not given to you from above" (John 19:11). Even the power that Pilate used to issue the crucifixion order and to have it carried out came from God Himself.

All earthly power has its origin in the power of God. It was God who created the earth with all its natural resources. A nation whose territory is rich in gold or oil will become a powerful nation through the wealth created by these precious commodities. But that power comes ultimately from God and belongs to God. How we utilize this power is our choice, and it can be used by people for good or bad because of the free will God has given to humankind.

Power and Authority

Power and authority are not the same thing. Even when we talk about God's power and God's authority, the two phrases are often used interchangeably. Authority is permission to use power. As the originator of all power, God has His own permission to use it. All power and all authority find their places in Him.

The one who has authority can delegate his authority to others to exercise on his behalf. This is what happened when Pilate used his authority as governor to order the Roman soldiers to carry out the execution.

When God created humans, He delegated authority over the earth to humankind through Adam (see Genesis 1:28). But Adam listened to the voice of the enemy and gave that authority away to Satan. As a result, Satan became the god of this world, the one to whom humankind submitted, and an interloping authority between God and man (see 2 Corinthians 4:4).

Through humankind's ungodly choices and the exercise of Satan's authority, many evil things came into the world, including sickness and disease. Clearly God had both the power to heal people and the authority to deliver them from the powers of darkness that had caused such personal devastation in the lives of man.

But fallen man now had neither the power nor the authority to do these things. Because God had already given man free will and trusted him with the exercise of authority on planet earth, man's condition required both a human and a divine answer. The stage was set for the coming of the Messiah. He was God's restoration plan for humankind from the very beginning (see Genesis 3:15).

The fact of Jesus' power and authority was evident throughout His ministry. After He had forgiven the sins of the paralyzed man, for example, the Pharisees began to accuse Jesus of blasphemy and to question His authority. "Who can forgive sins but God alone?" (Luke 5:21). Jesus responded by healing the paralyzed man so that the Pharisees would "know that the Son of Man has authority on earth to forgive sins" (Luke 5:24).

After Jesus had delivered the man who had manifested a demon in the synagogue at Capernaum, "all the people were amazed and said to each other, 'What words these are! With authority and power he gives orders to impure spirits and they come out!'" (Luke 4:36).

Both power and authority were essential components of Jesus' ministry. When Jesus sent the disciples out on their first mission trip to go and preach the Kingdom of God and to heal the sick, He needed to equip them for the task (see Luke 9:1–2).

Luke tells us that He gave the disciples two things that were essential for the mission: His power and His authority. The power would be needed to heal the sick, and His authority would be needed to set the captives free from the powers of darkness. To bring healing and deliverance, they needed both His power and His authority.

Ultimate Power and Authority

Whoever is in authority has permission to use whatever power is at his or her disposal. When the people of the United States vote in a new president, for example, they are also voting that person in as the new commander-in-chief of the nation's military personnel and equipment. They are giving that person authority over all of the armed forces.

At the end of Jesus' time on earth, just before He returned to heaven to await the time of His Second Coming, He told the disciples, "All authority in heaven and on earth has been given to me" (Matthew 28:18). Whoever has all authority also has the ability to use all the power at his disposal. The authority has been given to Jesus by His Father; therefore, all of the power of the Godhead is at His disposal.

When Jesus comes again, people will "see the Son of Man coming on the clouds of heaven, with power and great glory" (Matthew 24:30). As John shared in his prophecy, there will be the sound "like the roar of a great multitude in heaven shouting, 'Hallelujah! Salvation and glory and power belong to our God'" (Revelation 19:1). And we can join with the heavenly hosts in saying, "Hallelujah! For our Lord God Almighty reigns" (Revelation 19:6).

75

Trusting God

The most important personal lesson we can take from this teaching about the omnipotence of God is simply that no one has a higher authority level or more power than Him. And because the all-powerful One is also the all-loving One, we can trust Him completely with everything we are and everything we will be in the life to come. When He is Lord of our future, we have nothing to fear. His power is above every other power.

Just as the day came when Jesus the Messiah came into the world the first time, the day will come also when He will appear in power and great glory. For those who trust in Him, that will be a day of much celebration and thanksgiving. For those who have rejected Him, it will be a day of great distress and mourning (see Revelation 1:7).

SUMMARY

All power comes ultimately from God. There is nothing in all creation that is not empowered by Him. The power of all earthly authority comes from God, and the day will come when every knee will bow and every tongue will confess that Jesus Christ is Lord (see Romans 14:11).

PRAYER

Thank You, Lord, that all power is in Your hands. I recognize that while evil men may misuse and abuse Your power for a season, I have nothing to fear, for my eternal future is safe in Your hands. In Jesus' name, Amen.

GOD IS ALL-KNOWING (OMNISCIENT)

We have already considered the omnipotence of God. He is the source of all power. All authority is ultimately in His hands. Now we are going to look at another vital aspect of the character of God: His omniscience. In other words, God's ability to know all things.

To understand the word better, we will break it into smaller parts. *Omni* means "all," and *science* means "knowledge." When we put these two Latin words together, it means that God has all knowledge. He knows all things, and nothing can be hidden from His sight.

A generation ago it might have been hard for people to imagine how it could be possible for God to know all things with absolutely nothing escaping His notice. In one generation, however, information technology has made such staggering advances that no one thinks of the unlimited availability of knowledge as being remarkable.

We live in a day when it seems like the sum total of all the world's information can be researched and read on an internet-connected phone that we access while walking down the street. We can zoom in on almost any square mile of real estate courtesy of Google Earth, and we can talk to almost anyone from almost any location on the planet.

If these things are possible for fallen man, then it takes a minor step of faith to believe that awareness of where each and every human being is, what they are doing and what they are saying is no big deal for the Almighty.

God's Omniscience

When Scripture tells us that not even a sparrow falls to the ground without our heavenly Father knowing and that every hair on our heads is numbered (see Matthew 10:29–30), we realize that God's knowledge of all things is unlimited.

Jesus extended the omniscience of God to the words we speak when He said that "everyone will have to give account on the day of judgment for every empty word they have spoken. For by your words you will be acquitted, and by your words you will be condemned" (Matthew 12:36–37). Not only does God know what we have said throughout our lives, but all our words from the realm of time are also recorded for eternity.

If eternity records our words, what about our thoughts? It is a fact that everything we ever do begins as a thought. We can choose to think about anything we like—good, bad or neutral. Some thoughts may arrive in our minds as temptations from the enemy, but if we choose to dwell on them, they become sin.

Jesus illustrated this principle when He explained that as far as God is concerned, an ungodly thought that is entertained willingly becomes a sinful act—even if it never goes beyond the thought. Jesus issued a huge challenge to men when He said, "Anyone who looks at a woman lustfully has already committed adultery with her in his heart" (Matthew 5:28). For men, the visual image of a woman can so easily become a source of temptation for sexual desire and lust. If that was not the case, there would be no market for pornography.

The last of the Ten Commandments says, "You shall not covet" (Exodus 20:17). That means you must not think desirously and lustfully about anything that does not belong to you—whether that something is your neighbor's spouse (husband or wife), their house, their car or anything else.

A saying that has been attributed to Frank Outlaw, who founded a supermarket chain, expresses the possible progression from thoughts to actions and beyond in the following way:

> Watch your thoughts; they become words.
> Watch your words; they become actions.
> Watch your actions; they become habits.

Watch your habits; they become character.
Watch your character; for it becomes your destiny.[1]

No wonder Paul urged people to think only about wholesome things. "Finally, brothers and sisters, whatever is true, whatever is noble, whatever is right, whatever is pure, whatever is lovely, whatever is admirable—if anything is excellent or praiseworthy—think about such things" (Philippians 4:8).

For if we think about such things, there will be nothing to fear from the omniscience of God when we stand before Him on that final Day of Judgement when the Book of Life is opened and our words and actions are examined (see Revelation 20:12). For those whose sin has not been forgiven and cleansed by the blood of Jesus, the omniscience of God and the fear of His judgement will be related closely. Jesus said, "For there is nothing hidden that will not be disclosed, and nothing concealed that will not be known or brought out into the open" (Luke 8:17).

Why God's Omniscience Matters to You and Me

There is absolutely nothing in your life that God does not know about. Paul tells us that on that final day everything will be brought to light. There will be great rewards and much rejoicing for those whose lives withstand the testing fires of God's judgement (see 1 Corinthians 3:13–14). God will not forget all those times you served Him with loving obedience to His Word in the secret places of your life.

He will also not forget the tears that you shed when you went through tough times or sacrificed your own desires so that His will and purposes could be fulfilled. He will not forget every time you did this so that others could have the opportunity to come to know Jesus as their Lord and Savior.

Psalm 126:5–6 puts it this way: "Those who sow with tears will reap with songs of joy. Those who go out weeping, carrying seed to sow, will return with songs of joy, carrying sheaves with them." The sheaves can be understood to mean the harvest of souls that have been reaped for the Kingdom of God as a result of seeds of God's truth that we have sown.

My dad died many years ago. Even twenty years later, I still come across someone who owes his salvation to the seeds Dad sowed throughout his life. I have no doubt he will have a harvest of many sheaves in eternity. What a wonderful objective for each one of us to have—to be a sower of seeds that will produce a harvest of sheaves in eternity.

I have sat with many people as they have poured out the stories of their lives. In most cases they have come for help and prayer because of what has happened to them. The resulting consequences have become too great to bear. They cannot keep the pain and pressure trapped inside the cauldrons of their emotions any longer, and that often causes them to become victims of depression or various other psychological conditions. Our all-knowing God understands because He knows the trauma they have experienced.

Sometimes as a result of seeking comfort for their trauma in the wrong places, people have fallen into sin. At the time they knew no other way to cope with the inner turmoil. Addictions to alcohol or drugs, wrong relationships or the constant failure to overcome life's obstacles are the inevitable consequences of abuse, physical and sexual violation, deprivation and all other forms of cruelty. Often they feel bad and totally unlovable because of the things they have done.

When I explain to such people that God knows everything that has happened to them and that He understands the pain and suffering they have endured, there can be two very different reactions.

Some people feel relieved that God knows every detail. They find peace in knowing that those who were responsible for causing their suffering will have to give an account before the throne of God for what they did. The knowledge that God noted and recorded those things that were done to them, that He felt and understood their pain and that He has remembered their tears brings them great comfort and encouragement. (The Scripture passage 2 Kings 20:5, for example, tells us how God saw King Hezekiah's tears.) As a result, they can begin to receive His healing on earth, and they can also look forward to the joys to come in eternity with God where there will be total and perfect healing.

But other people react differently when they realize that God knew exactly what was happening to them. They feel a deep-seated anger directed at God.

They say, "If God knew exactly what was going on, why did He not stop it from happening? If He is all-powerful, why did He not use some of

His power to intervene and stop the person from doing such cruel things to me?"

Free Will and Suffering

If God really does know everything, why does He not intervene to prevent suffering? This is a very good question, and one that many people ask as they wrestle with the unfairness of life and with their own suffering.

The fact is, as we saw in the early stages of our journey to freedom, God has limited Himself in the way that He operates on earth. He gave both authority over the earth and free will to humans. As a result of wrong choices, evil is in the heart of man. When people do evil things, others become victims and suffer the consequences. It might be that people become the victims of horrendous wars, as in the world wars of the last century, or it might be that they become the victims of personal abuse and violation.

A majority of the many references to evil in Scripture refer to the evil that rises from the hearts of humankind. Yes, Satan is evil, but it is humans who choose to do the evil things. Most suffering is a consequence of those evil choices. Jesus experienced that same suffering when He became the sacrificial victim at Calvary.

God understands the pain that is caused when others hurt us, but if He were to intervene to prevent it, it would mean reversing the decision He made at the creation of humankind to give humans free will and authority over the earth.

God grieves over the pain and suffering that people experience because of man's inhumanity to man. His love for us is limitless and unconditional. His grace and mercy are beyond our understanding. For those who have responded to the eternity that God has placed in the hearts of every man and woman, the sacrifice of Jesus on the cross covers all of their sins. In eternity they will know total healing. Their suffering will be an experience of their earthly history. Indescribable joy will be their redeemed inheritance.

Not only is God omniscient, He is also fair. He knows what is in the heart of every person and longs for the day when time as we know it is folded away. That is when we can all participate with all the redeemed of the Lord and with our wonderful Savior in the glory of heaven. On that day there will be no more suffering and no more tears.

> "'He will wipe every tear from their eyes. There will be no more death' or mourning or crying or pain, for the old order of things has passed away." He who was seated on the throne said, 'I am making everything new!'"

Revelation 21:4–5

SUMMARY

There is nothing that is hidden from the eyes of God. He knows all things. God's omniscience is nothing to fear for those who are in Christ. For those who have rejected Him, there will be a day when God's knowledge of them will be brought into the light. People will be judged by their own thoughts, words and actions, and God will be seen as righteous and just.

PRAYER

Lord, help me to live each day in Your presence, knowing that I cannot hide anything from You. Help me to recognize when the enemy is prompting me to sin, and help me to choose to walk in Your ways all my life. In Jesus' name, Amen.

GOD IS IN ALL PLACES (OMNIPRESENT)

In the last two chapters, we have seen how God is all-powerful (omnipotent) and all-knowing (omniscient). We have begun to understand how important it is for believers to recognize that these are unchanging and unchangeable characteristics of the living God.

There is one more of these *omni-* characteristics that is vital to our knowledge of God and our relationship with Him. The meaning of the second part of the word in *omnipresent* is a little more obvious. The word expresses the truth that God is present in all places. There is no place you can go that will take you out of His presence.

David recognized the omnipresence of God, and he expressed his feelings about this in Psalm 139. He shared his wonder at the omnipresence of God—the fact that God is everywhere and that there is nowhere man can possibly go that would be outside of His presence.

> Where can I go from your Spirit? Where can I flee from your presence? If I go up to the heavens, you are there; if I make my bed in the depths [hell], you are there. If I rise on the wings of the dawn, if I settle on the far side of the sea, even there your hand will guide me, your right hand will hold me fast.
>
> Psalm 139:7–10

Jeremiah expressed a similar thought when he wrote in his prophecy, "'Who can hide in secret places so that I cannot see them?' declares the LORD. 'Do not I fill heaven and earth?' declares the LORD" (Jeremiah 23:24).

What Does God's Omnipresence Actually Mean?

As there are two sides to every coin, there are two equally accurate answers to this important question. The first answer relates to the presence of God outside of man, and the second relates to the presence of God within man.

It is not possible for God to create something and not have access to what has been created. The whole universe was created by God, and it lies within His grasp. Wherever one might be within God's universe, God is there.

Before the creation of man but after the creation of the world and the universe, Genesis 1:2 tells us that "the Spirit of God was hovering over the waters." He is present within His universe—all of it. There was no possibility, for example, that when the Apollo astronauts landed on the moon they would discover that this was a place uninhabited by God. Most astronauts relate that their visits into space were profoundly spiritual experiences that affirmed their belief in God.

The same would apply if the planned mission to Mars (or anywhere else in the universe) ever took place. God made everything, and His presence pervades every star, every planet and the space between them.

In my office is a model car. It is a replica of a car I used to own. I can put that model car in the palm of my hand. The whole car is then embraced by my presence. Imagine for a moment what it must be like for God. He created the whole universe, and it sits within the palm of His hand, just as the model car can sit within the palm of my hand. The whole universe is enveloped by God's presence and is contained within God. Nothing lies outside of His presence.

When Jesus was encouraging the disciples to really trust Him with their futures in the Father's house, He said, "Don't you believe that I am in the Father, and that the Father is in me?" (John 14:10). If nothing in the whole universe is outside of God, and Jesus and the Father are one, then there is nowhere in the whole universe we could go where Jesus would not be. That is why it is possible to have access to Father God at all times and in all places.

The second answer to our question relates to the presence of God within man. In an earlier chapter, we saw that God put a life-giving spirit into every human being. No one, not even the vilest of criminals, is without that signature of God in their hearts. As Ecclesiastes 3:11 says, "He has also set eternity in the human heart."

When the apostle Paul was addressing the learned men of Athens about creation and about God's presence within us, he said to these unbelieving people, "God did this so that they would seek him and perhaps reach out for him and find him, though he is not far from any one of us" (Acts 17:27).

If something of God is inside every single one of us, then it is totally impossible for any human being to go anywhere without having the presence of God within them. Wherever we are, God is. And even if it were possible for us to go outside of the universe, we would still be in touch with the presence of God within us. In summary, everything God made is within Him, and wherever we are, God is.

The Manifest Presence of God

Omnipresence does not mean, however, that the immediacy or awareness of His presence cannot vary from place to place. In times of revival, people talk about the manifest presence of God as being an almost tangible reality. It feels like something you can sense in your spirit and almost feel in the air that you breathe.

I am writing these words in the Outer Hebrides of Scotland. Seventy years ago, the Hebridean revival took place. In that revival there were times and seasons when the presence of God was so evident that people were coming under conviction of sin without anyone even preaching a sermon.

This was no organized charismatic event. People would gather in the church and remain late into the night for an unannounced meeting. They were drawn simultaneously by the presence of God—even to the extent that their homes were shaken, as happened in the beginning of the Church (see Acts 4:31).

These are not imaginary stories to excite vulnerable people, but real-life experiences that forever marked the lives of those sober Hebridean individuals. I know they are true, because I knew some of the people who were involved. Right up until the time that they died, they were still experiencing the impact that the reality of God's manifest presence had made on their lives.

Does this mean that God is not present when people are not experiencing Him like this? Not at all. But it does mean that God can and does on occasion satisfy the desire for His presence in those who seek Him with undivided hearts.

Why This Matters to Me

The omnipresence of God is a profound truth about the nature and character of God. The fact that none of us can ever escape from the presence of God is both terrible and wonderful news. For those who have rejected Him it is terrible news, and for those who love Him it is wonderful news. It is also wonderful news for those who are searching for Him (see Psalm 145:8) and for those who are facing any kind of difficulty (see Isaiah 43:2).

Revelation makes it very clear that the day will come when the almighty, all-powerful God will bring the era of time as we know it to an end. When that happens, all humanity, without exception, will appear before His throne. Sin in the heart of man will be judged, and there will be a division made between those whose names are in the Book of Life and those whose names are not (see Revelation 20:11–15).

The judgement of God for the sins of humankind fell upon Jesus at Calvary. He died for all. As John expressed it clearly, it was only "to all who did receive him, to those who believed in his name, he gave the right to become children of God" (John 1:12). Not to anyone else.

We are all deserving of judgement. For those who are in Christ, however, the punishment has already been carried out through Jesus. He paid the price for our sin. Our restoration to Him as children of the living God is an awesome privilege.

When this happens, I believe we who are in Christ will all be worshiping Jesus as never before. No wonder that in his prophetic vision John saw so much worship happening in heaven.

The twenty-four elders fall down before him who sits on the throne and worship him who lives for ever and ever. They lay their crowns before the throne and say: "You are worthy, our Lord and God, to receive glory and honor and power, for you created all things, and by your will they were created and have their being."

Revelation 4:10–11

Those who have not accepted Christ will see the freedom they could have had, but there will be no opportunity for them to move from the place of condemnation to the place of release. They will be in His presence, but in the timelessness of eternity, they will find no escape from the place of eternal separation and judgement.

Oh, how people will wish then that they could escape from the presence of God. Those who died believing that life ends at death will regret for eternity their rejection of so great a salvation. Those who have argued throughout their lives that the universe appeared accidentally out of nothing and that the whole of creation is an accident of evolutionary change will wish they could escape from the presence of their Creator.

But what joy for those who are in Christ. The new heaven and the new earth beckons those who decided to trust the Savior who went ahead to prepare a place for each of us.

SUMMARY

There is no escape from the presence of God. His omnipresence is at the same time a comfort for those who know and love Him and a terrible indictment of those who have seen all the evidence of His presence but have chosen to ignore Him.

PRAYER

I am so glad, Lord, that there is nowhere I can go that is outside of Your wonderful presence. Help me always to be conscious of this amazing truth as I choose now to trust You with everything I am and everything I will be in eternity. In Jesus' name, Amen.

GOD OF COVENANT

Later we will be looking in more detail at the different covenants that God established with His people. Each of them is significant and important. For now, we are just opening up the subject of covenant love—love that brings great encouragement and security to the people of God at all times and in all stages of their personal journeys.

The Nature of God

In our study of the nature and character of God, we have seen that He is holy and eternal, that He is Creator, that He is Father, Son and Holy Spirit, that His whole nature is described by agape (totally selfless) love, that He is all-powerful and all-knowing, and that we can never go outside of His presence. We have established theological truths. We have seen the vital relevance of each of these truths in our daily walk of faith with the living God.

We now want to take our understanding of the nature of God a little further as we look at the concept of covenant love and discover the significance of the Hebrew word *hesed*. Words are useful only if we understand what they mean, so we will discover together why this Hebrew word is so important.

Hesed Love

The word *hesed* does not have any direct translation in English. It is one of those words that exists uniquely in one language, but in other languages requires many different words to reflect its complete meaning. It is what we might call a rich word. It is a word with a lot of significance, meaning and interpretations, but it does not have an exact equivalent to any one word in English. In the Bible, the word is translated in different ways according to the context. What does this mean?

Imagine you are trying to describe a magnificent cut diamond that is on display and is shimmering in the light of the sun. As you move your head from one side to another the light seems to vary in its intensity. As you walk around the diamond, it sparkles in a hundred different ways. You need different words to describe what it looks like according to where you are standing.

Imagine if there were one word that could encompass and describe all the many amazing patterns of beautiful light emanating from the one diamond. It would be a very useful word. Then imagine that God is like the many-faceted diamond. He is shimmering with love that is emanating from His heart. If you were asked to describe what you were seeing in English, you would need many different words to express the wonder of God's love: generous, kind, selfless, patient, truthful, hopeful, enduring, persevering, and more. In Hebrew, however, just one word describes all that you are seeing—*hesed*.

Hebrew was and is the language of the people of God. It is no surprise, therefore, that Hebrew does have one wonderful word that fulfills this very purpose. When *hesed* is used in the Bible to illustrate different aspects of the nature of God's covenant love, the translators had to use different words in an attempt to illustrate what the original Hebrew writers were trying to say. Here are some of the words that are used: graciousness, loving-kindness, tenderheartedness, generosity, mercy, steadfastness and faithfulness.

When you put all these words together, they create a beautiful picture of what God is like. Who would not want to love and trust someone with such characteristics? When we remember that the character of God cannot ever change, we know it is always safe to trust Him.

Hesed Love and Discipline

There are times in the Bible when God has had to act in order to bring discipline and correction into the lives of His people. Sometimes that discipline meant exile and punishment. The writer of the Hebrews expresses this principle clearly: "God disciplines us for our good, in order that we may share in his holiness" (Hebrews 12:10).

Even when He disciplines us, it is still an act of His hesed love. In His mercy He does not want us to go so far from His heart that we reject the God who loves us so much. He wants us to be able to share in His holiness. Amazing!

When I took our dog, Harris, for walks, I always made sure he was on his leash. When he was young I made the mistake of walking him with no leash near a field of sheep. He chased the sheep. To him it was a big game, but the sheep were not enjoying it. He was behaving badly, and I was very embarrassed. I had to apologize to the farmer.

Harris was not a bad dog, but he did have a weakness. For his own good, we could not risk walking him in the countryside off his leash. The discipline of his leash was essential for his own safety and everyone's well-being. As an act of loving-kindness, I always kept Harris on a leash. As a result, we did not have problems. I often thought how nice it would feel to let him off his leash, but I knew it was better for him to know my love with the restriction of the leash than to experience punishment for what he had done off his leash.

Many Christians have weaknesses that we sometimes call *besetting sins*. These are sins individuals are vulnerable to, and they have to be especially on their guard to avoid. Does God still love us even though we may have such weaknesses? Yes. Does God sometimes have to place restrictions on our lives for our own good? Yes, I believe He does. He does not want those weaknesses to get out of control and deprive us of relationship with Him.

I once knew someone who had a real problem with television. He found himself unable to stop watching pornographic programs from satellite TV. He was out of control. He would go back to God and ask Him constantly to take away the desire, but God's response was to ask him to get rid of his television. He had a weakness, and as long as it was possible for the weakness to be fed, he was never going to get to a place where his relationship with God would be the most important thing in his life.

Before I entered the work of Ellel Ministries, I owned a business that specialized in antiquarian books. I loved old books dearly, and I could lose myself easily in the antiquarian book world. After I sold my business, the Lord spoke to me very clearly and told me not to go into an antiquarian bookshop until He released me to do so. I knew that God wanted me to give all of my attention to His call on my life and the developing ministry. For me, books could be a big distraction, as they absorbed much time and money.

Over the years, I saw many bookshops on my travels that I would have loved to explore. Fifteen years passed before I sensed the release of the Lord to go into such a bookshop again. When I did return to browse in an old bookstore, I enjoyed looking at the books without feeling the desire to be running an antiquarian book business again. What had been a weakness and could have become an addiction was now a thing of the past. This was a necessary restriction for a season in my life. God had to keep me on His leash.

The apostle Paul had a weakness. We are not told exactly what it was, although it may have been his pride. It is referred to in 2 Corinthians 12:7 as a thorn in his flesh. Three times he pleaded with the Lord to have it removed, but on each occasion the Lord encouraged him by saying, "My grace is sufficient for you, for my power is made perfect in weakness" (2 Corinthians 12:9).

The God of Covenant Love

We now have two wonderful words to describe the love of God—*agape* (the totally selfless love through which God wants to bless others) and *hesed*. Together these two words give us a very deep understanding of the loving nature of God and describe for us the heart of covenant love.

It was important that we spent some time realizing how much love is at the heart of God. Within Ellel Ministries we use the phrase "Bringing the heart of God to the heart of man" to describe what God has called us to do as we minister to and teach God's people. Many of those seeking help through Ellel Ministries have never known such love through their human relationships. Discovering the true nature of God's love for them is an amazing and life-transforming revelation.

The word *covenant* is used regularly throughout Scripture to describe the different seasons of relationship God had with His people. The most common usage is when the Old and New Covenants are being referred to. The Old Covenant refers generally to the relationship that God had with His people in the days of the Old Testament, and the New Covenant refers to the new relationship that God wants to have with His people through Jesus.

Later in our journey, we will look in more detail at the significance of the different covenants. When people talk about a covenant, most have only a vague idea of what the word means. Usually that meaning includes some sort of legal agreement.

This is understandable, because in traditional legal practice the word covenant is used to describe the special conditions or restrictions that are attached to a piece of property. An example of this would be conditions of a property that cannot be changed even when that property changes hands.

The very first property I owned had a covenant attached to its title deeds. It gave the local water authority absolute right to walk on my land to inspect the stream that flowed through it. There is a law of trespass in most countries that says that people cannot come on your property without permission. If they do so, they are trespassing. They are breaking the law.

But if a covenant is attached, such as the one mentioned above, the terms of that covenant are above the law of trespass. There was no way I could forbid a representative of the water authority from coming on my land because his rights were protected by a covenant.

When I sold the property, the covenant was not the subject of a new legal agreement for it could not be changed. The covenant was attached to the land. Those who signed the legal agreements through which the land changed owners had to accept the covenantal conditions.

This is an important principle that applies not only to legal situations, but also to the spiritual conditions that are attached to the relationships that God established between Himself and His people. In Scripture, a covenant is not a legal agreement that has been negotiated between God and man. God did not sit down with humankind to discuss the terms of a working arrangement for living on planet earth. Humankind did not have a legal representative try to negotiate the best possible terms for his client with the landlord.

There was nothing to negotiate, because humans had been made by God. The simple fact is that the conditions under which humankind could occupy planet earth were not up for negotiation. They were established as a direct consequence of the nature of God, which, as we have seen, was to love, bless and have relationships with His creation.

The First Covenant

The covenant that was first established between God and man contained one condition only: "You must not eat from the tree of the knowledge of good and evil" (Genesis 2:17). The world had been created by God for man. It was an act of hesed and agape love. The nature of God established the nature of all of God's covenants, and every one of God's covenants was established between God and man so that humankind might be blessed.

When Hosea was bringing a word from the Lord to the people of his day, he said, "As at Adam, they have broken the covenant; they were unfaithful to me" (Hosea 6:7). When Adam and Eve chose to listen to the temptations of the evil one and to eat from the Tree of Knowledge of Good and Evil, they discovered the consequences of violating God's covenant of blessing. They broke the commandment God had given them and were unfaithful to Him.

When people break a commandment of God, they will discover that there is a law attached to breaking the covenant. It is through sin that the negative aspects of the law are discovered. If people obey the commandments, they will never need to find out the consequences of being unfaithful to God. They will, instead, discover the laws of blessing that flow from obedience to God's commandments.

The law Adam discovered was that whoever you obey ultimately controls you. Adam had been given authority over the face of the earth. When he obeyed Satan, Adam gave away his authority. As a result, Satan became the god of this world.

Every covenant that God established between Himself and His people was an extension of that first covenant. Through covenant, God made provision for humankind to enter into the hesed blessings that He had prepared for humankind to enjoy.

Back to the Beginning

At the end of time, those who have been redeemed out of the hand of the enemy will rejoice as they are able to enter into the glory that was prepared originally by God for His creation. This is because of the hesed blessing of the New Covenant. It will be like going back to the beginning as God intended originally.

Between now and then we are living with all the complexities and difficulties of a fallen world. I do not pretend it is easy. It is not. As Peter said, we are living in a world where the devil, like a prowling lion, wants to devour God's people (see 1 Peter 5:8). None of us are strong enough to alone resist the devil. Our place of security is in God only, for He has a higher authority than the devil. Only He can shut the mouths of the lions (see Daniel 6:22).

We will finish today's chapter by quoting the prayer of commitment that John Wesley made as an expression of his response to God's covenant love:

> I am no longer my own, but thine. Put me to what thou wilt, rank with me with whom thou wilt. Put me to doing, put me to suffering. Let me be employed for thee or laid aside for thee, exalted for thee or brought low for thee. Let me be full, let me be empty. Let me have all things, let me have nothing. I freely and heartily yield all things to thy pleasure and disposal. And now, O glorious and blessed God, Father, Son and Holy Spirit, thou art mine, and I am thine. So be it.[1]

This was John Wesley's place of total security. It was reached through surrender to his loving God. It is the place that we should seek to be in also. It is only in the security of God's covenant love that we can experience fully His blessings while living in a fallen world.

SUMMARY

The loving nature of God is at the heart of all God's covenants with humankind. God did not need to promise He would keep His covenant, for

He never changes and cannot be unfaithful to Himself or His people. We can always trust and depend on Him.

PRAYER

Lord, help me to receive Your hesed love and to understand that I can always trust You, for Your love means You will never betray me. Thank You for being a God of covenant love. I rejoice to know that Your grace is sufficient for every one of my days. In Jesus' name, Amen.

ANGELS AND DEMONS

Thinking we can ignore the spiritual realms is as crazy as thinking a fish can swim without water.

ANGELS AND ARCHANGELS

What a blessing it is to hear how people's lives are being challenged and changed by understanding and applying the foundational truths in God's Word that form the basis of our journey to freedom. Every time I hear of what God has done, I rejoice at His amazing love. I know that the God who has brought healing to one will also bring healing to many.

Proverbs 9:10–11 tells us that "the fear of the LORD is the beginning of wisdom, and knowledge of the Holy One is understanding. For through wisdom your days will be many, and years will be added to your life." This is a wonderful promise that tells us that the more we understand about God the more we will receive blessings, one of which will be the adding of years to our lives. This is one of the reasons why we are studying JOURNEY TO FREEDOM and increasing our knowledge of God one step at a time. We are now moving on to look at what the Bible teaches us about the spiritual realms.

Experiences of Angels

On one occasion while I was preaching, I missed a key point in my teaching notes. One of our team realized what was happening and began to pray fervently. As she looked up from her prayer, she was amazed. She saw an angel tapping me gently on the shoulder. While I was aware of nothing supernatural transpiring, I looked down at that very moment and saw the item in my notes I had overlooked. I began to tell a story that fully illustrated the missing point.

I grew up listening to stories of missionaries who served God in China and East Asia with China Inland Mission. On one occasion two missionaries crossed a range of mountains to take some money that had been donated to the mission to the nearest bank. They camped overnight, and the following day they deposited the money in the bank.

Outside of the bank they were accosted by a man who claimed to be the leader of a local gang. The gang had followed the missionaries over the mountains with the aim of robbing them while they slept. As the gang got closer to the missionaries, however, they saw twenty-three soldiers guarding their camp. They could not approach to get to the missionaries because of the guards. The brigand wanted to know where the soldiers had come from. One of the missionaries told him that they had no soldiers—only the protection of God.

Many months later when this missionary was home on furlough she shared this story at a prayer meeting that my great uncle had organized. Uncle Will checked the detailed records he always kept and discovered that at the very time the missionaries were crossing the mountains, twenty-three people in America had gathered to pray for her work in China. The angels had been deployed because of the intercession of the saints back home. If angels are deployed by God as a result of our praying, then we need to take more seriously our commitments when we say we will pray for people.

Angels and the New Age

A few years ago, I was surprised to see books on angels beginning to appear in some of the secular bookshops in North America. At first glance, it seemed as though the world was catching up with the angelic realities within the Bible. On closer examination, however, I was not only disappointed, but I was also profoundly disturbed.

What was happening was that the New Age world of spiritualism, occultism and clairvoyance was tapping into the ungodly side of the spiritual realms. They were describing what they were experiencing as encounters with angels. Since then, there has been a veritable explosion in New Age occultism. It is so prevalent that when I keyed the word *angels* into the Amazon bookstore search engine, it listed over 115,000 separate references to books and related items. Angels, or at least counterfeit angels, are now big business.

There is, however, nothing new under the sun. Two thousand years ago the apostle Paul warned that "Satan himself masquerades as an angel of light" (2 Corinthians 11:14). That is one of his primary means of deceiving the world. He looks or behaves like an angel of God and deceives people into thinking that the false is true. There are false angelic beings behind all of the heretical sects and the thousands of false religions. Satan has deceived many people into thinking that his deceptions are truth.

New Age ideas were virtually unknown in my youth. Rationalism was the ruling philosophy of life, and anyone who believed in spiritualism or occult practices was spurned equally by believers and most unbelievers. But such rationalism, which followed the supposed enlightenment of a century earlier, created a spiritual vacuum in the human heart. A vacuum cannot remain unfilled for very long.

Humanity was not satisfied with the dryness of rationalism, and we began to search for new answers. Mainstream Christianity had been re-jected by the rationalists, and now rationalism itself was being rejected. A new generation arose that believed in the supernatural. It arose from the flower-power environment of music, sex, drugs and Eastern mysticism that became dominant in the culture of the Western world in the 1960s and 1970s.

Young people were ripe for the picking, and the explosion of New Age therapies, beliefs and practices filled the vacuum rapidly. Even Hol-lywood got involved. They used advances in special effects to portray the supernatural in such a way that it blurred reality and fantasy. A new era of spiritual deception began to take hold of the world in business and medical circles.

As a result of the New Age surge, it is quite acceptable today for a doctor's practice to offer a whole range of alternative New Age therapies. People look in a thousand different directions for answers to the issues of life when they have rejected the One who is the answer to every question of life.

Angels have now been brought out of the closet, and people who would have rejected such titles as *Messages from Your Angels* and *The Angel Therapy Handbook* as being mumbo-jumbo are taking in a flood of deception like blotting paper soaking up a vast pool of ink.

My wife and I once took a journey on a train. For the whole trip, we listened to a young professional woman telling her older friend about her journey to spiritual enlightenment. It began with orange-blossom perfume from an aromatherapy shop that gave her a spiritual high. She progressed from there through a whole cycle of increasingly more dangerous New Age and occult practices that dealt with all her fears. By the time we reached our destination, she was telling her friend how she had progressed to the point of practicing witchcraft in a coven.

Satan draws people in through whatever door he can. Once people's eyes have been blinded by the god of this world, they are trapped. Satan is not a creator—he is a copier. His false angelic realm is effective only by copying the real thing. This brings us back to our subject—true angels.

A banker has to study what real bank notes look like in order to pick out the false ones. In the same way, it is vital that we gain a scriptural understanding of the real angelic realm. We need to know how to identify false angels and false spirituality in order not to be trapped into believing the lies of the enemy.

Angels—according to the Word of God

Satan does not bother to imitate anything false—he builds up his own world system by copying the real one. And angels are definitely real. Western, rationalistic people may find it hard to cope with the idea of spiritual beings that cannot be seen or heard, but the New Agers have their own version of the angelic realm. It is not one, however, that is submitted to God in obedience to the Lordship of Jesus Christ.

In Scripture, angels are a natural and real part of spiritual life. There are some three hundred references to angels in Scripture. One of them refers to the angels who came and ministered to Jesus in the wilderness following the ordeal of being tempted and tested by the ultimate false angel, Satan (see Matthew 4:11).

Before he was renamed Satan, Lucifer used to be part of the angelic hosts (see Isaiah 14:12). He was one of the highest angels in rank and authority, probably of similar rank and authority to the archangels Michael and Gabriel. In order to understand how to discern the work of the enemy, to be equipped to resist him at all times and to stand against his plans and schemes, we need to understand how real angels operate and serve God. There is a significant amount of information about this in scriptural accounts.

The demonic realm is opposed to the work of God; therefore, if we see how angels operate and function under God's control, we will understand something of how demons do the work of Satan. The demonic realms appear to be organized and deployed in much the same way as the heavenly angels.

The first chapter of Hebrews, which majors on the nature and character of Jesus as being greater than the angels, concludes with a question that the writer proceeds to answer immediately: "What are the angels, then? They are spirits who serve God and are sent by him to help those who are to receive salvation" (verse 14 GNT). In other words, angels are spirit beings whose present principal responsibility is to serve God by helping believers. That means they are on our side.

Only angels of the highest rank are named in Scripture. Michael, the archangel (or chief angel) and Gabriel (who appears to be the chief messenger angel) are the only ones whose names and roles are illustrated or described. There are, however, many references in the Bible to a heavenly order of spiritual beings. This implies that angels have varying degrees of power and authority.

Paul states that "God created everything in heaven and on earth, the seen and the unseen things, including spiritual powers, lords, rulers, and authorities" (Colossians 1:16 GNT; see also Ephesians 1:21; 1 Peter 3:22).

There are also references in Scripture to other angelic beings referred to as the cherubim (see Genesis 3:24; Ezekiel 10; Revelation 4:6–9) and the seraphim, who Isaiah saw during his life-changing experience of seeing into the presence of God and realizing the extent of his own uncleanliness (see Isaiah 6:1–8).

The Archangel Michael

There are two major references to Michael in Scripture. It is clear from these that Michael is a warrior angel. The first of these passages describes

Michael as "Israel's guardian angel" (Daniel 10:21 GNT). He is the one who is responsible for watching over the interests of God's chosen people.

The earlier part of Daniel 10 describes how the angel who was sent in answer to Daniel's prayer (presumably Gabriel, who had made previous visitations to Daniel) ran into heavy opposition and had to do battle with the "angel prince of the kingdom of Persia" (verse 13 GNT).

This angel prince was not an angel in the service of God, but rather a fallen angel who had joined Satan's rebellion against God. He had been stationed by Satan as a spiritual ruler over that nation. The battle was so severe that Gabriel had to send for reinforcements, and it was Michael who came to his aid. Regardless of how high in rank the prince of Persia was, he was no match for Michael.

The second major reference to Michael describes how he did battle with Lucifer in heaven and expelled him along with all the other angels who joined in the rebellion against God, including the angel prince of Persia. "He was hurled to the earth, and his angels with him" (Revelation 12:9).

When Michael, the mighty warrior angel who had already defeated all of the hosts of Satan (Lucifer), appeared on the scene over Persia, the outcome was a foregone conclusion. After the battle was over, Gabriel was then free to complete his task and meet with Daniel. Gabriel began his message by apologizing for the delay. Daniel had been fasting and praying for 21 days—exactly the same time span that it had taken for Gabriel to get through to him. None of us have any idea what may be happening in the spiritual realm when prayers seem to be slow in being answered.

The angel who appeared at the resurrection was undoubtedly a high warrior angel, if not Michael himself. First, he rolled the stone away. "His appearance was like lightning, and his clothes were white as snow," and when the Roman guards saw him, they "were so afraid that they trembled and became like dead men" (Matthew 28:3–4 GNT).

My team and I have, on occasion, been conscious of what could only have been angelic help during the process of ministering deliverance to people and setting them free from the powers of darkness that had gained influence in their lives.

Demonic powers hanging desperately on to their footholds in the person's life have screamed in fear at Scripture that describes angels.

And when we have prayed to the Lord to send angels to help us in accordance with Hebrews 1:14, the demons have sometimes cried out "No, not them!" There have also been occasions when the person being delivered has had his or her eyes opened to see into the supernatural and has described both the angels and the battle that ensued. This has always resulted in a mighty deliverance taking place.

The Archangel Gabriel

Gabriel appears to be the chief messenger angel commissioned by God to communicate directly with His people on exceptional occasions. Sometimes he even manifests to the individual involved. His usual initial pronouncement is "Do not be afraid" (Luke 1:30; 2:10). This is a comforting command for those who might otherwise be in a deep state of shock.

Gabriel interpreted a vision for Daniel (see Daniel 8) and brought him understanding on difficult matters (see Daniel 9). As previously mentioned, it is presumed that it was Gabriel who came in response to Daniel's prayer (see Daniel 10).

In the New Testament, Gabriel was entrusted with telling Zechariah that he was to be the father of John the Baptist (see Luke 1:11–20). He was also responsible for telling Mary that she was to be the mother of Jesus (see Luke 1:26–38). Clearly, these are major events in God's timetable that required an unmistakable visitation with the goal of leaving the recipient no doubt whatsoever that God has spoken.

There are numerous other instances in Scripture of messenger angels appearing to communicate with believers in this way. An angel appeared to Samson's mother, for example, to advise her that even though she was presently childless, she would conceive soon (see Judges 13:3).

In Genesis 18, two angels warned Abraham and his nephew, Lot, about the impending destruction of Sodom and Gomorrah. In Judges 6 an angel appeared to Gideon and commissioned him as the Lord's agent for the rescue of Israel from the Midianites. And in Acts 10 Cornelius saw a vision in which an angel of the Lord told him that his prayers had been answered.

Clearly, messenger angels have a strategic role in directing God's people and in answering their prayers. I suspect that God instructs angels to intervene and provide angelic guidance in response to our prayers more frequently than any of us might imagine.

Having begun our look at the angelic realms by finding out about the archangels Michael and Gabriel, we will look next at what Scripture tells us about all the other things that angels do.

SUMMARY

Angels are spiritual beings. They are servants of God and are sent by Him to help those who are receiving salvation. The chief archangels Michael and Gabriel have many other angels serving with them carrying out the commissions of God. Satan is a deceiver and seeks to imitate the angelic realm in order to deceive the world into worshiping him.

PRAYER

Thank You, Lord, for angels and for the times when, unknown to me, You have sent them to protect me. Help me to understand the reality of the angelic realms so that I will be able to discern those times when the enemy may try to deceive me with false ideas. In Jesus' name, Amen.

GOD'S PLAN FOR THE ANGELS

In our first study of the angelic realms, we began to gain understanding from Scripture about what is right and what is wrong in terms of the interaction between the angelic and human realms.

Hebrews 1:14 makes it very clear that God sends the angels "to serve those who will inherit salvation." That phrase means those who are already redeemed out of the hand of the enemy as well as those who have not yet received salvation.

In Matthew 18:10, Jesus makes specific reference to angels when talking about children. He refers to "their angels in heaven" and says that they "always see the face of my Father." This means that the angels take their instructions from Father God only. We see that God assigns guardian angels to humans and that the angels look continually to God for direction. They do not take their instructions from us. If fallen humans had authority over angels, we would be tempted to use them as a spiritual extension of our self-centered and sinful objectives. Angels, therefore, take their instructions from God alone.

The fact that God assigns angels to help us does not mean, however, that angels exist only to serve us. They were created by God originally to serve Him, and as part of their service to God, they can also be assigned to serve humankind. The emphasis of Scripture here is extremely important.

It is God who sends them—they are not available for us to use as some sort of spiritual toy.

More about Angels and the New Age

At this point we can begin to see the subtle difference emerging between a godly and scriptural understanding of the angelic realm and the distortions of the New Age and occult realms. If you look carefully at New Age books on angels you will see that the main thrust of their emphasis is always how you can tap into the angelic realm for your own benefit without ever referencing God. This is always wrong.

This emphasis is obvious from the titles of books such as: *How to Hear Your Angels, Introduction to Connecting, Working and Healing with Angels, Messages from Your Angels* and *Spiritual Guidance from Your Personal Celtic Angel*. In all of these cases the authors are deep into New Age philosophy. One author is described as running the foremost New Age business in his country, and another is described as a lifelong clairvoyant. Undiscerning people could be deceived easily into thinking these are mainstream Christian titles. Since the Bible talks about angels, they must be okay.

The reason people buy such books is that they are looking for spiritual answers to the cries of their hearts. Rather than going to the source of life, they are pointed by Satan in a different direction. He fills the spiritual vacuum with his version of spiritual reality. This will always lead people into deception. Satan focuses on the vulnerable and hurting. He leads them into greater bondage that has the effect of isolating them from the real spiritual answers that are found only in Jesus.

Because this is important, let me emphasize afresh the fact that at no place in the Bible is it ever suggested we should initiate contact with the angels and start using them for our own purposes, even if that purpose might seem to be good. When people do that, they will always be dabbling in the murky supernatural realms of the New Age and occult worlds.

Angels are deployed by God, not by man. Yes, we can ask God to send His angels, and we might even have some remarkable encounters with real angels as a result—there are many such accounts within Scripture and within Christian history—but that does not give us license to go beyond God's boundaries of safety for His people.

The simple fact is that when people start dabbling in New Age and occult angelic realms, they are not dealing with angels, but rather with demonic beings. These demonic beings are in the service of the enemy and are masquerading as angels of light. Not surprisingly, the concept of sin (as opposed to what New Agers might perceive as right and wrong) is unknown in New Age philosophies. Demons are not going to make people aware of the absolutes of the Almighty or of the real problems within their hearts.

For all of the above reasons, it is vital that we gain a solid understanding from Scripture of how the angels of God operate. We must be able to discern the difference between the real and the false. Let's take our study of angels a little deeper and put down some solid scriptural guidelines for understanding the angelic realms. But before we do so, there is one more topic I need to mention.

False Angels and the Church

One of Satan's primary means of undermining the spiritual authority of God's people in the Body of Christ is to make them tolerant of things that look as though they might be good but in reality are not. If people have not been trained in the foundational truths of the Word of God that we are working carefully through, it becomes very easy to import New Age angelic beliefs and practices, and even occult practices, into the Church without realizing that it is wrong.

Sometimes people are deceived by false beliefs because they seek angels to fill their spiritual needs. Satan has done a good job of making angels seem more relational or cuddly than God, who they may see as remote and cold. The answer is not for them to take comfort in false beliefs, but to seek God's healing for their relationships with Him.

In his letter to the Thessalonians, Paul said,

> The coming of the lawless one will be in accordance with how Satan works. He will use all sorts of displays of power through signs and wonders that serve the lie, and all the ways that wickedness deceives those who are perishing.
>
> 2 Thessalonians 2:9–10

Paul also warned Timothy about such things when he said that "some will abandon the faith and follow deceiving spirits and things taught by demons" (1 Timothy 4:1). Paul was speaking about people who were inside the Church—not outside of it. You cannot abandon a faith that you have never had. We need to be on our guard not to allow a doctrine of demons to take root in the belief system of the Church simply because it seems okay.

Ministering Angels

Earlier we identified two primary categories of angelic beings—the warrior angels under Michael and the messenger angels under Gabriel. Another major category of angels is the ministering angel. Scripture does not tell us the name of their archangel, or ruling angel, but of all the angelic beings, the ministering angels are probably the ones who have given humans the most attention through their Christian journeys. Most of us will have been unaware of the angelic agency involved, but many of us will be able to remember times when it has seemed as though we were being carried through tough times in ways that were beyond our control.

This is what happened to Jesus immediately after His forty days of fasting and prayer in the wilderness. This was the period during which Satan had tested him severely. Matthew said that "angels came and attended him" (Matthew 4:11). In 1 Kings 19 an angel is seen providing sustenance for Elijah in the wilderness. It seems that ministering angels have a specific purpose of bringing encouragement, personal blessing and provision to God's children. There are many ways in which they function.

We face much spiritual opposition as Christians. Angels play a strategic role in encouraging us and lifting our spirits during these times of opposition. I am reminded of the story in John Bunyan's *Pilgrim's Progress* when Christian, the main character, was at the house of the Interpreter. He was amazed at a fire that continued to burn brightly in spite of cold water being poured continuously on it. The key was the man (who was really an angel) on the other side of the fire who was pouring on oil that kept the fire burning in spite of the water.

On one occasion when I was teaching, I experienced a particularly heavy anointing of the Holy Spirit. God was ministering deeply into people's lives. After the meeting, one of those present said that halfway through the teaching her eyes had been opened to the supernatural realm, and she had seen a ring of angels all around me. One by one the angels came forward and poured oil into me to give out to the people. She said that after each such incident I would start teaching something new and relevant to the people present.

It was a very humbling experience to hear this lady's account of what she saw, and it is an experience in which I rejoice. I was completely unaware of what was happening in the angelic realm, but I was aware that it seemed as though the teaching was flowing particularly easily and powerfully that night. I was teaching things that I had definitely not put into my notes.

What Else Do Angels Do?

In addition to the three broad categories of angels described above—warrior angels, messenger angels and ministering angels—we can gather from Scripture a number of other aspects of the character of angels and understand something of the various roles they fill.

1. *They always worship God* (see Revelation 5:11–14). Worship, adoration, submission and obedience are all different facets of the same thing. Whatever we worship will always have the primary influence over our hearts (see Matthew 6:21). In contrast to the fallen angels who rebelled against God, the choice of the angelic realms to be in total submission to the worship of God and Jesus ensures that their conduct will always be as servants of the Most High God. A truly loyal servant would never want to usurp the authority of his master.

2. *They rejoice in the works of God* (see Job 38:7). Within any love-based family, there is always a sense of rejoicing and personal thrill when a member of the family does something special. As a child, I thought that my dad and mom were the best in the world. I thought it was wonderful when Dad did something special, like winning a photography competition in a national newspaper. I celebrated when my older brother did something special in his career. Equally, they all rejoiced when I did something good. I blossomed

under the encouragement of their approval. Rejoicing in the things members of the family do is part of what love is all about. When the angels rejoice in the works of God, they are making a profound statement about the love they have for God and for everything He is and does.

3. *They always execute God's will* (see Psalm 103:20). Angels never hesitate or resist doing the will of God. Their sole existence is to love and serve Almighty God. When He asks them to do something, obedience is instant. They do not question the wisdom of God. They submit to it.

4. *They have influence over the affairs of nations* (see Daniel 10; 11:1; 12:1). Angels can be given positions of delegated authority by God where, in submission to Him, they carry out His plans and purposes in the spiritual realms. Their areas of authority can be small or large according to the instructions they have been given. When we choose to submit our will to the will of God, it is at that point, I believe, that God allocates angelic beings to serve Him. By serving us, they are really serving God. If we do not want to serve God, then we do not. It seems that the angels do not have the same authority. I believe that is because of the free will that God gave to humans in the first place.

5. *They watch over the interests of churches* (see Revelation 2–5). In Revelation 2 and 3 there are seven letters written by Jesus and recorded by John that were sent to seven churches in Asia Minor. Each letter begins with the words "to the angel of the church." Just as an angel may be given authority to serve God over an area or a region, they can also be given authority to serve God over churches and Christian ministries. The extent to which they are able to help us in our churches is, I believe, related directly to whether or not we want Jesus to be Lord of the church. Sadly, there are many churches that have become man-centered religious clubs with no desire for Jesus to be Lord. It is doubtful an angel would be able to protect the people of a church in that kind of situation. In the letter to the church at Ephesus, God said that unless the people repented of falling away from their first love, their lampstands would

be removed. Perhaps the lampstand represents God's angel over the church. Whatever it means, it was certainly a serious implication.

6. *They assist and protect believers* (see Hebrews 1:14; 1 Kings 19:5). Elijah was supported and ministered to by an angel who brought food to him. There are many stories of extraordinary and sometimes miraculous things that happen for God's people when they seek to walk in God's ways. Within Ellel Ministries we have experienced many such instances that could be understood only as angelic intervention. On one occasion when I was driving my car, the driver's door suddenly flew wide open. I took my foot off the accelerator and applied the brake while I tried to grab the door handle. The car stopped suddenly. A fraction of a second later a young child on a tricycle came down a hill and shot out into the traffic at the exact spot I would have been had the door not flown open. Undoubtedly, I would have killed that child. I wonder who opened the door of my car to make me slow down?

7. *They are used to punish God's enemies* (see Acts 12:23; 2 Samuel 24:16; Isaiah 37:36). There are many examples in the Scriptures when angels were used by God to carry out grave judgements on those who stood in opposition to the people of God. In Acts 12:23, Herod took upon himself the glory of the people and made himself out to be God. He was struck down immediately by an angel and died. Perhaps that is also what happened to Ananias and Sapphira when they cheated on God over their giving (see Acts 5:1–11). If we could see behind the scenes in all the events of history, I think we would all be amazed to see the extent to which angels were acting in judgement on behalf of God.

8. *They perform extraordinary acts on behalf of God's people* (see Acts 12:6–10; Daniel 6:22; Exodus 23:20–23). I love the story in Daniel 6 about how he was protected when he was in the den of lions. It says that because Daniel was innocent of any wrong before God, He had sent His angel to shut the mouths of the lions. This was an extraordinary act. Humans kept the lions hungry so that they would devour quickly any prisoner given to them for execution.

9. *They minister personally to each one of God's children* (see Matthew 18:10). This passage speaks about each one of God's children personally having an angel who takes its instructions from the face of God. What comfort this brings to know that God, in His loving mercy, has provided us with angelic support. Another very important Scripture that provides great encouragement to all believers is, "For he will command his angels concerning you to guard you in all your ways; they will lift you up in their hands, so that you will not strike your foot against a stone" (Psalm 91:11–12). It is clear from this that it is God who commands the angels and not us. As long as we do not start treating our angel (or angels) as our own spiritual servant independent of the will and instructions of God, I believe that God wants to bless and encourage each one of us with the provision of angelic support.

Psalm 91:4 says that God will "cover you with his feathers," and mentions that we are "under his wings." Some have said that this may be referring to the wings of a guardian angel who is under the authority of God. This may be the case, because angels truly are under God's authority. Ultimately, it does not matter how God affords us His protection. What really matters is that God's Word tells us that He will keep us from falling and that "his faithfulness will be your shield and rampart" (Psalm 91:4).

Now that we have an understanding of what Scripture tells us about the angels of God who are under His command, we are better equipped to look at how the enemy's dark angels can operate. We should be more prepared to differentiate between the things that are of God and those that are not.

SUMMARY

The angels of God are spiritual beings who are His servants. They worship and serve Him constantly. The angels are deployed by a loving God to carry out His will and purposes, both in the world in general and in our lives.

PRAYER

Thank You, Lord, for the provision of angelic beings to love and serve You in this fallen world. Thank you that they act in my best interests according to Your instructions. Lord, as I choose to love and serve You in every way I can, I ask that You provide me the loving protection I need to carry out Your will in my life. In Jesus' name, Amen.

LUCIFER—AND HIS FALL FROM HEAVEN

After looking at the positions and work of the angels, we are now going to explore the reality behind all of the deceptive powers that are at work in the world. These powers try to lead humankind away from the living God and cause people to worship a false God.

You may be thinking, *Why do I need to know about this? I would rather just learn about God.* If that is how you feel, I understand. Who wants to spend time studying falsehood when there is so much truth we need to know? But if we do not know our enemy, we run the risk of falling into his traps and coming under his influence and authority. Paul was careful to explain to the Corinthians that he was not unaware of Satan's schemes because he had no desire to be outwitted by the enemy (see 2 Corinthians 2:11).

I enjoy fly-fishing for salmon. Most years I will come back from a vacation in Scotland with a number of salmon to put in my freezer. The only reason those salmon are in my freezer is because I deceived them. With a small artificial fly, I tempt the salmon to snap at the bait. Ten minutes later, the salmon is on the bank of the river and headed for my freezer. If that salmon had been more discerning and had seen what was passing in front of it, it would not have been tempted and hooked.

Satan is like the very best salmon fisherman. He knows exactly what sort of fly to use to tempt us, and he does everything he can to make us snap at his offers. Once he has caught us, he will try to extract us from the river of life and place us in his freezer. It is vital that we understand his methods and his ways so that we can learn how to avoid them.

Some theologians find it amusing that people like you and me believe that Satan exists. But the world also likes to make fun of people who believe that what Jesus said was true and that the Bible is the Word of God.

When commenting on the mess the world is in, Ronald Knox, who was a very astute and learned Anglican and then Roman Catholic priest at the beginning of the twentieth century said, "It is so stupid of modern civilization to have given up believing in the devil, when he is the only explanation of it!"[1]

Jesus had personal encounters with Satan. If we are to dismiss Satan as being a figment of religious imagination, we would also have to dismiss Jesus as being the embodiment of truth. To believe that Satan does not exist would mean that we would have to believe that Jesus was deluded and wrong.

I have seen thousands of people released from the bondage of Satan's control. Their lives were transformed completely as a result. I have no doubt that Satan is real.

Archibald Brown, who was a Baptist minister from England, said, "The existence of the Devil is so clearly taught in the Bible that to doubt it is to doubt the Bible itself."[2]

Lucifer's Fall

In our study of the angelic realms thus far, we have looked at two of the archangels referred to by name in Scripture: Michael and Gabriel. The third one who is named was referred to originally as Lucifer. We know him better as Satan, for that is his usual name throughout Scripture. As we will see later, many other names are also used to describe his character.

The name *Satan* means simply "adversary" or "one who opposes." Satan is God's adversary, and he has opposed God since the moment he chose to use his free will to rebel against the Almighty. His original name, Lucifer, which can be translated as "morning star," "day star," "son of the morning" or "the bringer of light," is referenced in Isaiah 14:12.

Satan is a fallen angel who sought to elevate himself above his status. As an archangel, he would have been an awesome, magnificent, splendid and very beautiful creation of God. It is probable that Lucifer was one of the highest of angels.

Isaiah said that Israel would one day take up a taunt against the king of Babylon (see Isaiah 14:3–15). Most commentators interpret this passage to be describing the origin of Satan who vowed to make himself like the Most High.

> You said in your heart, "I will ascend to the heavens; I will raise my throne above the stars of God; I will sit enthroned on the mount of assembly, on the utmost heights of Mount Zaphon. I will ascend above the tops of the clouds; I will make myself like the Most High."
>
> Isaiah 14:13–14

For a little further reading on this topic, look up Ezekiel 28:12–17. This is a similar passage in which the prophet addresses the spiritual power behind the king of Tyre.

Scripture does not tell us if there was anything else behind Satan's rebellion. We know that he chose to use his free will to try to overthrow the Almighty who had made him in the first place. He wanted to take the worship of heaven for himself. God took notice of what was going on in the heart of Lucifer. It would have been unacceptable for the heavenly realms to remain polluted by the sin of rebellion. This left God with no option but to summon Michael and give him orders to gather together all of his warrior angels and go to war. There was no way that this angel who had chosen to use his free will to oppose his Creator could be allowed to remain in heaven.

Revelation 12 describes the ensuing battle in heaven when Michael, who was the archangel and chief warrior angel, was deployed with his warrior forces against Lucifer and his rebellious angels. "The great dragon was hurled down—that ancient serpent called the devil, or Satan, who leads the whole world astray. He was hurled to the earth, and his angels with him" (Revelation 12:9). Earlier in this passage the author mentions a third of the stars being swept down to earth (see Revelation 12:4). This is understood generally to mean that a third of the heavenly host responded to Lucifer's beguiling words and was thrown out of heaven with him.

From then on he was no longer called *Lucifer*, which means "bringer of light." He was renamed Satan and was now God's adversary who would for evermore be hostile to Him and oppose His will.

Jesus added His own personal, eyewitness testimony to the accounts of Satan's expulsion from heaven. When talking to the 72 who had returned full of joy because they found that the demons were subject to their commands, Jesus put their exuberance into a right context (see Luke 10). He reminded them that He had all power and authority in the first place.

Jesus was in heaven exercising His own authority when Satan was expelled. He had the power and authority to expel Satan from heaven, but He also has the authority to delegate His power to those He chooses on earth. John tells us that those "he gave the right to become children of God" are those who "receive him, to those who believed in his name" (John 1:12).

As children of God we have delegated rights. Therefore, Jesus was able to say to the 72 that He had given them authority over "snakes and scorpions and to overcome all the power of the enemy" (Luke 10:19). Jesus linked His authority to cast Satan out of heaven with the authority He had given the disciples to cast servants of Satan (demons) out of people.

Jesus felt it was necessary, however, to remind them that it was far more important that they rejoice because their names were written in heaven rather than rejoicing because they had authority over demons. They had power and authority over the enemy because their names were written in heaven (see Luke 10:20). This is a serious reminder to all of those who want to be obedient to the commission to cast out demons.

Satan and all his rebellious angels were thrown down to earth. He took residence here and began to exercise his own spiritual authority. This is a domain that, for the time being, is under his control. Jesus referred to Satan as the "prince of this world" or "ruler of this world" (John 12:31 NIV, GNT). Paul stated that the "god of this age has blinded the minds of unbelievers" (2 Corinthians 4:4). Both Jesus and Paul recognized the present position that Satan holds in the hierarchy of earth's spiritual powers. We err badly if we are dismissive of the reality of Satan, of his kingdom, of his power or of his authority.

I am not advocating that we should pay him any respect in the sense of offering homage. God the Father has rescued believers "from the dominion of darkness and brought us into the kingdom of the Son he loves"

(Colossians 1:13). But we place ourselves in grave danger if we are not aware of the wiles of the enemy or if we do not recognize what power and authority he has. As Paul instructs us, "Our struggle is not against flesh and blood, but against the rulers, against the authorities, against the powers of this dark world and against the spiritual forces of evil in the heavenly realms" (Ephesians 6:12).

One of Satan's temptations to Jesus in the wilderness was the offer of the world on a plate.

> The devil led him up to a high place and showed him in an instant all the kingdoms of the world. And he said to him, "I will give you all their authority and splendor; it has been given to me, and I can give it to anyone I want to. If you worship me, it will all be yours."
>
> Luke 4:5–7

When Satan said that the kingdoms of the world had been handed over to him, he was referring to what happened in the Fall. Man, through his sinful choice, handed over the authority God had given him to Satan. We will be looking at that important event more carefully later on our journey.

The amazing thing about the temptation of Jesus was that He did not deny that Satan had the right to make Him such an offer. Jesus could have accepted the offer, but the price would have been too high. It would have meant a total role reversal with Jesus bowing down to Satan instead of every knee bowing to Jesus. Paul declared every knee will bow to Jesus—that includes Satan's (see Philippians 2:5–11).

Ultimately, the force of this temptation was to offer Jesus the chance to win back the world without going to the cross. It was an attractive proposition on the surface. There are many people who would like to achieve great spiritual objectives and make a name for themselves without visiting the cross of Calvary. But Jesus knew that without the cross there would be no eternal hope for redeemed sinners. He confronted Satan with a quote from the book of Deuteronomy: "It is written: 'Worship the Lord your God and serve him only'" (Luke 4:8).

Understanding the position that Satan holds currently in this world aids us considerably in our understanding of the incarnation, death and resurrection of Jesus. Jesus established the eternal and unique precedent of independence from the power and grip of Satan. He lived for 33 years in a world that was under the control of Satan, but He did not sin. If Jesus had sinned even once, His mission would have failed.

The wonder of salvation is that we are the ones who benefit from His sinlessness. When Christ is in us (after we have been born again of His Spirit), we are in the same position before God that Jesus was, for our sin is covered by His glory. The shed blood of Jesus through His sacrifice on the cross is sufficient, and we are redeemed out of the hand of the devil. What amazing grace!

William Gurnall's Great Book

We are going to end this stage of our journey to freedom with a quote from William Gurnall's great book. Gurnall was a seventeenth-century Englishman, a scholar of Cambridge University and the rector of the parish church at Lavenham in Suffolk. He died in 1679. Before he died, his great book on the Christian's armor against the work of Satan had been printed in six different editions.

John Newton, the converted slave trader, said that if he was confined to one book besides the Bible, Gurnall's *The Christian in Complete Armour* would be his choice. Spurgeon, the great nineteenth-century preacher, said, "Gurnall's work is peerless and priceless; every line full of wisdom . . . the best thought-breeder in all our library."[3]

If you are still wondering why it is necessary for us to spend time in finding out about Satan and how he operates in this fallen world, then listen to these words from Gurnall's book:

> If Satan can entice you to sin for what he assures you is a worthy prize, you are in serious trouble, but the worst is yet to come. Once he has you sitting at his table, he will begin in earnest to teach you the tricks of his trade. This diabolical dealer will show you how to slip your sins under the table, telling you no one—not even God—will see. He has been teaching this trick since Adam, who thought he could hide behind a fig leaf. What did Joseph's brothers do when they had left him for dead but hide their deed under the coat they had bloodied? And how did Potiphar's wife respond when Joseph turned away from her adulterous gaze? She hid her sin (again in his coat) and accused him of her own wickedness.

Beware of playing such games of chance with God. No coat is large enough to hide your sin; no hand is quick enough to slip it under the table and miss the all-seeing eye of God. If He does not call you to account for it in this life, you can be sure you will answer for it in the next.

There are many dangers of playing the devil's games, but an obvious one is that you may come to like them. With William Gurnall's words in our minds, let us prepare ourselves to know our enemy and be equipped to serve the living God.

SUMMARY

Lucifer was created by God as a very high angel with enormous power and authority in the heavenly realms. When he rebelled against God, Michael cast him and all the other rebellious angels out of heaven to earth. He is now called Satan and continues to oppose God and the people of God. In order to overcome him in our daily Christian walk, we need to understand his tactics and learn to withstand his attacks on our lives.

PRAYER

Thank You, Jesus, that You resisted every one of Satan's attacks and that he had no hold over You. Thank You that Your sinlessness is my only hope of eternal glory with Father God in heaven. Help me, Lord, to learn to resist the enemy and serve You only all of my days. In Jesus' name, Amen.

FROM **LUCIFER** TO **SATAN**

Even the world's greatest dramatist, William Shakespeare, knew a thing or two about the devil and his ways. In *Hamlet* he said, "The devil hath power to assume a pleasing shape."[1] And in *The Merchant of Venice* he wrote, "The devil can cite Scripture for his purpose."[2] There are many, many quotes from Shakespeare that show what a depth of scriptural knowledge he had.

Both of Shakespeare's sayings above are profound in their truthfulness. If temptations did not seem appealing, no one would be interested in them. Satan is no fool. He does not show us the consequences of falling into sin. We discover them afterward when it is too late. It sometimes seems as though the devil sends his demons to Bible school—they seem to know Scripture so well. They can quote passages out of context and mislead people into thinking certain actions are supported by the Word of God.

An atheist can read the Bible and know every word that is in it, but that does not make him a believer. It is a heart transformed by the living presence of the Lord Jesus that can understand the significance of those words.

Sigmund Freud was the man who is credited largely with laying the foundation stone of modern psychology and psychiatry. He knew what was in the Bible, but he was ignorant of the truth it contained. This is what he said: "Demons do not exist any more than the gods do, being only the products of the psychic activity of man."[3]

With such a spiritual foundation for much of modern psychiatric practice, it is not surprising that, in general, psychiatry does not have answers for the spiritual conditions that beset the minds of humankind. I thank God for the chemical discoveries that have helped psychiatrists be able to control many of the presenting psychological conditions that people experience. While it is a good thing to control their distressing symptoms, people need to be healed of the deep inner issues that gave rise to the symptoms.

Only a spiritual answer can resolve a spiritual problem. My experience in ministry has taught me that people's lives can be transformed only by having solid spiritual foundations and loving obedience to the truths of God's Word. Sometimes people need to continue with the medication that is keeping them afloat while they are working through the spiritual issues. Being healed spiritually is what will bring them ultimately to a place of freedom from the need for prescribed drugs. It is important that the doctor who put them on medication can see when there is no longer a need for the medication. When that healing has taken place, medication can be reduced or stopped.

I have not changed my belief that people need to know Jesus as savior, healer and deliverer. We need to know Him in every aspect of His being. In the past, however, I might have been too hasty in wanting to rush to minister to people. As a result, I sometimes made the mistake of assuming people were in a different place before God than they were.

I wish now I had taken more time with individuals to make sure the foundational truths were anchored securely in their lives before trying to minister healing and deliverance to them if they had inadequate foundations. This is why I am passionate about people reading through JOURNEY TO FREEDOM.

What Is Satan Really Like?

Most of us have been called by several different names at different stages of our lives. We all have the names we were given by our parents, but we are often called by affectionate personal names or nicknames. These are sometimes used as a description of the sort of person that we are. Such names can be either complimentary or uncomplimentary, and they are often descriptions or distortions of some aspect of our character or physique.

Names in the Bible have enormous significance. There are, for example, over 200 different names for God used throughout Scripture. Each one of them shows us something different and special about His character. Each name opens up a door of understanding about the character and nature of God. Names such as:

- The Lord Almighty
- The Lord Who Provides
- The Lord Who Heals
- The Lord Who Sanctifies
- The Lord Our Peace
- The Lord Our Righteousness
- The Lord Our Shepherd
- The Lord of Hosts
- The Lord Everlasting
- The Lord Who Sees

All the names ascribed to God are names of blessing for God's people. In contrast, when we see the names that are used in Scripture to describe Satan, we discover that those names describe what he has done to bring curses on the human race. They express his nature. They tell us what he is really like.

Regardless of how glossy the wrappings around the temptations Satan puts in front of us may be, his real character will be exposed eventually. In the extraordinary film *Chitty Chitty Bang Bang*, the obnoxious child collector tricks children into getting in a decorated cart that offers all sorts of fancy and exciting attractions. The moment the children enter the cart, however, iron gates slam shut behind them, and they find themselves not inside a children's wonderland but in a prison on wheels that rushes them off to the dungeons.

Satan is a bit like that with his temptations. People become victims of their own desires when the gates slam shut. They find out what the real character of Satan is only when they are trapped. We can give thanks that, even then, there is One who is able to deliver us out of the hands of the enemy—it is the Lord Jesus. Looking through Scripture for the names of Satan and their meanings alerts us to his real character. The names teach us about the filth, depravity and evil intent of Satan, the prince of demons.

- Abaddon (or Apollyon the Destroyer)—Revelation 9:11
- Accuser of the Brethren—Revelation 12:10
- Adversary—1 Peter 5:8
- Angel of Light—2 Corinthians 11:14
- Antichrist—1 John 4:3
- Beelzebul (dung god)—Matthew 12:24, 27
- Belial (worthless or perverse)—2 Corinthians 6:15
- Condemner—1 Timothy 3:6
- Deceiver—Revelation 12:9
- Devil (accuser, slanderer)—Matthew 4:1
- Dragon—Revelation 12
- Enemy—Matthew 13:39
- Evil One—Matthew 13:19
- God of This World—2 Corinthians 4:4
- King of the Abyss—Revelation 9:11
- Liar and Father of Lies—John 8:44
- Lucifer—Isaiah 14:12
- Murderer—John 8:44
- Oppressor—Acts 10:38
- Prince of the Power of the Air—Ephesians 2:2
- Roaring Lion—1 Peter 5:8
- Ruler of the Demons—Matthew 12:24
- Ruler of the World—John 12:31
- Satan—Matthew 4:10; Zechariah 3:1

- Serpent—Genesis 3:1; Revelation 12:9
- Tempter—Matthew 4:3
- Thief—John 10:10
- Wolf—John 10:12

Satan's Ultimate Objectives

Satan has always been in rebellion against God, and he has sought to attract worship to himself and turn people away from God. His tactics have not changed since the beginning of time. He still uses age-old, well-tried temptations that have led men and women into sin generation after generation.

Pride, power, sex, wealth or false religion is at the heart of most of his tactics, and in most cases they are dressed up subtly enough for public consumption. For fallen men and women, greed, self-pleasing and lust for power create fertile grounds in which Satan can sow his seeds of rebellion. In serving any false gods, people are bowing their knees unwittingly to Satan. He does not mind that people are ignorant of what they are really doing.

Deception is his stock in trade. Once people have been deceived and have taken the bait, the progression of temptations that can follow is endless. James' advice to "resist the devil" is effective practical guidance for everyday living (James 4:7). If we do not resist, we lay our lives wide open to the demonic. Peter said something very similar when he told us "be alert and of sober mind . . . resist him, standing firm in the faith" (1 Peter 5:8–9).

Satan hates to see people live long, fulfilled lives in the service of God. The sooner a person's life is terminated, the less opportunity there is for salvation to be accepted. At a recent Christian gathering, I asked the body of Christians present how many of them had ever contemplated suicide, however fleetingly. Over 60 percent of them admitted to having had suicidal thoughts. The progression to self-destruction is down a well-worn path that begins with deception.

Once people have believed the deceptive lie that they are worthless, useless or rubbish, which is in direct contradiction to the truth of God's Word (see Psalm 139), they become vulnerable to being deceived. Conflict arises between our God-given sensitivities to the truth of the Lord and the feelings and beliefs by which we are gripped.

Distress is the next stage of the downward spiral, with the need for heavier medication to keep individuals on an even keel. At this point the person's life is so controlled by their conditions and the consequential medications that life begins to lose its purpose.

For some, critical despair sets in. This is but a hair's breadth away from suicide attempts. Satan is a filthy fighter. He hates God so much that he will stop at nothing to destroy those God created. How different he is from God, who loved people so much that He sent His Son to die for them (see John 3:16). Satan has never forgotten how he was defeated by Jesus at Calvary. That is why he works to the limits of his capacity to keep people from finding out the truth, which is that in the name of Jesus they can be set free. He works overtime to discredit the ministry of deliverance as well as those who are working to bring healing through deliverance to God's people.

Evangelism, healing and deliverance are urgent commissions to be fulfilled by the Church of Jesus Christ. They are not optional extras that we might choose to practice occasionally. If we cease from evangelism, we cease from following Jesus. If we fail to minister healing and deliverance, we leave people in a bondage from which Jesus died to set them free. We also ignore a command that Jesus gave to the Church within the Great Commission (see Matthew 28:18–20).

God and Satan—the Key Differences

Before moving on, it is worth noting five significant contrasts between Satan and God.

1. *God is Creator.* Satan is a created being (see Ezekiel 28:13–15).
2. *God is omnipresent—present at all times and in all places.* Satan is limited in both time and location (see Job 1:6–7). He can only carry out his work through the agency of demons and evil spirits who are under his command.
3. *God is omniscient—there is nothing that He does not know.* Satan and his forces are limited in knowledge (see Acts 19:15).

4. *God is omnipotent—His power is unlimited.* Satan's power is limited and restricted within the confines that God has allowed (see Job 1:6–12).

5. *God is eternal—there is no beginning or ending to God's Kingdom.* Satan's time is limited. One day Jesus is coming again as King of kings and Lord of lords (see Revelation 19:16). At that time, Satan's rule and reign will come to an end and the scenario of Revelation will commence. Hallelujah! Satan and his demons know the Scriptures well. The prophetic words in the Bible that tell of the end for Satan and all of his fallen angels are feared and hated by the demonic powers.

Revelation 20:7–15, Hebrews 2:14–15 and Matthew 25:41–46 are all very encouraging sections of Scripture for God's people. From experience, I can assure you that quoting these passages of Scripture out loud is the most effective method for undermining the rights of demonic powers. Demons know the truth and authority of these passages. We, as Christians, need to know them as well.

In the next stage, we will look at how Satan's kingdom operates, and we will start to equip ourselves to understand the ways of the enemy. That way we can strengthen ourselves and be on our guard against all the tricks of the great deceiver. We do not need to be depressed by the works of the enemy. We can rejoice in who we are in Christ. Here are some encouraging words for you from a sixteenth-century monk, John of the Cross: "The devil fears a soul united to God as he does God Himself."[4] Rejoice—the devil is afraid of you!

SUMMARY

The reality of Satan is evident in all the works of darkness that we see across the world. The names of Satan describe his nature and his character, but the enemy fears those who are joined to Christ. No matter what the enemy throws at you, you are secure if you remain united with Jesus.

PRAYER

Thank You, Lord, that You resisted all the temptations of the enemy and that You remained in authority over him throughout Your life. Thank You that Your victory has shown me the way of salvation and victory over the evil one. Help me to recognize his temptations and resist him at all times. In Jesus' name, Amen.

SATAN'S POWER AND **AUTHORITY**

A little later, we will be looking in more detail at the consequences of the Fall, what happened when man chose to agree with Satan, and what happened when he discovered that he had come under Satan's authority.

We saw from Scripture some of the names of Satan that are used in the Bible to describe his character and nature. I have known believers to be more frightened of the devil than they should be. This is true especially when they learn that he is our adversary.

But be encouraged by Charles Spurgeon's view on this—he is *comforted* by the fact that Satan is our adversary. This is what he said:

> There is something, however, very comforting in the thought that [the devil] is our adversary—I would sooner have him for an adversary than for a friend! O my Soul, it were dread work with you if Satan were a friend of yours, for then with him you must forever dwell in darkness and in the deeps—shut out from the friendship of God! But to have Satan for an adversary is a comfortable omen, for it looks as if God were our Friend, and so far let us be comforted in this matter.[1]

Yes, we do need to recognize he has power and authority and that he is the god of this world. We need to be careful that we do not give him rights in our lives by treading on his territory. But we have nothing to fear, for Jesus said, "Take heart! I have overcome the world" (John 16:33).

Satan's Kingdom

Satan reigns as the ruler of this world only because man gave him that position. Authority over planet earth was given originally to man, but man gave it away. Instead of humankind ruling the world under God, Satan became the ruler of the world in rebellion against God.

Even though Satan is described correctly in Scripture as the ruler, prince or god of this world (see John 12:31; John 14:30; 2 Corinthians 4:4) that does not mean by any stretch of the imagination that he has powers equal to God's power. Satan is not equal and opposite of God. That is the heresy of dualism. Satan is a created being who fell from his place in glory. He is not omnipotent, omniscient or omnipresent. He would love nothing more than for people to believe that he is all three and in a superior position to the Almighty. Satan's primary sin in the heavenly realm was pride (see Isaiah 14:12–15), and he has not changed in his nature. This particular leopard will never change his spots.

As a created being, Satan is limited by location (see Job 1:6–7). He tries to give the appearance of omnipresence by letting people think that the demonic powers that are encountered in different parts of the world are Satan himself. But Satan needs his army of demonic helpers to create and maintain this illusion of omnipresence. Without them he could have little influence across the world.

As a high angel, Satan must have had considerable power before he was thrown out of heaven. His power is not a power that can be trifled with or treated lightly—but he is not omnipotent (see Job 1:6–12). When he was thrown out of heaven, he kept his power but lost his realm of authority in which to use it. He was able to regain authority to use it by taking over the domain that God had first given to man.

The way Satan can add to his power is only by tempting man into doing things his way. When sinfulness becomes more widespread, it increases the power at Satan's disposal. But do not be alarmed; remember that Jesus said, "All authority in heaven and on earth has been given to me" (Matthew 28:18). No matter how much Satan might want to display his power,

God's authority and omnipotent power is always higher than anything Satan can muster.

Satan's knowledge is also limited—he is not omniscient (see Acts 19:15). He depends on the knowledge gathered by his demonic agents to discover what is happening around the world. He does not know the secret things that God has yet to reveal. Amos 3:7 talks about God "revealing his plan to his servants the prophets" and not to anyone else.

I believe the things that God reveals to His servants should remain secret until the right time for them to be made public. There have been many things over the years that God has shown me prophetically about the work of Ellel Ministries that I knew He required me to keep secret until their times of fulfillment.

If secret things are exposed to the world ahead of time, it can give the enemy an opportunity to undermine and oppose the things of God and obstruct the purposes of God. Keeping one's battle plans secret is the number-one rule of military engagement. Make no mistake, the Body of Christ is at war, and the enemy of souls is trying constantly to upset the battle plans of the Church. These teachings on the tactics of the enemy are to provide you with knowledge and insight to hold in your heart. They are not here to make you feel paranoid or subject to more fearful bondage.

While I do not believe the enemy can have access to the secret place of communion that all of us should have with God in our spirit, he does have an absolute right to know about anything we do that is ungodly. We can have no protection against the enemy there. Once we open the door to a particular area of sin, the enemy knows all about it (see Genesis 4:7). He can come knocking on that same door again and again. He tries to turn a one-off sinful experience into a well-worn pathway that turns eventually into a rut from which we cannot get out.

I once saw a road sign at the beginning of a particularly bad rural road that said, "Choose your rut carefully—you will be in it for the next 25 miles." Ruts are like that. Once you are in them, it is very hard to get out of them. Sinful life patterns are much the same. It is better not to get into them in the first place.

Satan's kingdom is a powerful kingdom, but it is a kingdom with severe limitations. Satan does try to deceive people into thinking he is an alternative god. Once people have swallowed such lies, they become wide open to the demonic powers. These powers can hold them under the bondage of this false belief. His reign as king of this world is extended only by a hierarchy of demonic power. It is likely that the angels who fell with him from heaven and who were already in the higher echelons of angelic authority have now taken up positions as princes over nations under Satan's world system.

For the time being, Satan is god of this world. But his time and his various abilities are limited. He is not worthy of our worship, but he continues to deceive much of the world into following after him. They do not always know they are worshiping Satan when they are doing the works of darkness. Satan does, nevertheless, receive that worship, and he benefits from the added power it gives him. Christians can have victory over him and his forces in the name of Jesus, but they must be on their guard constantly. As Peter says, "Your adversary, the devil, prowls around like a roaring lion, seeking someone to devour" (1 Peter 5:8 NASB).

The Powers of Darkness

We have already seen how one of the ways Satan is referred to in Scripture is as "ruler of the kingdom of the air" (Ephesians 2:2). If Satan is the ruler and there is a "kingdom of the air" under his authority, what are the powers in this kingdom that are under his control?

Satan has all of the angels who joined in the rebellion in heaven and were thrown down to earth by Michael under his control (see Revelation 12:9). We have established that Satan is not omnipresent. Without the assistance of other powers of darkness, he is limited in what he is able to do. He does have charge over a very large number of fallen angels. Most commentators believe Revelation 12:4 is telling us that one third of the heavenly beings rebelled with Satan and followed him out of heaven. But just how many is a third of the heavenly beings?

The size of the heavenly host is referred to in Revelation 5:11. Various translations of this verse refer to the number in various ways. The Revised Standard Version and New American Standard Bible translations use the words "myriads of myriads, and thousands of thousands." The King James Version says, "ten thousand times ten thousand, and thousands of thousands." The Good News Translation refers to it as "thousands and millions of them." What is clear is that a countless host of angels is involved. If they represent the number of angels that were left after a third had been expelled, then we are also talking about a huge number of fallen angels who are serving Satan in rebellion against both God and man.

Fallen Angels

Paul implied strongly that the fallen angels who rebelled with Satan had been organized around the world into a hierarchy of satanic power. In several passages, he described a supernatural force that he faced in his day-to-day ministry. He knew this was the real enemy.

The most specific of these references highlights the spiritual battle lines. "For our struggle is not against flesh and blood [human beings], but against the rulers, against the authorities, against the powers of this dark world and against the spiritual forces of evil in the heavenly realms" (Ephesians 6:12).

Paul was under no illusion. He believed that even though his ministry was to human beings made of flesh and blood, the reason the battle was tough could be attributed far more to powers in the spiritual realm. It was more than the mere resistance of the human mind to the truth of the Gospel. He warned us to take up the full armor of God so that we may be able to stand firm against whatever Satan and his demonic powers would throw at us (see Ephesians 6:13–18).

Paul's comments are consistent with Daniel's experiences recorded in Daniel 10. As a prisoner serving the emperors of Persia, Daniel came before God in fasting and prayer. He prayed for three weeks before an angel came in answer to his prayers.

When the angel arrived, he accounted for his 21-day delay by describing some of the battle that had taken place in the spiritual realm. He had been in combat with the angel who was the prince of Persia. With assistance from the archangel Michael, the angelic prince of Persia was overcome. Daniel's prayers had initiated the aerial combat. His experiences on the ground were a result of what had been happening in the air.

We should not worry much about all of the different levels there might be in the hierarchy of demonic power. There is only one fact that should concern us, and that is that Jesus is above all powers and all authorities. Those who are in Christ are secure in Him (see Ephesians 1:21–23). The best way of staying out of his grip is to keep doing the things God has given us to do.

If you stop pressing on with your destiny to fight the enemy when he attacks, you can be in danger of taking your eyes off your goal. It is best to keep going forward. As you do, you will see that the enemy is unable to prevent you from achieving God's objective for your life.

Next, we will turn our attention to learning how to resist the devil and to live in the victory of the cross by seeing how Satan operates at a personal level. I once read that all of the kings throughout history have sent their people out in battle to die for them, but there is one King who said that He would die for His people. That King is your King and my King. It is a privilege to be loved by such a God. As we learn about the devices of the enemy, let us never take our eyes off the victory of our King Jesus.

SUMMARY

Satan is not all that he wants us to think he is. He wants us to think that he is above the Almighty, but we who are in Christ know that all things are under the feet of the One who has overcome both the world and the works of the evil one. Satan may be our adversary, but that confirms that we are safe in the security of the One he opposes.

PRAYER

Thank You, Lord, that You overcame Satan at the cross. Because I am in You, I have nothing to fear from the powers of darkness. Help me to recognize the times when Satan tries to deceive me so that I can live for Christ without giving Satan any ground in my life. In Jesus' name, Amen.

SATAN AND HIS KINGDOM

*Satan is only irrelevant to those
who are unconcerned about where
they will spend eternity.*

SATAN'S ROLE

In the last two stages of our journey, we took time to look at the spiritual realms. This was to find out what the Bible says about angels and to learn what angels do. We saw how Lucifer, who was one of the highest angels, chose to rebel against Almighty God. He and all of his rebellious angels were thrown out of heaven by Michael's angelic army. Revelation 12 describes the battle, and Luke recorded Jesus' words as He testified that He had personally seen the event (see Luke 10:18).

It would be tempting to move on and begin to look at more wholesome topics than the enemy's activities, but unless we know our enemy and how he operates, we will never be effective or successful in winning our personal fights against him. We will not be able to have faith for the big battles if we are losing the war at a personal level.

Bad News—Good News

The bad news is that at the moment we declare the Lordship of Jesus in our lives, we become a focus for Satan's attention. Satan is not unduly concerned with churchgoers who are lukewarm in their commitment to Jesus. Sadly, some people seem to regard church as a Sunday social club where you can meet with your friends. Such people pose no threat to Satan's kingdom of darkness.

But he is very concerned with those who have come to maturity in Christ and who have made Jesus the unconditional Lord of everything they are and everything they do. These believers are in a position to exercise authority over the works of darkness in their lives. Satan, therefore, will do everything he can to oppose them and to minimize their effectiveness as soldiers of Jesus Christ. He will try to undermine their spiritual integrity and to penetrate every weakness in their defenses.

But here is the good news—the ultimate victory has already been won by Jesus. By faith we can choose to enter into it. We do this by living under the authority of Jesus. We do not try to fight a spiritual battle in our own strength with ineffective weapons. James showed us the way when he said, "Submit yourselves, then, to God. Resist the devil, and he will flee from you" (James 4:7).

Sometimes I have heard people quote only the second half of this important verse. They tell others to resist the devil with the assurance that he will flee from them.

But the result of that advice is that people come back saying things like, "It didn't work. I resisted him, but the devil didn't flee from me!" It is important to read and understand the whole verse. We should emphasize the phrase "submit yourselves to God" as the primary instruction from this Scripture passage. We cannot expect the enemy to be influenced by our resistance to him if we have not submitted ourselves to God's higher authority.

Psalm 91 expresses the principle so well, beginning with the statement, "Whoever dwells in the shelter of the Most High will rest in the shadow of the Almighty. I will say of the LORD, 'He is my refuge and my fortress, my God, in whom I trust'" (verses 1–2).

Some people desire with all of their hearts to submit themselves to the authority of God, but they struggle to achieve this because Satan has a prior hold on their lives of which they are not aware. Satan will hang on to whatever control he has so that he can operate in secret and keep people in bondage. They do not have any understanding of what the demonic powers are using against them. Asking the Lord to expose darkness and reveal the enemy's secrets is an important prayer to keep in our spiritual armory.

A man I prayed for just could not understand why it was that no matter how much he prayed and determined not to sin again he would constantly find himself going to places where he picked up sexual partners. He was heartbroken by what kept happening to him. He was deeply repentant and desperate but was beginning to think that God either could not or would not answer his prayers.

One day he discovered a stack of pornographic magazines that had belonged to the father he loved. This was a deep shock to him. At the same time, however, it gave him a clue as to what had been going on in his own life. The next time we met for prayer, he was able to speak out his forgiveness of his father and ask God to cleanse all of the demonic power that must have infiltrated him as a child through this impure covering. Spiritual influences had come to him through his father's sexual sins.

When we prayed for the ability to resist sexual impurity, the ministry was different. It was as if God had pulled out a very deep root that had been operating in his life since his earliest days. The enemy had been able to use this demonic hold that was hidden away in secret to speak things into his mind as if they were his own choices. In reality, it had been the suggestions of the enemy that he had been obeying. He had not realized the extent to which his personal choices were being directed by the generational demonic power within.

From that moment on, things were different. The next time temptation came, he was able to resist it. Knowing how the enemy had used the generational influence from his father had helped him to maintain his stand against temptation and grow strong in this previous area of weakness. He was able to renounce generational sexual sin and take authority over it in Jesus' name. The change in him was tremendous. There were still his own habits that needed to be broken, but without the demonic empowerment and with the Holy Spirit's enabling, this was no longer the impossible task that it had seemed to be previously.

A lady and her husband had been longing for a child. They had prayed hundreds of times, had been anointed with oil in their church fellowship and had gone through all of the possible medical processes available. Still, nothing had happened. As I was talking to them, the Lord made me aware of witchcraft that had been practiced in her mother's generational line. This was something that she readily admitted was true, but because she did not realize this could be relevant to their inability to conceive, she had never thought it necessary to pray about this aspect of her family history.

Within a few minutes, she had been delivered from a spirit of death that had held her in bondage and that had made it impossible for her to conceive. Within ten days—after eleven years of childlessness—they conceived their first child. They now have three children. Once the satanic secret had been revealed, it was possible for her to submit everything to the Lordship of Jesus. She was able to be delivered from the hold of the enemy and to see the fruit of being set free.

Satan's Rule—Powerful but Limited

Satan's reign is powerful, but it is limited. He is limited by time. When Jesus comes again, Satan's reign will be over. He is also limited in authority. He has to operate through the ungodly actions of humankind. This is because authority over the earth was given originally to humans. When we use our own power to do things that please Satan, we further empower Satan.

I traveled recently from one country that had had a cruel and severely oppressive history into a neighboring country that had experienced a great deal of religious freedom. I was immediately conscious of a change in the spiritual atmosphere. I was sensing something that could not have been measured but was certainly felt. There was a different ruling spirit in operation.

The account in Daniel 10 of a war taking place in the heavenlies between the demonic prince of Persia and the angelic messenger of God highlights the principle. The demonic prince of Persia had been empowered by the activities of people in the ungodly Persian regime. This ruling territorial spirit did everything it could to prevent the angelic support from getting through to Daniel while he was within the ruling spirit's territory.

It is possible to move from one region of a country to another region within the same country and discern a spiritual change. Christian leaders often tell stories of the different prevailing spiritual climates in the towns in which they have ministered.

An American couple we minister with from time to time told us that they experienced a dark foreboding presence while driving through a certain valley in Scotland. Several days later, while they were enjoying a historically-based Scottish novel, they realized that when they had felt the dark presence, they had been passing through the place where a group of soldiers, who were largely of the Campbell clan, had taken advantage of the hospitality given them by the Macdonald family. The Campbells rose in the night and massacred over thirty of the Macdonalds in their homes. It was a terrible betrayal of trust. The American couple had perceived the curse on the land even though they had known nothing of the history of the area.

Satan also tries to use our sin as an opportunity to take spiritual authority over churches, schools, companies, organizations and even areas or regions. When teaching in local churches around the world, we have learned to undermine the authority of any ruling spirits that Satan may have placed over those churches. We do that by working with those in spiritual authority in that particular place to deal with any known spiritual issues there might be. This might include repentance over issues such as division, sexual sin, occult activity, etc. The result has often been a dramatic increase in the effectiveness of the ministry in that place.

One testimony we received after such a church visit was that the church life and its evangelism were so transformed that the congregation doubled within twelve months. Satan can only use authority he has been given. We need to take that authority away from him through repentance and cleansing prayer. Once a place has been thoroughly cleansed, it is necessary to keep it free from satanic influence by holy living and by regularly praying cleansing prayers.

How Does Satan Operate?

Satan will always seek to oppress, afflict and occupy human beings with evil spirits. These evil spirits are working constantly to fulfill his objectives. Satan is not omnipresent. He has to depend totally on the spiritual beings under his control. We may refer to them in general terms as the *powers of darkness*. They do have power, and they hate the light that comes through Jesus Christ.

There appears to be no difference between the terms *demons*, *evil spirits* or *unclean spirits* in the gospel accounts. The descriptions of the effect they have in the lives of the demonized are similar. Whether or not they are different from fallen angels is unclear from the scriptural accounts and is largely irrelevant. What matters is that although they are all under the authority of Satan, Jesus has a higher authority.

When it comes to dealing with them, Paul uses the analogy of a Roman soldier's shield, or a shield of faith. We are to fend off attacks from spiritual enemies with shields of faith (see Ephesians 6:16). The picture is protection from something that is likely to penetrate our defenses unless dealt with effectively. Jesus, Himself, held up the shield of faith when He quoted Scripture as His defense against the devil's temptations in the desert (see Matthew 4:1–11).

It would appear from the scriptural accounts that the powers of darkness vary in size, power and authority. In my years of ministry, I have encountered evil spirits that lift off easily, and then I have also encountered those who seem much stronger and have many more footholds in a person's life. Sometimes my ministry partners and I have wondered whether we are dealing with a single demon or a collection of spirits that are bound together and are, therefore, able to hold on more tightly to the ground they have taken in the person's life.

The bottom line is that because Satan was defeated by Jesus at Calvary, no spiritual power under his control can stand against the power of the name of Jesus. Whatever opposition the demons put up, they have to submit to the authority Jesus has given to His Church.

That is really good news—indeed it is the message at the heart of the Gospel. Paul wrote, "Christ in you, the hope of glory" (Colossians 1:27). This is the position we adopt with respect to the powers of darkness.

When under the control and domination of the powers of darkness, we face eternal separation from God. But because Christ is in us, we benefit from His victory and have a rightful share in the glory that is to come. Because we are in Christ we no longer come under "the elemental spirits of the universe" (Galatians 4:3 RSV).

SUMMARY

Satan has power and authority, but it is limited to what was given originally to him by humankind at the Fall and by what continues to be given to him through the sinfulness of humankind. No power or authority that Satan holds is greater than what we have through the victory that Jesus gained over the enemy on resurrection morning.

PRAYER

Thank You, Jesus, that You did not give in to any of Satan's temptations and that there is nothing that he may throw at me that You have not already dealt with. Help me to always remember that it was Your victory and Satan's defeat that released Your people into eternal freedom. In Jesus' name, Amen.

SATAN'S FORCES

Many years ago, I tried to help a lady who had some issues that looked as though they might have been caused by emotional problems. In those days, I had very little understanding of the way Satan works in people's lives, and I had even less experience in dealing with it. I was totally taken aback when she began to manifest some very aggressive behavior. Today, I would recognize instantly that kind of behavior as being a demonic reaction to the presence and power of the Holy Spirit. She certainly was not filled with the peace of God that I thought should have been present as a result of my prayers for her.

I telephoned a friend who I thought would have answers because he lectured at a Bible college. He came, but then quickly left as he realized that he could not offer me any help. This was something new for him as well. I only wish I had known then what I have learned since about the ways of God and the ways of the enemy.

I have learned over the years how important it is for us to have an understanding of how the enemy works. In times of war between nations, the intelligence services are vital to the success of a campaign. If you have no knowledge of what your enemy is doing, you can be taken by surprise at any moment. Major battles have been lost because of a lack of good information about the enemy's tactics, resources and battle plans.

We need to know how the enemy works and what he does so that we will be better equipped to understand some of the things we encounter in people's lives—including our own. Once we have recognized and understood a problem and its source, it is much easier to deal effectively with it.

The Characteristics of Demons

While there are many unanswered questions about the origin of demons, we do not need to be ignorant of their characteristics. There are a lot of scriptural references to these character traits, as well as many observations that have been made by people around the globe who have been involved in deliverance ministry. We should not dismiss the confirmed testimonies that have come from different observers in different countries when they are consistent with Scripture.

Demons Are Alive

Demons are not just ideas or indefinable forces that operate from within the minds of humankind. They are living, functioning spiritual beings with minds, characteristics and wills of their own. They are dedicated to the service of Satan. All of this is implicit in the gospel accounts of the encounters Jesus had with demons.

It is important to remember that demons can only inhabit a person when the person (or their ancestors) have given them the right to do so. When there is a battle to cast out a demon, it usually means that to some degree those rights are still operating. As we saw previously, submission to God's authority is absolutely vital (see James 4:7).

Jesus never treated a demon as anything else but a living entity who was in opposition to the interests of God and man. He was not surprised when they spoke through the lips of a demonized person (see Luke 4:34). He was not taken aback when they challenged Him with either statements or questions from a knowledgeable and intelligent source: "What do you want with me, Jesus, Son of the Most High God?" (Luke 8:28). Jesus said:

> "When an impure spirit comes out of a person, it goes through arid places seeking rest and does not find it. Then it says, 'I will return to the house I

left.' When it arrives, it finds the house unoccupied, swept clean and put in order. Then it goes and takes with it seven other spirits more wicked than itself, and they go in and live there. And the final condition of that person is worse than the first."

Matthew 12:43–45

It is obvious from the above passage that Jesus knew that a demon is alive, it has a will of its own, it has intelligence and it can choose to live somewhere. In this scenario, it thinks that the place it has just come from might still be vacant and might be worth going back to. It has enough wisdom to curry favor with higher demonic powers (more wicked than itself) by introducing them to a new home.

But the knowledge that demons have is limited. In the book of Acts, the demon that spoke out to the sons of Sceva said, "Jesus I know, and Paul I know about, but who are you?" (Acts 19:15). The demon did not know who the sons of Sceva were.

All demons recognize and know Jesus. This is not surprising as Jesus was present when all the powers of darkness were cast out of heaven. Many times I have seen demons recoil in fear at the name of Jesus or when they have seen the presence of Jesus in members of our ministry teams. They cannot stand Jesus' love for a person in need. They also cannot stand the authority that believers have because of the presence of Jesus in them.

Demons can react with emotional responses. They certainly seem to have feelings of their own. James tells us, "The demons also believe—and tremble with fear" (James 2:19 GNT). By saying that the demons believe, James was not saying that demons trusted in God. Instead, he was recognizing that demons are well aware of the truth about God. They are believers in God in the same way that I am a believer in Satan. I know about him, but I certainly do not trust or depend on him.

This passage highlights something very important. True belief must be more than an assent to truth. Belief must be accompanied by trust and personal commitment to Jesus Christ. That kind of belief is saving faith. It is faith in Jesus now and for all eternity.

Many people are deceived into thinking that because they believe in God, they are part of His Kingdom. But without repentance from sin, heart commitment and personal trust, belief in God is no different from the belief that demons have in the reality of God. The demons tremble with fear because they know that they are on the losing side.

There have been times when we have been praying for people and encountered demons. We have seen demons express the whole range of emotions that people also feel. Sometimes there is a deep anger at being exposed. At other times they whimper pathetically at the thought of being cast out of a home they have occupied for such a long time. We have come to realize that some people whose emotions are out of balance or even out of control are like that because demons are controlling their feelings.

The fact that demons are living, spiritual beings does not give us any reason to be sympathetic toward them. We should not take any notice of their entreaties when they plead for permission to stay or promise to be good if we will not cast them out.

Demons Are Disembodied

Demons do not have bodies of their own. They can express themselves most effectively through occupying the body of a human being. This is the case with all of the ruling territorial spirits. They use the earthly authority that God gave humans to be able to carry out their demonic orders.

God never intended men and women to be occupied by evil spirits. He did, however, plan that we could know the presence of the Holy Spirit within us. When we worship God by doing those things that please Him, the Holy Spirit empowers us from within. But when we worship Satan by doing those things that please Satan, then he is able to send evil spirits to take up residence in us. He uses the capacity God gave us to receive the indwelling Holy Spirit for his own purposes. When this happens, Satan is contravening God's intentions for His creation.

A dimension of deliverance ministry that is vital for us to understand is that even when people die, demons do not. This is because demons are disembodied creatures. They are unaffected by the deaths of their hosts. They have to leave the body of the deceased, but they are then free to carry on their work in someone else's body. When death occurs, demons may transfer directly to someone else. They have direct access to their new host through such things as generational sin, occult practice or an ungodly soul tie with a previous sexual partner.

A man I once knew was out walking his dog. He suddenly became aware of his mother and felt terribly burdened. Shortly after returning home, he received a telephone call from a friend in South Africa who relayed that his mother had just died. During her life, she had been involved in occult practices. Scripture tells us that in such cases the sins of the fathers can be visited on the children (see Exodus 20:5). That is exactly what happened. When we prayed for him, he was completely delivered from the demonic burdens that had suddenly come upon him at the moment his mother had died.

Demons Are Able to Speak

There are numerous examples in Scripture of demons speaking through the mouths of the people they are occupying. At Capernaum, right at the beginning of Jesus' ministry, a man stood up in the synagogue and shouted to Jesus, "What do you want with us, Jesus of Nazareth? Have you come to destroy us? I know who you are—the Holy One of God" (Luke 4:34).

Jesus was speaking with such authority that He amazed the people who were there. The demon was exposed and forced out into the open as a result of what Jesus was saying. Then Jesus went on to take authority over the demon and set the man free. The effect on the gathering at Capernaum that day was electric. Jesus expelled the demon from the man, and during the process of deliverance the man was thrown down onto the ground by the demon. The crowd was amazed and said, "With authority and power He commands the unclean spirits and they come out" (Luke 4:36 NASB).

Their amazement was not that Jesus had commanded the unclean spirits to come out, but that they actually came out when He commanded them. They were used to the Jewish exorcists attempting to expel demons with much noise but with little success. The demon's behavior gave Jesus an important opportunity to teach them.

There was a time some years ago when I was preaching in a church and was beginning to teach about the power of the name of Jesus over all of the powers of darkness.

Suddenly a man stood up in his pew and started shouting, "Shut up! Shut up! Shut up!" The demons within him could not stand what was being said.

He tried to tear a Bible into small pieces to throw at me, but the Holy Spirit fell upon him. He, like the man in Capernaum, was thrown down to the floor and ended up lying between the pews. As I continued preaching, members of the team then took him to another room and prayed for him to be delivered of the evil spirit. The effect on the congregation was remarkable.

Later that day, there was a somewhat challenging discussion about whether or not Christians could have demons. In the middle of the debate this man got up, came to the front, took over the microphone and ended the discussion with one of the most brief and profound statements on the subject I have ever heard.

"Now listen," he said, "I've worked in ministry for the last few years. I've been born again for five years, and I didn't think I had a demon, but I did. And now I don't. So there!" With that he returned to his seat and saved the whole meeting hours of fruitless theological discussion.

Christians can have demons—but Jesus can set them free. Demons cannot possess or own a born-again believer who has been bought with the price of the shed blood of Jesus and is owned by Him, but believers can certainly have demons—the demons do not possess the person, but they can have an influence over them.

When we bought our very old house and moved in, we took possession of the property. The house had woodworm in the roof timbers. The woodworm did not possess (own) the house—but the house definitely had woodworm. When Jesus comes into our lives, we become His possessions being bought with the price of His blood. Even so, we may still need healing and deliverance as God starts to clean us up from the inside out.

Given the opportunity, demons will always try to deceive you with lies. When the enemy tries to tempt us with things that look attractive but that are contrary to what Scripture says, we know that he is lying. He usually presents us with a so-called benefit so that we will consider his offer. Occasionally demons will try to speak out through people. The Holy Spirit's gift of discernment helps us to recognize what God is saying and to differentiate between things that are not of God. The gift is called discerning of spirits (see 1 Corinthians 12:10).

First and foremost we need to discern what the Holy Spirit is saying to us, and then what the human spirit of a person might be saying. We also need to be able to tell what may be coming from the demonic. But we should not try to use demons to get information, because we might be further deceived by what they say. The inner witness of the Holy Spirit will help us avoid being led astray by a false witness that comes from the enemy.

As far as Scripture is concerned, there is no record of any demon speaking a lie directly to Jesus or speaking a lie when someone was ministering in the name of Jesus. In those circumstances, the demons were always obliged to speak the truth.

The main caution I would add here is that you should never seek information from a demon for any other purpose than to evict it. To seek information unrelated to the process of deliverance is bordering on mediumship.

If You Want to Know More

I have been careful to put only enough information about deliverance ministry in JOURNEY TO FREEDOM to ensure that the training gives you a thorough grounding in the subject without overwhelming you with more than you need. If, however, you are one of those who is actively involved in a healing and deliverance ministry and need to know more, I suggest that you get hold of a copy of my book *Healing through Deliverance* (Chosen, 2008). It is about 600 pages of comprehensive information on the subject.

SUMMARY

Knowing our enemy is a vital part of preparation for spiritual warfare. The Bible gives us many clues as to the characteristics of demons. These clues help us to understand how demons operate so that we can be forewarned and forearmed.

PRAYER

Thank You, Lord, for the authority You always demonstrate over all the powers of darkness. Help me to be aware of what the enemy is doing when it is essential for what You have called me to do. But more importantly, help me to be even more aware of Your love, power and authority as I seek to serve You day by day. In Jesus' name, Amen.

SATAN'S OBJECTIVES 18

There are at least six objectives that Satan has for your life:

1. to keep you locked in darkness with him for time and eternity,
2. to keep you from understanding the truth about how he operates,
3. to keep you from discovering your power, security and authority as a child of the King,
4. to keep you from finding out how, in Jesus' name, you can overcome him,
5. to limit your potential as a citizen of the Kingdom of God, and
6. to rob you of your destiny.

Our objective for JOURNEY TO FREEDOM is to teach the precious foundational truths of the Kingdom of God so that you will not only know and understand who you are in Christ, but so that you will also enter into the destiny God has prepared for you (see Jeremiah 29:11; Ephesians 2:10).

How Satan Uses Demons

In the previous stage of our journey, we found out from Scripture about some of the many different things that the angels are responsible for and how they operate. As fallen angels, the demonic powers of darkness operate in the spiritual realms in a similar way, but they are under the control of a different master.

From what we already know about angels, we can deduce how the demons might operate. We know that demons directly oppose the work of the angels. There are several different Scripture passages that depict the sort of battles that take place in the heavenlies.

1. Demons always serve and worship Satan.

While the angels of God worship Him constantly (see Revelation 5:11–14), the demons, in contrast, offer all of their worship to Satan. This is not because they love him but because they are held in bondage by a regime of fear and terror. Punishment and retribution are hallmarks of Satan's kingdom.

I remember very well when a spirit was being cast out of someone who had been involved in satanic things. The demon was in abject fear. This was not just fear that we were going to use our authority in the name of Jesus to throw it out of the home where it had been for a long time. It was also the fear of having to face the higher power it was under after failing in its mission.

2. They rejoice in the works of Satan.

The angels of God always rejoice in the will and works of Father God (see Job 38:7). They love Him and know that He can always be trusted. The demons, however, have a vested self-interest in helping Satan achieve his objectives. Since they made the choice to join in Satan's rebellion before being thrown out of heaven (see Revelation 12:9) they know there is no way back. The outer darkness of Hell is their only possible eternal destination (see Matthew 25:41).

Even though serving Satan has been their downfall, they cannot escape his control. They have no option but to rejoice in everything Satan does in the hope that their master can put off the inevitable conclusion to the end of all things. They might believe, as Satan probably believes, that he will turn the tables on Jesus at the very end. That certainly would seem to be the impression given by John in Revelation 20:7–10.

C. S. Lewis, the author of the Narnia stories, also wrote a book entitled *The Screwtape Letters*. If you have never read it, please try to get hold of it. *The Screwtape Letters* is a book that chronicles correspondence from a senior devil to a junior devil. They discuss how much progress is being made in trying to keep a human being away from faith in God. It is fantasy, but it is very close to the reality we know exists in the life of a Christian believer. It is a great read and very enlightening. In the whole of the twentieth century, C. S. Lewis stands out as one of the authors with a tremendous but rare insight into the spiritual realms.

3. They always execute Satan's will and wishes.

The angels of God always and instantly respond to the wishes of Father God (see Psalm 103:20), and the demons always and instantly obey the will of their master, Satan. This means that they are committed to

- attacking God's special creation—human beings,
- keeping people out of God's Kingdom, and
- opposing believers who are determined to live their lives under the Lordship of Jesus and who have a heart for being obedient to God's will.

4. They are strategically involved in the affairs of nations.

Whereas the angels who are placed by God over nations are deployed by Him in response to the intercession of the saints (see Daniel 10), Satan places his ruling spirits in positions over the nations according to the way those in authority over the nations behave. Leaders who consistently oppose the will of God have the effect of giving Satan the right to position ruling spirits over their nations. These ruling spirits will hold them in the bondage of satanic control until the acts that gave the enemy rights are confessed and repented of by those in authority.

5. They oppose the interests of churches.

It is clear from the letters of Jesus to the seven churches, written down by John in Revelation 2 and 3, that angels are given special responsibility for watching over the affairs of churches. Many Christians naïvely believe that they are free from Satan's influence and attacks inside their congregations. In reality, however, that is the place where Satan seeks to exercise the greatest influence by keeping God's people from entering into true relationship with Him and from discovering what He wants them to do.

The enemy can gain influence within our churches through spiritual rights given to him through sins committed on the property that have not been repented of and cleansed, through unresolved sin within the present and past leadership of the church or through beliefs that are contrary to the Bible that have been held by leaders in spiritual authority. Even beliefs such as Christians cannot have demons can have a debilitating effect on the fellowship, can restrict the effectiveness of prayers for healing and can eliminate the possibility of having a successful deliverance ministry.

I was once ministering deliverance to a lady, but for some unknown reason I was unable to make progress. The demon kept manifesting on her face, but it would not leave. This went on until the Lord prompted me to bind the demon over her church that had convinced the leadership that Christians would never need deliverance. This wrong belief was paralyzing the healing ministry in the fellowship. As soon as that spirit was bound, the woman received deliverance.

While Satan will tempt all believers to sin, he has a huge interest in tempting leaders in order to gain high-profile negative publicity. When a key Christian leader is caught in some major scandal—especially in the financial or sexual arena—the effect is devastating.

While the Holy Spirit always wants to move a fellowship forward to do the works of the Kingdom, a few missiles that are aimed carefully at the weaknesses that leaders already have can undermine the work of a fellowship for a generation. In recent years there have been a number of such high-profile cases, and the effect has been devastating to the Body of Christ. They have produced justifiable taunts of hypocrisy from the media claiming that Christian leadership is no better than anyone else.

6. They oppose the work of believers.

While angels have an assignment under God to serve and protect believers (see Hebrews 1:14), their authority to do so is limited by the desire of the believer to truly shelter under the covering of the Most High (see Psalm

157

91:1). If we do not desire God's protection, we will not get it. Demons have an assignment under Satan to tempt believers out from under God's protection. They will try deliberately to get believers to do things that are contrary to God's will and that are revealed clearly in God's covenant and commandments.

Wherever believers are seeking to be obedient to the will of God and to move forward under the anointing of the Holy Spirit, demons will seek to undermine what God is doing through them. The words that Satan used to deceive Adam still have their capacity to charm (see Genesis 3). He still tells believers to enjoy themselves because the consequences will not be nearly as bad as God has said.

The enemy might say something like "You have been going through a tough time recently. You deserve a bit of pleasure. God will really understand." It is Genesis 3 all over again. But as soon as the temptation has been indulged, the enemy will pile on the guilt and shame before he leaves you alone with your sin. He is a dirty fighter—always has been and always will be.

But Satan is not concerned about those who are just religious, whatever their particular brand of religious expression may be. Religion that is outside the anointing of the Holy Spirit is of no particular threat to Satan's kingdom. It is clear that God hates religion and forms of religious expression. They are not what He desires for His people (see Isaiah 1). If God hates something, you can be sure that Satan gets excited when we place a high priority on doing that very thing. Religious spirits who take over people's minds and introduce their own false belief systems are some of the toughest to dislodge.

Satan is also behind those who love to criticize every church they go to. There are those who give the impression that they are the only ones with the ear of God; therefore, they know exactly what a church should be like. I love the quote from C. S. Lewis's *The Screwtape Letters* when the senior devil is talking to his junior devil in training:

> Surely you know that if a man can't be cured of churchgoing, the next best thing is to send him all over the neighbourhood looking for the church that "suits" him until he becomes a taster or connoisseur of churches . . . The search for a "suitable" church makes the man a critic where the Enemy [God] wants him to be a pupil [disciple].[1]

7. *They will do all they can to attack God's children (Satan's enemies).*

Angels only act to bring blessings to God's people. That is the opposite of the demonic strategies that are dreamed up by the planning department of hell. The personal attacks may include such things as sickness, accidents, financial problems and relationship breakdowns. Indeed, they will take advantage of any weakness or any unhealed issue in a Christian to gain a foothold.

The main objective of all sorts of continuous attacks against God's people, especially leaders, is not necessarily to put a brick wall in front of them so they cannot move forward. It is to gradually wear them down so that they choose to give up the fight. If Satan can get us to use our will to cooperate with him, then we will do his work for him.

When it seems as though the attacks are continuous, it is not the time to give up—it is the time to press forward to victory. The enemy can see that victory is coming, and his last throws of the dice will be to try to make you give up.

8. *They perform extraordinary acts on behalf of Satan and his kingdom.*

There are many extraordinary acts in Scripture carried out by angels. An angel, for example, opened the prison doors to let Peter out of jail (see Acts 12:6–10) and another caused the sudden death of King Herod (see Acts 12:23).

But the Egyptian magicians were capable of duplicating some of the miraculous signs that Moses did in front of Pharaoh (see Exodus 7–12). Satan's agents have power, and they will use it to deceive people whenever they can. This is the power behind all of the extraordinary things that were practiced by the Egyptian magicians and that are practiced today by a whole range of occult and New Age practitioners.

Everything from voodoo operations, spoon bending and spiritualism to sudden storms and extraordinary weather patterns. They are all in Satan's repertoire. There are many deceptions operating in Satan's kingdom. The people of God need to have discernment. Scripture says that in the last days even the elect may be deceived (see 1 Timothy 4:1). We have been warned.

9. They "minister" personally to each human being.

Just as God would give to each child an angel (see Matthew 18:10), Satan tries to use demons to lead each child astray with what the spiritualists would call a guiding spirit. We recognize this simply as a demon. The job of such a spirit is to do everything possible to turn a person away from God. The spirit's job is to deceive each person into joining false religions, participating in the occult or believing New Age teachings. The goal is for the person to do any ungodly thing that is contrary to God's will and purpose.

It is important to remind ourselves that Satan is not equal and opposite to God. God is far, far greater, and there are twice as many angels as demons. It is good to remember, too, that we are not powerless victims of the enemy. We have all of the weapons of spiritual warfare at our disposal (see Ephesians 6:10–18; Romans 8:37–39), and as we continue on in our journey to freedom we will become increasingly more proficient at using them to take the enemy's ground.

SUMMARY

The way the demons operate to oppose believers is the reverse of how the angels work to help those who are receiving salvation (see Hebrews 1:14). If the enemy is opposing us, we do not need to be discouraged. We should be determined to press on to victory.

PRAYER

Thank You, Lord, for showing me how the enemy operates. I have no desire to walk in his ways, and I ask You to forgive me for all the times I have given Satan authority in my life through making wrong choices and listening to his temptations. I choose now to exercise godly authority in my life and my family. I choose to trust You, whatever the circumstances. In Jesus' name, Amen.

SATAN'S DEFEAT AT THE CROSS

I have on many occasions heard Christians say, "I don't have to worry about Satan anymore—he was defeated at the cross." The way they say it can sometimes sound very disparaging of those who are being intentional not to give Satan any room in their lives. Their arguments can sometimes sound very convincing.

They make it sound as though Satan retired from active service and went away on vacation after the cross. This is the reason we need to understand clearly why we should be concerned about his activities, how the cross was the eternal answer to Satan's power in eternity and that he still has a measure of authority and power on earth.

This topic has already been covered earlier in the book, but I want to bring this information together so that we will understand fully how wonderful the victory of the cross was and yet why we still have to keep our guard up against the enemy.

What Actually Happened to Satan When Jesus Died?

The short answer to this interesting and critical question is—absolutely nothing. Even though he had failed to overcome Jesus, he was still in his place on the throne of this world. But here is the long answer.

Satan was the god of this world, the ruler of this world and the spiritual controller of this world before Jesus died. And he was still all these things after Jesus' death and resurrection (see 2 Corinthians 4:4; John 12:31; John 14:30). As we saw earlier, it was humankind who gave Satan his authority over planet earth. As long as there are sinful men and women on the earth, Satan will remain in the position of authority that he was first given by Adam.

"But," I hear you saying, "What about the victory of the cross? It does not sound like much of a victory if nothing actually changed as a result." Who said nothing changed? All I said was that Satan's position as the god of this world remained unchanged.

There was only one Man who fought the toughest of Satan's temptations, resisted them all and won His ultimate battle over the enemy. That was Jesus' battle and not ours. Before the Fall, Adam was sinless. When he was tempted, he fell into sin, and the whole of the human race also became tainted with sin. Jesus is sometimes referred to as the second Adam because, like Adam in the beginning, he was also without sin. As a sinless man, Jesus was a huge threat to Satan. He was targeted by Satan from the moment He was born—from the attempt to kill Jesus in the massacre of the innocent babies in Bethlehem through all the temptations in the wilderness and various attempts on His life throughout the three years of His ministry.

This sinless human being had a greater authority than Satan and was the ultimate threat to Satan's kingdom of darkness. He moved in the authority that God had given to humankind on the earth. If Satan could have taken Jesus' life as opposed to Jesus choosing to give it up then Jesus would have come under Satan's control. When a shooting takes place, the person who fires the gun controls the life of the victim. Satan wanted to be in charge of Jesus' life.

Death and Hell Defeated

Jesus told us that eternal death in hell was the punishment that had been prepared for Satan—not for humankind (see Matthew 25:41). But when humankind chose to sin and go Satan's way, it was as if humankind got on board a bus that Satan was driving. The name of the destination displayed on the front of the bus was hell. Anyone who joined Satan for the ride would finish up at the same destination as the driver. The whole human race got on board.

Father God knew from the very beginning that because He had given humankind free will, man would choose to go his own way. Man would choose Satan's way and would be headed for certain death. He would be separated eternally from God in hell. It was His love for humankind that made Him resolve to provide a way of escape (see John 3:16).

Death became humankind's destiny after the huge, wrong choice was made. Death was the just consequence of making the choice. God's rescue plan was to send His Son to live and die as a man in the place of humankind. He was to bear the just consequence of humankind's sin and open up a way back to heaven (see Romans 6:23).

One of the songs I learned as a child has stuck with me all these years:

> There's a way back to God from the dark paths of sin;
> There's a door that is open and you may go in;
> At Calvary's cross is where you begin,
> When you come as a sinner to Jesus.
>
> E. H. Swinstead, "There's a Way Back to God"

The fact is that Jesus was not killed by Satan. Jesus resisted all the temptations Satan used to lure Jesus to come under his authority. Jesus voluntarily chose to die for the sins of humankind while remaining in a totally sinless state (see John 15:13). Satan knew that if a totally sinless person were to die without ever having come under his control, the curse of death would be broken. At this point Satan changed his tactics. Instead of trying to kill Jesus, his last temptation was to invite Jesus to make a magnificent display of great power and come down off the cross (see Matthew 27:40). This was something no one had ever done before. What a display and performance that would have been.

By this time Satan was petrified that Jesus would die a sinless man. If that happened, there would be nothing that could stop Him personally from overcoming death and being raised from the dead. Death was not the inheritance of Jesus, and the resurrection would be certain. That was a horrendous thought for Satan.

If Jesus escaped the clutches of death, there would be nothing Satan could do to stop a way of escape being opened up for humanity. That is exactly what happened. One of the greatest signs that this had been done was the tearing of the curtain in the temple (see Matthew 27:51). The curtain had symbolically separated humankind from God under the provisions of the Old Covenant. We will be learning more about covenants later in our journey to freedom.

Jesus' Victory

At that point Jesus had endured death and had come through on the other side. The resurrection was the glorious sign of His personal victory. Isaiah's prophecy had come true. "He will swallow up death forever" (Isaiah 25:8). Paul took up a similar theme when he said, "Death has been swallowed up in victory. Where, O death, is your victory? Where, O death, is your sting?" (1 Corinthians 15:54–55).

Even though Satan had not been able to overcome Jesus, he was still for the time being the god of this world. He still had all the authority on earth that he had previously been given by man at the Fall.

At that moment, Satan's days of authority were numbered. His authority and power did not change immediately, but a day was now set in God's diary of time and eternity for the return of Jesus—not as the babe of Bethlehem, but as the King of kings and Lord of lords. The consequence of His victory at the cross would not only be seen and understood by the whole world, but the just sentence on Satan and his kingdom would then be carried out. The time of Jesus' coming is only known to the Father. Scripture tells us that not even Jesus or the angels in heaven know when it is going to be (see Mark 13:32).

In the meantime, Satan has exactly the same power and authority on the earth as he had previously. You need to be aware of his devices and be on your guard constantly against his temptations and attacks. It is true that Jesus overcame death and Satan's power on the cross, but those temptations and attacks will still come—and probably with increasing measure as the days hasten on. When people ask me when I think the Second Coming will be, the only safe answer to give is that today is one day nearer than it was yesterday. World events are moving so quickly that it is hard to imagine that the coming of the end of the ages will be a long way away.

What Did Change at the Cross?

What changed at the cross was that from that moment on there was a way that opened up for as many as chose to believe to enter into life in all its fullness (see John 1:12). When we receive His salvation, we enter into Christ and He enters into us. A divine exchange takes place—the consequences of our sins are covered because Jesus covered them for us. In exchange, we receive His victorious life. It is a miracle and a privilege. When we are joined together with Him, everything He suffered for us and experienced for us becomes ours by faith.

Because Jesus died, those who believe in Him and are in Him have also died. Paul put it this way: "I have been crucified with Christ" (Galatians 2:20). He also said he was buried with Him and raised from the dead in Him and was, therefore, alive forevermore in Him. Paul declared that his life was now hidden with Christ in God (see Romans 6:3–5; Colossians 3:3).

What changed because of the cross was the status of all who believe. It was as if believers were let out of jail. Those who had believed before Jesus rose from the dead were also able to get out of jail. All believers were able to enter into the freedom from the curse of sin and death that had come through the Fall (see Hebrews 11:39–40).

What about Satan Now?

Do we or do we not need to be bothered about Satan? In reality, the answer to this critical question is both no and yes. When we are born again and redeemed out of the hands of the enemy, we have nothing to fear in eternity. Our physical death will simply be a transition from life on sinful earth to life in the glorious reality of heaven's paradise. From that vantage point we can laugh at Satan because we have escaped his clutches (see Psalm 124:7; 2 Timothy 2:25–26).

During our time on earth, we are in Christ (see 1 Corinthians 1:30), and Satan cannot stop us from doing the things that God has called us to do.

We are living now in the reality of Jesus' higher authority, and in eternity we will be free forever from Satan's influence on our lives.

But remember that even though you are born again, you still have a carnal, sinful nature. You are still prone to sin and are vulnerable to temptation. Satan is a thief and a robber (see John 10:7–10) who will do everything he possibly can to deprive you of the blessings God has stored up for you.

I have heard people say, "I do not need to bother about Satan, because Jesus said, 'No one will snatch them out of my hand' and 'No one can snatch them out of my Father's hand'" (John 10:28–29).

Those words are certainly in the Word of God, but we also have free will. After we are saved, if we use our free will to make ungodly choices and walk in Satan's ways, we are putting ourselves in grave danger. As long as we choose to remain in the Father's hands, nothing can touch us.

We read in 1 Timothy 4:1 about people who abandon the faith they once had, and we see the dangers of returning to a sinful way of life after having been saved. We see also in other passages of Scripture that there is no room for complacency (see Hebrews 5; Hebrews 6; 2 Peter 2). We must not make light of Satan's continued temptations of the saints of God. In fact, Peter tells us the opposite when he warns us that the devil is like a roaring lion who wants to devour us (see 1 Peter 5:8). Paul also urges us to wear our spiritual armor at all times to defend ourselves against the fiery darts of the evil one (see Ephesians 6:10–18).

SUMMARY

Even though Jesus was victorious over Satan on the cross, Satan is still the god of this world. Our sins are forgiven, and we are released from the punishment for our sins because Jesus paid the price of death on our behalf. We can enter into His victory. Through His power and authority, we can resist temptation and fulfill the destiny God has stored up for each one of us. But we need to be on our guard at all times and not let pride, lust or self-interest lead us into behavior that restores Satan's authority over our lives. Satan may have been defeated by Jesus, but he still has a massive amount of power and authority through the ongoing sinfulness of humankind.

PRAYER

I am so grateful, Jesus, that You overcame Satan on my behalf. Without You there would be no escape. Thank You, Lord, for Your wonderful love and Your amazing gift of a redeemed life—for ever and ever. In Jesus' name, Amen.

SATAN'S ETERNAL DESTINY— AND OURS!

I love books—especially books about real people who lived real lives. I love discovering what people believed, what they did, what motivated them and what they achieved. I sometimes wonder what the libraries of heaven will look like.

I especially love reading about some of the great saints of history who trod paths of faith and courage. One of these saints was Thomas Brooks. Thomas Brooks was a nonconformist preacher who was born into a Puritan family. On several occasions, he preached before Parliament, and he was active as a pastor in London during the terrible days of the Great Plague and the Great Fire in 1665 and 1666.

He wrote many devotional books, and in his pastoral work he came face-to-face with the work of Satan in the lives of those he served. His summary of Satan's work is a classic. He compares the nature of Satan and the wages Satan pays as the false god of this world with the nature of the living God and what He pays.

> Satan promises the best, but pays with the worst; he promises honor, and pays with disgrace; he promises pleasure, and pays with pain; he promises profit, and pays with loss; he promises life, and pays with death. But God pays as he promises; all his payments are made in pure gold.[1]

The Truth

Evangelism is sharing the truth about God with those who do not know Him and praying that the Holy Spirit will draw the sinner to the Savior. I believe one of the most powerful ways of revealing the truth about God is to open people's eyes to the reality of Thomas Brooks's observations. If the world could see the end from the beginning, Satan's tawdry limitations would be exposed for what they really are.

In every issue of today's papers, there is irrefutable evidence that confirms what Thomas Brooks said. We see sin's consequences, which lead to a harvest of pain, suffering, sickness, disease, war and death. The world has been blinded by the god of this world, and politicians think that one day they will be able to resolve all of the world's problems through new initiatives, social engineering, military intervention, medical discoveries or financial handouts. The world and its politicians are very deceived.

Tragically, even much of the Church has joined with the world's ignorance of the enemy's activities. They have proclaimed Satan as a myth that was only believable by an unenlightened generation. Charles Baudelaire, who was a French poet, said, "The cleverest ruse of the Devil is to persuade you he does not exist."[2]

Jim Packer, a distinguished twentieth-century theologian, added, "The natural response to denials of Satan's existence is to ask, who then runs his business?—for temptations which look and feel like expressions of cunning destructive malice remain facts of daily life."[3]

Satan's business is certainly thriving in a very broken world. All pretense of sexual morality has disappeared from society and government. Drugs, occultism, violence and promiscuity are the stuff of entertainment, tragic deaths result from wild drunken driving and sexually transmitted diseases are rampant. If the world could see the reality of who is behind it all, people would run to the Savior. There is no other answer.

Satan's Future

I often skim through a book to assess whether or not I want to spend time reading all of it. I usually read the first few pages and then turn to the last chapter. If I am excited by the ending, I buy the book. I have news for you:

I have read the last chapters of *the* book, and the ending is very exciting and very good. And if this book was new to me, I would definitely buy it. It is very good news indeed.

We may read the papers and watch the TV news and hang our heads in dismay, but regardless of the mess that we see in this world, we can share the glorious news that the last chapters of Revelation confirm to us that Satan's days are literally numbered (see Matthew 25:41). Even in these days of waiting for the last chapters to unfold, we can take great encouragement from Paul's words: "For though we live in the world, we do not wage war as the world does. The weapons we fight with are not the weapons of the world. On the contrary, they have divine power to demolish strongholds" (2 Corinthians 10:3–4).

We have the weapons now to resist the enemy and to build the Kingdom of God even in the midst of a world that has rejected God and is doing Satan's work for him. Satan hates believers who truly exercise their spiritual authority, for there are no other people on the face of the earth who have the capacity to remind him of what awaits him at the end of time.

Only believers can live in this victory, because the ultimate victory was won for them by Jesus at Calvary. We can, therefore, overcome Satan through the authority we have in Jesus when our lives are submitted to Him. The daily victory that believers can have over the enemy is a constant reminder to Satan and all the powers of darkness of what happened when Michael threw Satan out of heaven (see Revelation 12:7–12). It is a reminder of what happened at the cross. It is a reminder that this will one day be repeated before the whole universe as "that ancient serpent, who is the devil, or Satan" is chained and bound and thrown into the Abyss for a thousand years (Revelation 20:2). We will return later in our journey to freedom to look at what Revelation tells us happens next.

For now, we take comfort in the fact of scriptural prophecy. What God has said, He will do. At the very end of all things, the devil who deceived everyone, including those who served him, will finally receive the judgment he deserves (see Revelation 20:7–10).

Our Hope and Destiny

All those who have received the Savior and claimed their right to be restored to relationship with Father God (see John 1:12) will know the joy of eternal life with the redeemed of God. They will be completely free of their carnal natures and all of the influence of Satan and his demons. This message is implicit in every book of the Bible and is evident on every page of the book of Revelation.

The joy and relief in the heart of John is clearly expressed in his prophetic words as he describes what the Spirit was showing him, of those exciting Satan-free days that are yet to be:

> Then I saw "a new heaven and a new earth," for the first heaven and the first earth had passed away, and there was no longer any sea. I saw the Holy City, the new Jerusalem, coming down out of heaven from God, prepared as a bride beautifully dressed for her husband. And I heard a loud voice from the throne saying, "Look! God's dwelling place is now among the people, and he will dwell with them. They will be his people, and God himself will be with them and be their God. 'He will wipe every tear from their eyes. There will be no more death' or mourning or crying or pain, for the old order of things has passed away." He who was seated on the throne said, "I am making everything new!" Then he said, "Write this down, for these words are trustworthy and true." He said to me: "It is done. I am the Alpha and the Omega, the Beginning and the End. To the thirsty I will give water without cost from the spring of the water of life. Those who are victorious will inherit all this, and I will be their God and they will be my children."
>
> Revelation 21:1–7

In this fallen world, Satan has given humankind a false inheritance. It is different from the true inheritance for those who know and love the Savior (see Ephesians 1:3–14). This is His provision for you and for me—and the enemy will have no part in it. All of Satan's promises will have been seen for what they are: lies and deceit. But, as Thomas Brooks reminded us, the promises of God are like pure gold.

We may have endured severe trials at the hands of the enemy, but rejoice, "Blessed is the one who perseveres under trial because, having stood the test, that person will receive the crown of life that the Lord has promised to those who love him" (James 1:12). What an encouragement this is to press on in the race of life knowing the reward that God has laid up for us all—and Satan will have no part in it.

SUMMARY

Satan's destiny was sealed the moment he rebelled against God. Jesus' victory over Satan was completed at the cross with His death and resurrection. When we enter glory, we will be entering into the fullness of what that victory meant. We can now overcome the works of the enemy in our daily walk with God and look forward to eternity with Him.

PRAYER

Thank You, Lord, for Your amazing and wonderful plan of salvation. Thank You for Your unconditional love and for the fact that Satan is defeated. Thank You that we can look forward to enjoying eternity in heaven with You. I am so, so grateful. Help me to live knowing the reality of eternity in my heart. In Jesus' name, Amen.

MAN—GOD'S SPECIAL CREATION

*Unless I discover who I am, I will never fulfill
the destiny God intended for me to enjoy.*

CREATED FOR GLORY

It is time to take stock. We need to look at the map and see how far we have come and then step forward into a new phase of our journey to freedom. We need to understand the relevance of all of the truth we have been looking at as it relates to the lives we are now living.

As God's children, we have a huge but very exciting challenge on our hands. We are made in the image and likeness of our wonderful God (see Genesis 5:1) but also live in a fallen world controlled by a determined enemy of souls (see 2 Corinthians 4:4). How do we turn the desire that God puts in our hearts to love and serve Him into a reality that is evidenced by us living lives that are truly transformed by His presence? Our challenge is to turn the understanding we have gained about our spiritual foundations into achieving His objectives for the rest of our lives.

Many people who come to Ellel Ministries in need of personal help or training have those objectives in mind. They want their lives to really count for the Kingdom of God. They are either looking to Him for help with their own issues, or they are looking for training so they can serve others in the Body of Christ. But almost all who come realize quickly that there are areas in the gardens of their own lives that need the attention of the Gardener.

Let's review exactly what JOURNEY TO FREEDOM is all about and where we are going together in this walk of faith. Amazingly, God has chosen to manifest His glory through His disciples on planet earth (see John 17:6–10).

We can easily look forward to enjoying the glory of God in heaven, but it is the desire of God to show the world something of His glory through the redeemed lives of His children. That includes you and me.

Getting Healed without Prayer

In the early years of the ministry, we developed many different courses that covered different aspects of healing and discipleship. One of our leaders decided to put all these courses together into a more systematic pattern. As a result, the Modular School was born. This is a school that is run in most Ellel Centers and is used regularly to introduce the ministry to new locations.

As this school became established, I began to notice something quite amazing. People were getting healed without having asked for specific prayer. As the cycle of ten weekend courses was completed over a twelve-month period, some of the areas of healing that people were reporting were of real significance. The testimony times at the end of the schools were quite remarkable. Long-term issues, problems and conditions were being resolved often without any specific prayer. This has become a well-established pattern, and we confidently expect people's lives to be changed and transformed as they take in and apply the truth of God's Word.

We found that while people may have heard similar teaching before, they had not been in an environment where they were expected to apply the truth in their own lives and to trust God with the outcomes. We were watching miracles take place one step at a time. That is exactly what I am expecting to happen as people progress through JOURNEY TO FREEDOM.

Miracles—One Step at a Time

Here is an example of what we saw in our training classes. A person had experienced a problem with unrelenting fear. He had prayed for years to be released from it. He had others pray for him. Nothing happened. He was still just as fearful, and he was beginning to think that God either did not want to heal him or was unable to heal him.

Then he completed the unit of the Modular School about acceptance and belonging. He began to appreciate and receive the unconditional love of Father God into his heart. It is this love that provides great security to our inner being. Once his heart was anchored in the love of God, he could discover the truth of the Scripture that says, "There is no fear in love. But perfect love drives out fear" (1 John 4:18).

Examples like this happened repeatedly. People got healed of their fears by discovering the reality of the truth of God's Word. They found their absolute security in the God they now knew really loved them. They experienced the healing process one step at a time.

When you have taken enough steps and then look back at where you have come from, you may well exclaim, "It's a miracle!" Not because a sudden miracle has taken place, but because the issues that underpinned the problem have been systematically removed through acquired knowledge of the truth. Almost imperceptibly, healing has occurred.

The Truth That Will Set You Free

There is a very profound verse in John's gospel in which Jesus tells the disciples what to expect if they hold to the teaching He is giving them. The words *hold to* mean much, much more than just listening to the words. For if you hold on to something, you are depending on it. People can often really understand what is true but be reluctant to trust themselves to it.

The old story of the famous tight-rope walker, Blondin, illustrates this well. He had walked backward and forward on a high wire across the Niagara Falls that links Canada and the USA. He pushed across a wheelbarrow that contained a sack of potatoes. After the accumulating crowd cheered enthusiastically, he asked a man in the crowd if he believed he could wheel a man across in the barrow.

"Oh yes," said the man.

Blondin said, "Well, jump in the barrow and let's go." Not surprisingly, the man who had professed that he believed that Blondin could do it was not willing to trust Blondin with his life.

That is exactly where a lot of people are in respect to the application of the truths we have been learning together in JOURNEY TO FREEDOM. It is possible to believe them without trusting the God who has revealed them to us.

I once rescued a boy from a swollen river. It had been raining very hard, and he was stranded on a rock in the middle of the torrent. For his life to be saved, he had to hold on tightly to the rope that I managed to get to him. I dragged him to safety across a raging flood of water. Just believing in the rope or believing in me was not enough. For his life to be saved, he had to jump into the water and hang on to the rope for dear life.

It is the image of hanging on to His teaching (like hanging on to a rope) that Jesus was communicating when He said, "If you hold to my teaching, you are really my disciples. Then you will know the truth, and the truth will set you free" (John 8:31–32).

That is why we are tackling the subject of healing and discipleship from the bottom up instead of from the top down. It would be easy to look at all sorts of healing needs, focus our attention on the symptoms and then pray for healing. This is what happens on many occasions when people ask for prayer for healing but do not receive healing. It is not surprising, therefore, that real healing is relatively rare—people are praying for the wrong things.

I used to lecture on building technology at Manchester University. I made a specialty out of studying building defects. By far the largest number of major structural problems were caused by a building being too heavy for its foundations. If the foundations are inadequate, a building becomes unstable and may even collapse—sometimes with the loss of many lives.

Recently the private life of a well-known Christian leader was exposed after it was discovered that he had been visiting a prostitute. The result was devastating and had a calamitous effect on many people who thought they could trust this man as their leader. The building (of his life) collapsed, causing much damage to family, friends and congregations.

As the story was told, it was revealed that for years he had been struggling with temptations. What was obvious was that the inner foundations and securities of this man's life were a long way from what God intended. There was a deep inner void in his heart, and his need for comfort was being satisfied in all the wrong places. It is rare to find lasting answers to problems such as these without stripping away all the structures that have been built on inadequate foundations. The answer is not found normally by praying about the sexual problems, but by exploring the reasons why the heart of the believer is not secure in the comfort provided by the "God of all comfort" (2 Corinthians 1:3).

I know that some people feel that the teaching in the early stages of JOURNEY TO FREEDOM has been more basic than they had expected. But thirty years of experience teaching and ministering to people across the world—often to those with the very deepest of personal needs—has taught me that the spiritual foundations of a person's life are critical. Unless foundations are put securely in place, prayers for healing may be unsuccessful. Sadly, people can fall away from the faith disappointed, disillusioned and thinking that God has let them down.

In reality, it is not God who has let them down, but it is the enemy who has done everything he could to prevent them from having a full knowledge of the truth. This is often the case when they have not been taught the essential foundations for living a godly life—the vital principles that are missing from the teachings of many congregations. It is as if people have been building the walls of their lives with stones, but the stones are held together by mortar that does not contain enough cement. When the rains (of pressure and testing) come, the mortar washes away and the wall collapses.

God brought me into this ministry by showing me the need for healing in people's lives. He then showed me all of the different ways of ministering that are important parts of the healing process. Now He has made me passionate about seeing people not only being healed and delivered, but also having their lives rebuilt on solid foundations. I want to help build such solid foundations in people's lives that for the rest of their days they are secure in God regardless of what storms the enemy throws at them.

Our human nature always wants quick fixes to our problems, but quick-fix solutions rarely contain permanent answers. There are types of concrete that are very quick-setting. They are great for mending holes in busy airport runways, but they do not last long. In time the whole runway will need to be dug up and re-laid properly. In many ways that is what JOURNEY TO FREEDOM is all about—digging up the runway of your life and relaying it properly so that it will withstand the pressure of the rest of your days.

Jesus was careful to say to His disciples, "I chose you and appointed you so that you might go and bear fruit—fruit that will last" (John 15:16).

Father God does not offer quick fixes that do not last. He offers a journey with Him that will sustain us for time and eternity.

A tree grows a little bit each year. With each growing season, a new ring is added to the trunk of the tree. When conditions are good with lots of rain and warmth, the growth rings are wide apart. But when there are hard times and little rain, the rings are very close together, making the wood harder and denser. Trees grown in harsh environments produce wood that is strong and will endure. And lives that are lived out on very solid foundations will remain secure and will still produce good fruit in tough times. My prayer is that living the principles laid down in JOURNEY TO FREEDOM will produce good fruit in people's lives.

It cost Jesus everything to bring to earth the truth that sets people free. It was not an easy task. Satan opposed Him every step of the way—from His birth in Bethlehem to the cross at Calvary. That truth is available freely for us now. Just as it was a tough walk for Jesus, it also requires determination for us to apply that truth in our lives. We have an enemy of souls who not only opposed Jesus but who will also oppose us. Satan knows that God's people who are set free to serve the living God are dangerous to the kingdom of darkness.

But I believe that through JOURNEY TO FREEDOM, God will build His strength into His people and will heal and restore them so that they will indeed be dangerous to the powers of darkness. I am praying they will be like Daniel, who said, "the people that do know their God shall be strong, and do exploits" (Daniel 11:32 KJV). And therein lies the key—knowing God. Unless we truly know God for who He is, we will never be strong.

Created to Share the Glory of God in a Fallen World

We are created beings who are made in the image and likeness of God. That is why we have spent so much time in this series learning about the nature and character of God—unless we really know Him, we cannot begin to know ourselves as we really are. And it is only as we are restored in His image and likeness that the true strength and character of God emerges in our hearts.

I am praying that God will strengthen your spiritual spine and that you will be as determined as Daniel was. I pray that regardless of how strong the opposition is, you will walk in obedience to the God who has created you. You are not an accident. You were created by God. Yes, men and women make choices as to the relationships that they create, but it is God who designs the embryonic human being that explodes into life.

Your life came from God. You were created by Him, and one day your spirit will return to Him (see Ecclesiastes 12:7). It is only in and through Him that you can both know your identity (who you are) and fulfill your destiny. If you try to achieve your destiny outside of Him, whatever you achieve will always be less than what God intended. It is only what God intended that will give you the greatest joy and the deepest eternal satisfaction.

I am sensing a deep excitement in my spirit as we start to climb the hills of God. There may be some mountains ahead of us, but the view from the top is glorious. The psalmist puts it this way:

> I lift up my eyes to the mountains—where does my help come from? My help comes from the LORD, the Maker of heaven and earth. He will not let your foot slip—he who watches over you will not slumber; indeed, he who watches over Israel will neither slumber nor sleep. The LORD watches over you—the LORD is your shade at your right hand; the sun will not harm you by day, nor the moon by night. The LORD will keep you from all harm—he will watch over your life; the LORD will watch over your coming and going both now and forevermore.
>
> Psalm 121

For centuries those words have been comfort to the souls of pilgrims on their journeys. We are on a journey together. May the psalmist's words be a comfort and encouragement to you as we discover more about who we are and what God wants us to be.

SUMMARY

The restoration of God's order in the foundation of our lives is vital for our security in God and for the fulfillment of our destiny. We are created by God in His image and likeness for a purpose. It is in knowing Him as He really is that we will discover ourselves as we really are.

PRAYER

Help me, Lord, to look carefully at the foundations of my own life. I do not want to build my life on good ideas and dangerous deceptions. I choose now to build my life on the Rock of Jesus Christ and to allow Him to restore me as He intended me to be. In Jesus' name, Amen.

MADE IN THE IMAGE AND LIKENESS OF GOD

We are created beings who were brought into existence by a God who does not just love us, but who actually is love. We have also learned that God is eternal, God is Creator, God is holy and God is the Trinity of Father, Son and Holy Spirit.

If these are the primary attributes of the nature and character of God, and if we are made in His image and likeness as we see in Genesis 1:26–27 and Genesis 5:1, then something of each of these characteristics will also be in the hearts of mankind. That is exactly what we discovered together when we recognized that something of the eternal nature of God is in every single human being.

Because God is love (see 1 John 4:8), humans are capable of expressing love also.

Because God is eternal (see Ecclesiastes 3:11), the human spirit is also eternal. Humans do not come to an end when their bodies die. The choices we make on earth within the realm of time determine how we will spend eternal timelessness.

Because God is Creator (see Genesis 1; Genesis 2), humankind is also creative. The primary evidence of the creative genius of humankind is being able to achieve everything that we do in all the realms of human discipline in every aspect of art and science. We reflect our Creator.

Because God is holy (see 1 Peter 1:16), that spark of God in our spirit that we call our conscience is an arbiter of right or wrong. This is not measured by the laws that are put in place by humans but by the ultimate standard of the holiness and righteousness of God. A pure conscience that is undamaged by the influence of consistently wrong choices is sensitive to the holiness of God. Without anyone having to teach us how to do it, our conscience gives us an immediate sense of guilt when we transgress God's eternal spiritual laws.

All of these attributes of God are present within humankind, but because of the sin that was introduced into humanity through the Fall, they are overlaid by the carnal nature. Even the apostle Paul struggled with doing what was right and not doing what was wrong (see Romans 7:14–20). As we review together the journey we have traveled, we are preparing the ground for God to start the work of rebuilding our lives on solid foundations of His truth.

The Trinity of Man

God is a Trinity of Father, Son and Holy Spirit. Man, with a trinity of spirit, soul and body (see 1 Thessalonians 5:23), is a reflection of the nature of God. Before the Fall there was an unbroken unity of spirit, soul and body within man. This reflected the unbroken unity of Father, Son and Holy Spirit. Jesus and His Father had a oneness that demonstrated how God intended the spirits, souls and bodies of humankind to work together in relational fellowship with each other and in submission to God (see John 14:5–11).

This was the unfallen state of humanity—perfect unity within and perfect relationship with God. It is this unity within us and with our God that we must strive for as we walk a pilgrimage of healing and discipleship as redeemed sinners.

Sin separates. First, sin separates us from God (see Isaiah 59:2). But sinfulness also causes division within an individual and between other humans. People try to bury their sinfulness, hide their sins from others and pretend to themselves that sinful things never happened. Sin operates according to one of the primary principles of warfare—divide and conquer.

If an army remains intact and fights together as one unit, it is very hard for an enemy force to overcome it. Its strength comes from its operational unity and integrity. But if an army becomes fragmented with one section out of touch with another or without one leader in control, disunity soon becomes evident. Disunity produces disorganization that leads quickly to dysfunction and, soon after, to defeat.

Satan knew that if he could get the flesh of man (soul and body) working together against the spirit of man, it would only be a matter of time before humankind would come under his authority and control. We will return to this important subject later when we look in more detail at the consequences of the Fall. For now, we need to keep these things in mind as we look at what God intended each component of the trinity of man to be.

The Spirit of Man

Scripture is very clear about the fact that humankind is more than a body. Paul prays that his brothers and sisters might be whole in spirit, soul and body (see 1 Thessalonians 5:23). David says, "Praise the LORD, my soul" (Psalm 103:1–2, 22; Psalm 104:1). This is David's spirit speaking to his soul and telling it to worship God.

And when Jesus was talking to the woman at the well, He said that those who worship God must worship Him in spirit and in truth, teaching that humans have a spirit with which they can worship God (see John 4:24). The words *in truth* refer to the part of humans that can make godly or ungodly (truthful or untruthful) choices.

At the beginning of Jeremiah, we read these awesome words: "Before I formed you in the womb I knew you" (Jeremiah 1:5). This is one of those verses where the Amplified version of the Bible helps us to understand what is being said. "Before I formed you in the womb I knew you [and approved of you]" (AMP). It is inconceivable that God would know and approve of Jeremiah and not know and approve of every other human being also.

Yes, Jeremiah was picked out for a very special task. The remainder of the verse describes how Jeremiah was separated, set apart and consecrated to be a prophet to the nations. That was his task. But first he, as a human being, was approved of by Father God.

This verse states without there being any possibility of confusion that God knew us even before we were conceived. It was not our physical being that He could have known.

Genesis tells us that the living soul comes into being at the fulfillment of our initial creation (see Genesis 2:7). There was a spiritual dimension to our being that God knew even before our conception. Ephesians 1:4 says, "For he chose us in him before the creation of the world to be holy and blameless in his sight." On this side of eternity, we will never understand fully what this means. One day, however, it will be clear, and we will understand outside of the limitations of human minds with revelation from God.

When people talk about Jesus, they sometimes refer to the fact that He came in the form of a man. This is exactly what Scripture says in Philippians 2:8. The full reality of this extraordinary statement, however, is not the incredible truth that Jesus took on the cloak of humanity and came to earth in the form of a man. The amazing aspect of the statement is that man was created in the image and likeness of God. Originally, we were made to look like Him, not the other way around.

In reality, there was no other form in which Jesus could have come. He came in appearance as Himself. The rest of humankind looks like Him. He did not have to be transposed into what was for Him an alien creature. When He came, He took upon Himself a body God had given to humankind. He came as wholly man and not just a spiritual being that looked like a man (see Romans 8:3; Philippians 2:8).

We are slowly creating a picture of the intrinsic nature of man. We are spiritual beings first—spiritual beings that were known by God even before our conception. In our spirits, we can enjoy fellowship with God, we can communicate with Him in prayer and praise (see John 4:24) and we can know the unparalleled joy that flows from being in harmony with Him (see Psalm 16:11).

You can have spiritual emotions as you view the events happening around you from God's point of view. You can see the beauty of God's creation, and your spirit can respond by soaring in thanksgiving as you are overwhelmed with the love, provision and mercy of God. In your spirit, you can have God-inspired experiences, conceive visions, hear the voice of God and dream about fulfilling your destiny.

The Soul of Man

But humankind is more than spirit, for we are tied into physical reality by our flesh. The flesh in Scripture does not refer to just the body—the flesh is the soul and the body together. We read of the sins of the flesh (see Colossians 2:11), but this does not mean that your body can sin independently of your soul. Your body cannot do something wrong without your agreement and instruction. The soul within you is in charge of your body, and when your body is involved in something sinful, it is doing so only because your soul has made a choice to use your body for that particular purpose.

Your soul is like the driver of a machine, and your body is the machine. The two together form *the flesh*. Within your soul is your mind, your emotions and your will. These three are the primary contributors to your behavior and what others may describe as your personality. With your mind, you think. With your emotions, you feel or respond. With your will, you make decisions. All three motivate the soul to use your body to carry forward thoughts and intentions into physical activity—both the good and the bad.

Free Will

Just as God is able to exercise His will freely, He gave humankind the wonderful gift of free will. This is both the most precious and the most dangerous thing that God gave us. Free will is precious because it is such an incredible privilege to have this God-ordained characteristic. We are able to use our will to make right choices and to be creative with the resources we have at hand.

Free will is dangerous, however, because people have learned how to use their free wills to make ungodly decisions and to break the covenant relationship God wanted us to enjoy with Him forever. Yet, if God had not given us free will, He could never have enjoyed relationship with us—as we will discover later. Free will and the capacity to enjoy relationship go hand in hand.

The Body of Man

You have a body. This is the part of your being that receives the most attention. Yet, in the overall scheme of eternity, it is the least important part of your creation because you only have a physical existence for a limited period of time. It is your body, from your first cry to the last breath, through which your humanity is expressed. The life of your body determines how long you are privileged to live on the earth. After death you will wait in paradise to receive your resurrected body for eternity (see I Corinthians 15:51–52).

Your body is the most amazing of machines—a billion times more complex than any computer or machine humankind could ever construct. It is a chemical processing plant, extracting the necessary good from food and eliminating the waste. It supplies oxygen to the bodily systems via an incredibly efficient breathing machine. The oxygenated blood is pumped around the body by a heart that beats faithfully about two billion times in the average lifetime.

Your brain and your sensory organs manage and control the machine, giving constant instructions to all the muscles and bones. A thermostat controls your bodily temperature within a very narrow band of efficient operation. Your sexuality makes reproduction and the continuation of the human race possible. What an incredible machine God has given you in which to live and move and have your being on planet earth.

When this wonderful body is working according to the maker's instructions, we say that we are well. When it is experiencing a malfunction, we say that we are sick. Under many conditions the body acts as its own healer, fighting off infection and self-repairing physical damage such as cuts and bruises. When the conditions appear to be beyond the normal capacity of self-repair, a sick body is then in need of medical treatment, supernatural healing or both.

We will soon return to look in more depth at both the nature of each dimension of our humanity and at the healing needs that are especially evident in each of these dimensions when things go wrong. But now, we must press on with understanding more about how God intended us to live in loving relationship with Him and with each other.

SUMMARY

Humans are made in the image and likeness of God and have within them a nature and character that is a reflection of God's nature and character. Understanding how God has put us together is an important foundational tool in our understanding of how to pray for healing.

PRAYER

Thank You, Lord, for the privilege of being made in the image and likeness of God. Help me, Lord, not to let You down by behaving in a way that is different from what You intended. I want to be a good and faithful representative of the living God during my time on planet earth. In Jesus' name, Amen.

CREATED FOR LOVE AND RELATIONSHIP, PART ONE

We have reminded ourselves of how God put us together as human beings in a way that is unique in the whole of creation. We are different from all of the animals because we are comprised of a spirit, a soul and a body (see 1 Thessalonians 5:23), and our soul is eternal.

Animals have life forces (perhaps similar to the spirit) and bodies, but they do not have an eternal soul that was created uniquely for them that lives on beyond their deaths.

But human beings do have eternal souls that were created uniquely for them by God. For the soul, bodily death does not mean the end of existence. It is the point of transition from eternal existence within the limitations of time to the realms of eternity beyond the limitations of time (see 1 Corinthians 15:53).

When Jesus said, "before Abraham was born, I am" (John 8:58), He was describing His place within the Godhead. He was stating that like Father God, He had always existed.

But His words also implied that eternal existence outside of time was like always living in the present without the historical and future dimensions of existence that the realm of time facilitates and requires. Eternity beyond death is a timeless existence and not an extension to everlasting time as we know it.

Agape and Hesed—Love and Relationship

We have already introduced into our journey to freedom an understanding of the nature of God's love as being *agape* love, the selfless giving of love from one to another. And we have also seen how the character of God is expressed in Hebrew by the word *hesed* that illustrates all the wonderful things about God that He wanted us to experience as He expressed His agape love toward humankind through a covenant.

We are now going to look at what it really means to be in a love relationship with God. That is why He made us. We were created by Him for both love and relationship. We have to look at these two aspects of humankind's existence together, for outside of relationship with those who also have the capacity to love us in a similar way, the very idea of love is meaningless. Love requires being in a relationship with others. It requires both giving and receiving by two parties or more.

Humans in Partnership with God

We are not only different from the whole animal kingdom in the nature of who we are, but also in the very reason for our existence. The whole animal kingdom was created by God to serve humankind. It was God's intention that humans should rule over the animals as part of their authority over planet earth (see Genesis 1:28; Genesis 2:19–20; Genesis 9:2).

The kind of enforced authority that humans were given over the animal kingdom does not allow for two-way loving relationships. We give animals loving care and affection, and from some of them we even obtain a measure of response. But that is not relational love in the way that God intended love to be. We were meant to share God's power and authority in a relationship of love.

It is true that we are dependent upon God as our ultimate provider of all things because He made us (see Acts 17:28; Colossians 1:17), but God's desire was more than simple dependency. He desired for our relationships with Him to be partnerships that include both giving and receiving love.

Because He made us, we are dependent on Him. If you really love some-one, however, you want to please them by doing what they want. In your relationship with God, you will want to obey Him. Obedience becomes the desire of your heart, not a response to slavishly enforced control (see John 14:15).

In a statement of remarkable honesty for such a proud and warlike man, Emperor Napoleon said, "Alexander, Caesar, Charlemagne and I myself have founded great empires; but upon what did these creations of our genius depend? Upon force. Jesus Christ alone founded His em-pire on love, and to this very day millions will die for Him."[1] Napoleon understood the difference between relationships that were created by force that could only be maintained by force, and those that were the fruit of love. Relationships based on love need no force other than love to maintain them.

God intended that man, using the power and authority that came from His love, would be a partner with Him. Watchman Nee, a wise Chinese theologian who suffered persecution for his faith, talked about Adam in his book *The Latent Power of the Soul*.

> If Adam was capable of managing the earth, his prowess was most certainly superior to ours today. He had power, ability and skill. He received all of these abilities freshly from the Creator. . . . The power which Adam had in that day must have been tremendous. He must have been a man with astounding ability. All his powers were inherent in his living soul. We may look upon Adam's power as supernatural and miraculous, but so far as Adam was concerned these abilities were not miraculous but human, not supernatural but natural.[2]

Adam was not only in an unbroken relationship with God, but he was God's partner as well. So much of what God had intended for humankind, including the dynamics of the original relationship, was lost after the Fall. Perhaps when Jesus comes again and reigns for a thousand years on earth the world will see what it could have been like if humankind had not made the wrong choice. It will be exciting to see the potential that God placed in humankind realized as the second Adam, Jesus Christ, rules and reigns on earth (see Revelation 20:4–6).

Affection and Comfort

The word *love* has so many different meanings that few people will understand its real significance in terms of relationship.

A person may say things like "I love my house," "I love my car," "I love my bed," "I love steak and chips" or any of a thousand other things that we sometimes describe as things that we love. As a child I had a soft monkey, and I loved my monkey. Our grandson has a toy rabbit that he will not go anywhere without. And I have farming friends who really love and care for their animals. None of these things, however, has the capacity to return love.

All such loves have only the potential to be one-sided expressions of a limited relationship. We may enjoy them enormously, but they are not love. Animals or possessions can be genuine objects of our affection, but all that they do is provide us with a measure of enjoyment and comfort. They will never provide us with the blessings of a mutual, two-way love relationship. They never respond to loving attention with equal love. The comfort they provide is always short-lived, and we need to get a fresh fix constantly. That is the case with all sources of comfort that are centered on the experiences of the flesh.

This is one of the main reasons people get addicted to cigarettes, alcohol, food, pornography or sexual activity. They are flesh-based sources of comfort. As such, they do give a measure of comfort (false comfort, but comfort nevertheless) that comes without any commitment to relationship. Prostitution thrives on providing comfort to men who do not want the responsibility of being in a right relationship or who do not want to let down their defenses. Being seen for who and what they are would feel too costly or too risky—for then they might have to start being accountable to others.

Real love needs a relationship through which it can be expressed. It also involves taking responsibility for one side of the relationship and being accountable to the other party for maintaining it. When people back off from responsibility and accountability in adult relationships, we call it abdication. If this develops within a relationship, the relationship starts to show signs of breakdown.

For many people, short-lived love substitutes are the only safe way they know to get a measure of comfort. These will never truly satisfy. This is one of the primary reasons that so many people are overweight or grossly overweight. They comfort eat because they do not know what real love is or do not have any understanding of how to give and receive love. Being obese can then become a barrier to other people accepting and loving them, thus perpetuating a vicious cycle of cruel self-hatred.

The constant need for comfort that is fulfilled in nonrelational ways has the effect of excluding other people from being involved relationally with them. Comfort is not love, and as a substitute for love it will only ever satisfy for a season—sometimes for a very short season at that.

It is difficult to have a meaningful heart relationship with someone who gives all their affection to something that you do not or cannot share with them. Their fixation or obsession with whatever is the source of their comfort becomes a barrier you have to cross in order to have any sort of relationship with them. The need for such false comfort often arises out of the absence of real love in their hearts.

I once knew a man with whom I might have had a good relationship except that he was obsessed with cats. Probably as a boy who was brought up in a loveless family situation, his cat had become his source of comfort. Fifty years later cats were still his source of comfort, and this precluded him from having any form of deeper relationship with others. I was not prepared to join him in his world of cats in order to develop the relationship. His obsession was an impossible barrier for me to cross.

It is only the experience of real relational love in our hearts that gives permanent comfort to our spirits and souls. That is why Paul describes God as "the God of all comfort" (2 Corinthians 1:3). It is His love that comes to our hearts through relationship with Him that is the ultimate source of real comfort. His love will comfort us when we are going through troubles and periods of anxiety, fear or loneliness.

All real love has its source in the one true God—the God who is love (see 1 John 4:8) and who has made us in His likeness (see Genesis 1:26–27). It is secure, God-centered, loving relationships as God intended from the beginning that provide the soul-satisfying human comfort that we all need.

One-sided relationships that are abusive, self-centered, controlling, manipulative, fearful or violent can never be expressions of true love. All such relationships are distortions of what God intended and are not examples of loving relationships. This is true even when the controlling partner says that he or she loves the other person. We have prayed with people who recoiled in fear when we said that God loved them, for that is what an abuser had said when he wanted to use their bodies. What they had experienced as love contained nothing loving, safe or kind.

When people have been treated cruelly, it often takes a considerable amount of time to help them discover what God is really like and for them to learn what love really is. It is not easy for some people to have to reject what they thought was love, because that was the only love they knew. It had become part of their identity and their security.

But be encouraged—the God who is love will wait patiently until you are ready to let down the defensive barriers that you might have erected. When you are ready you will discover a whole new world of loving reality as the God of love overwhelms you with His hesed kindness and comfort.

The Pain of True Love

True love in a fallen world does not come without the potential for pain. This special pain began in the heart of God when He saw humankind choose to listen to the temptations of Satan. The love relationship that God had experienced with Adam was a perfect joy to both him and God. God enjoyed those evening walks with Adam in the amazingly beautiful garden He had made to bless His creation (see Genesis 2:8).

God had placed His likeness in Adam and Eve—and it was very good (see Genesis 1:31). It must have been exciting for God to see the ones He had made exploring and discovering all of the gifts and abilities that they had been given. Then came the trauma of their rejection of Him even after everything He had done for them.

The searing pain of tragic loss must have cut right through His heart. The relationships He had longed for and was just beginning to enjoy could never be because humankind's sin had come between them. Satan had stepped into the gap to take control of the world God had made.

Without love there would have been no such pain. But God could not change His heart. He still loved His creation and longed for restoration of the relationships He had lost. This event was the genesis of the extraordinary story of humankind's redemption that culminated on the cross. The cross is the ultimate symbol of love expressed in pain.

It was not only the heart of God that felt the pain. Deep in the core of each human being is a heart that is crying out for the God who made it. We are searching for the only love that will ever satisfy our love-hungry souls. The pain of loss makes us look again to find the God who made us and who could again be the fulfillment of our hearts' desires.

Satan stands in the gap providing comfort substitutes of every type and nature to stop people from looking for the God of love. He uses every type of false religious experience to seduce the hearts of all who start the search to find the God who made them.

Satan resists every move of the Spirit of God to draw men to the Savior. No matter how hard he tries, the darkness cannot put out the light (see John 1:5). And one by one, the empty hearts of those who want to find Him will be filled with pure love as they discover that the One who made them still loves them.

It is always love that motivates the heart. It was the desire to love and to be loved that motivated the heart of God to create the universe and put man on earth in the first place. It was love that motivated the heart of God to send His Son on the most extraordinary rescue mission both time and eternity will ever see (see John 3:16). It is love that draws the heart of man to the heart of the Savior (see Jeremiah 31:3; John 12:32). It is love that restores our lost identity.

It is His love that shows us how to love. When we love others with the love that He gives to us, the world's population will catch their breath and run into the arms of the One who has never stopped loving them. They will at last discover why God made them in the first place.

The god of this world can offer nothing like that.

SUMMARY

All real love involves relationship. God desires not only to have a relationship of love with His people, but also to partner with them in the works of the Kingdom of God. We all need to experience comfort in our hearts. But ways of obtaining comfort that are outside of the plans and purposes of a relationship with God will always disappoint. When love is not returned it always causes pain—something that God understands completely because of humankind's rejection of His love.

PRAYER

Thank You, Lord, that I can love You because You first loved me. Help me to understand more about how to express my love to You in the relationship I now have because of Jesus. I am so grateful for the extraordinary love that held Jesus on the cross so that my Redeemer could express the love that Father God had for me. In Jesus' name, Amen.

CREATED FOR LOVE AND RELATIONSHIP, PART TWO

Having now understood that love and relationship are inseparable and that love without relationship is not what God intended, we can see that love without relationship is only a substitute for the real thing. We may be passionate about something and think that we really love that thing, but if it does not have the capacity to respond to us, there is no relationship. This is not what love was meant to be. I am passionate about Alvis cars, but I do not expect a love response back from my Speed 20. If I did, I would be waiting for a very long time. The deception I would be in would ensure that my heart would remain unsatisfied forever.

We may even have a fixation about another person and think we are in love with them, but if it is only a one-sided affection—even if it is an all-consuming passion—it is not a love relationship. One-sided love relationships, or unrequited love, will only cause pain in the long run. Without a relational response, the heart is never able to receive the love it craves and needs.

The real thing, however, is not a soft option of self-satisfying enjoyment. Responsive love is costly and requires commitment from both parties. That is the true nature of God's love. Even when humankind messed up, God remained committed to us. When we respond to God's love, we set out on a joyful pilgrimage hand in hand with God.

A love relationship with God may be joyful, but in a fallen world it is also costly. Every move we make in response to God's love for us is always against the flow of worldliness that originates in the carnal nature. It is taken advantage of by the enemy of souls. But when we learn to live in the victory that Jesus has won for us on the cross, the joy of the Lord will overflow from the core of our beings. Then we can be the happiest people on earth—whatever the circumstances of our lives. Out of the center of our beings will flow rivers of living water (see John 7:38).

As God's people, we have the joy of experiencing salvation now, as well as knowing that our salvation will be complete in heaven's glory throughout eternity (see 2 Timothy 2:10). We may also feel, however, as if we are going constantly against a tidal flow of ungodliness in the world around us. But let's rejoice. It is only dead fish that go with the flow. The living ones always have their noses facing upstream against the current. If a fish is held in flowing water with its head facing downstream, it will soon die. Let's keep swimming upstream against the current and live.

We ended the previous chapter by looking at the pain we experience when we are rejected by those we love, and we looked at the pain God must have felt when humankind rejected Him. We minister to large numbers of people who carry pain from rejection in their hearts. They live their lives being controlled by those hurtful experiences from the past.

I understand how some have been so hurt by the experience of what they thought was love that they do not want to risk the pain of another relationship—not even with God. I am thankful that God loved us so much that He risked the pain of being rejected again. Jesus was despised and rejected (see Isaiah 53:3), but He persevered because of love. Deep healing flows from the cross for those who have known the pain of rejection and who are still struggling with the consequences. Later in JOURNEY TO FREEDOM, we will look more closely at how to overcome and be healed from this pain.

The Sacrifice of Love

Real love in our heart will always motivate us to bless other people—especially those with whom we are in a right relationship. As we act responsibly within a relationship, there may be times when a measure of sacrifice is required. I believe that real love and sacrifice can never be separated completely. The very nature of love generates the desire to help and serve the ones you love. That means sacrificing your own interests and needs in order to bless others (see 1 Corinthians 13:4–8). Sacrifice without love, however, can be very manipulative and used as a means of controlling others through a misplaced sense of duty.

Phrases like "After all I've done for you" can be used to put guilt onto others so that they will do things for you. This is not the sacrifice of unconditional love (see Hosea 6:6). A good mother sacrifices her own desires on behalf of her children. If her children are in need of food and clothing, she will do without to ensure that their needs are met. If a child has real needs, a good father will deny himself the pleasure he might have had through spending money on himself. These kinds of sacrifices do not have to be thought about—they are a natural by-product of the love that God has put into the hearts of humankind for their children. It comes from that deposit of godliness that is contained within the heart of every human being. People do not have to be believers in God to act in a God-inspired way, for it is God who gave them His life.

The ultimate sacrifice is to give one's life on behalf of another (see John 15:13). Recently in Afghanistan a British soldier rescued a wounded comrade. The life of the rescued soldier was saved, but the hero lost his own life in a courageous rescue mission. Such impulsive heroism is applauded the world over.

But what Jesus did on the cross was not an impulsive act of spontaneous heroism in which He was unfortunate to have perished in the cross fire. His sacrifice was the plan of salvation that was worked out in heaven's realm before Jesus came to earth. He had chosen to die long before the moment of death. God knew not only what would happen, but also that only through the death and resurrection of a sinless man could the chains of death that were held by Satan be broken for all who believe (see Isaiah 53:10).

His was not just the ultimate sacrifice of one person dying for another, but the strategy of the Godhead designed to overcome Satan, the ultimate enemy of death. It was done to restore relationship between God and humankind. John 3:16 expresses it so powerfully: "For God so loved the world that he gave his one and only Son." Loss of the relationship between God and humankind created a pain so great that the pain of Calvary was a price that God paid willingly. The pain was worthwhile since it meant bringing us back into the fold of His relational love.

I pray that as you read these words you will catch something of the love that God has for all who are living in this broken world. I pray also that you will feel something of the pain that God feels as He looks at this world. He loves people so much, but they continue to choose Satan's way instead of receiving His gift of life.

Unless we share the pain that He has in His heart at the sight of generation after generation of His children running headlong into eternal death, we will never understand what evangelism is for. Evangelism is not about growing church membership—it is about restoring God's children to a relationship of love with Him. It is possible to be part of a big church and still not know what real love is.

Just spend a few minutes imagining what you would feel like if you had taken every single thing you had worked for within the span of your life and gave it away to rescue people in desperate need. There, in a huge pile, were all of the provisions you had made for them. It was the accumulated wealth of your life's endeavors. But instead of being appreciated and valued by grateful recipients, the people ignored all you had given. This was in spite of the fact that they desperately needed what you had offered. And not only were they ignoring the good things you had provided, but they were also looking in the sewers of life for some supposedly tasty morsel to stimulate their souls. How would you feel?

Take it a step further and imagine that you had also given your life for these people, and still they ignored your sacrifice. Allow yourself to weep the tears of God as you look at Jesus on the cross. Then cast your eyes on the countless millions in a self-sufficient world who are running headlong into selfish oblivion inspired by Satan. It is only when people clearly see the price paid for their salvation that they will be motivated to be evangelists.

I was privileged to learn these lessons as a child. My father never missed an opportunity to speak a special word from God to people he met. He would pray for the right opportunity to say a gracious word. Invariably, he would slip in a word of encouragement or challenge when he felt led by

God. The person receiving my dad's word may not have wanted to hear it, but it could not be ignored.

Like a fisherman, my dad was casting a fly on the waters of life. What joy there was when someone responded and was born again. Even the letters that my dad wrote to my mother before they were married were filled with accounts of God's hand on this person and that person. He wrote of the joy they would have together leading people to the Savior.

The Joy of Love

We have looked at the pain and sacrifice of love, but overriding the possible pain and sacrifice is the joy. It is not only the joy of serving the Lord, but also of being with the Lord in a loving relationship. It is being a partner with Him in the business of the Kingdom. The writer of the letter to the Hebrews captured this so perfectly when he said,

> Fixing our eyes on Jesus, the pioneer and perfecter of faith. For the joy set before him he endured the cross, scorning its shame, and sat down at the right hand of the throne of God. Consider him who endured such opposition from sinners, so that you will not grow weary and lose heart.
>
> Hebrews 12:2–3

The price was high, but the joy that was set before Him enabled Him to endure everything He went through. He looked forward to the joy of restoring back into relationship those who had rejected God, and He anticipated eagerly being able to express the Father's love to us. The path was hard and the opposition was tough, but there was joy ahead. The joy transcended all of the pleasures this world has to offer.

An athlete may be in training for four years for an Olympic race. For those years the athlete may only know the pounding of his own feet on the track as little by little he improves his fitness, his strength and, above all, his times. When the race is run, it is over in a moment. But as he crosses the finish line and takes the gold, he considers the medal, the adulation and the praise of the crowd as sufficient rewards for his years of hard training. Hebrews 12:1 uses this image to encourage us to "run with perseverance the race marked out for us" for the reward is great.

If athletes will train and work this hard for a medal—a scrap of metal of such little value in the eternal scheme of things—how much more should we persevere for the Kingdom of God? Set before us is the joy of an eternal relationship in which there will be no more pain (see Revelation 21:4). God wanted our human relationships to be built on the same divine principles of selfless love and sacrifice. Then we will know the joy that comes from the fruit of love in those relationships.

Guidance and Love

One of the issues that concerns believers is knowing the leading, direction and guidance of God. They recognize that God knows all things, and they know that the wisdom of God comes from hearing and obeying His voice. In essence, that is what guidance is all about—hearing and obeying God.

But what has surprised me on many occasions is the way many believers try to obtain the guidance of God for their lives without having any desire to learn to walk in the ways of God. They seem to be blind to the fact that they can only know the personal guidance of God if they have learned to walk in a true love relationship with Him and understand His ways. Only then will His guidance become the daily experience of their lives.

Sadly, many believers look at guidance like using a bit of magic to discover the most favorable path. This illusion is at the heart of astrology. The demons are very happy to oblige with all sorts of demonically inspired coincidences to deceive the vulnerable and, sometimes, even God's people. People sometimes ask me what God is saying they should do in the circumstances of their lives. I do not have a hot line to heaven about the way ahead for them. There may be rare occasions when God will use other believers to speak a word of guidance into a person's life, but generally that is only to confirm what the Lord has already been saying to the person.

The general rule for personal guidance is that the person who is living the life should be the one who is hearing the voice of God. The key to hearing the voice of God to show you the way ahead is being in a relationship with God, reading His Word daily and sensing the anointing of the Holy Spirit (see Isaiah 30:19–21).

Just as you can sense what someone you know and love is thinking, you will find the presence and influence of God having a supernatural impact on your thoughts as the Holy Spirit draws close. Many times I have experienced this, particularly when God has been guiding me about a new center for the ministry.

On one occasion I was taken to a potential property by one of our leaders, but as I entered the place it was as if I could sense God shaking His head. It was far too small for the work that God was calling into being. He then gave me a Scripture that confirmed to me that this was not the place.

Very soon after, we were shown a different and much larger property. As soon as we walked on the land, I felt the excitement of the Holy Spirit. I was sure that this was the place. Now we have ministered from here for over twenty years. We also discovered that the first owners of this property had dedicated the place to God and had prayed that one day it would be used to bring healing to God's people. Their prayers were answered.

Psalm 25:14 tells us that "the LORD confides in those who fear him." He gives guidance to those who are in a right relationship with Him. Looking to others to provide the guidance that we should be getting from God directly can be an abdication of our responsibility. It can be easier to ask someone else to hear God for us as it means that we do not have to work at our own relationship with Him. It also is an excuse to blame someone else in the event that his or her counsel did not work out the way we thought it would.

As our team has provided discipleship training for people seeking personal healing, their relationships with God have been restored. Often, amazingly, they become more aware of the voice of God along the way. In most cases it is not guidance that has been a problem for them, but the lack of a close relationship through which guidance can come. We need to be close to someone to hear what they are saying. And our relationship with God is no different—we need to be close to Him to hear what He is saying to us. The key to guidance is not receiving a word from a prophet, but rather the elimination of issues that stand in the way of a restored relationship with God.

Jesus knew perfect guidance—He only went where the Father told Him to go, He only said what the Father told Him to say (see John 8:28) and

He only did what the Father told Him to do (see John 5:19). How did He know what the Father wanted Him to say or do? The relationship He had with the Father was unbroken and had never been polluted by sin. He and the Father were in unity with each other in perfect relationship. Because of that, Jesus was able to hear the voice of Father God and receive perfect guidance from above.

And the wonder of the Gospel is that in Christ all believers can be in that same place of intimacy with the Father. What a privilege to be able to hear the voice of God and walk in His ways—what joy lies ahead for His saints!

A Final Thought

You may have noticed that nowhere in our discussion of love and relationships have we talked about the erotic love of marital relationship. This form of love is not common to all love relationships because it has been reserved by God to be expressed only within the covenant of marriage. Indeed, the word *eros* is not even mentioned in the New Testament. Not because erotic love in marriage is not something that God blesses, He does. It is because God wanted us all, married or not, to understand that the relational love that comes from a loving God is for every single one of us to have and to enjoy.

SUMMARY

Love and relationship are inseparable. Love without relationship is not love as God intended. God is love, and even in the Godhead there is relationship between the Father, the Son and the Holy Spirit. God created humankind so that He and they could enjoy the selfless love that comes from His heart. Sacrifice is an outworking of love, but so also is the joy that flows to our hearts from the heart of God. Guidance comes to humankind from God. It comes through having a restored relationship with Him.

PRAYER

Thank You, Father God, for the supreme love of Jesus. Thank You, Jesus, that You gave everything to win me back to You because You wanted to restore relationships with humankind. I am so grateful. Help me, Lord, to show Your love to those I know in this broken world. I pray others will be drawn to the Savior through the love I show to them. In Jesus' name, Amen.

CREATED TO WORSHIP

25

We first looked at the topic of worship when we studied the Lord's Prayer together. We saw then how God is the ultimate source of everything we are and everything we have—we owe our very existence to His gracious hesed love. Every breath we take is a reason to praise and worship Him.

Every time we respond to His love and do those things that please Him, we are not only partnering with Him in the work of the Kingdom, we are worshiping Him. And heartfelt worship of the living God attracts the Spirit of God so that our praises are filled with His Spirit. The more we live in the reality of doing the works of the Kingdom of God, the more He dwells in us by His Spirit.

True Worship

The greatest expression of worship is not in the enthusiasm and passion demonstrated when you sing songs of adoration to God—important though that may be—but rather it is in your day-by-day willingness to walk in His ways. That is true worship. That is what Jesus meant when He talked to the woman at the well about worshiping God in spirit and in truth (see John 4:24).

To worship God, who is spirit, you must relate to Him with the spirit He has given you. Unless, however, you are also worshiping Him with your soul and your body, there will be an inner discrepancy between what your spirit might be saying and what your flesh might be doing. That introduces division into the inner being and creates a gap that the enemy loves to exploit for his own ends.

Wholehearted worship involves every part of our being. If we are less than wholehearted, we are making ourselves vulnerable to the enemy's inroads into our inner being. King Amaziah is one of those who "did what was right in the eyes of the LORD, but not wholeheartedly" (2 Chronicles 25:2). His sad story is told throughout this chapter. As a result of his lack of whole-heartedness, he came to a place where he "would not listen" (verse 20), and eventually he "turned away from following the LORD" (verse 27).

The sad thing is that this man, who intended to do things that were right in the eyes of the Lord, lost everything because his worship of God did not extend to his obedience to God. He was deceiving himself. He lost his protection and rebelled against God in disobedience. In the end, he lost his life to evil men who murdered him. Worshiping God less than wholeheartedly is a serious matter.

D. L. Moody, that great American evangelist, said, "Many a professing Christian is a stumbling-block because his worship is divided. On Sunday he worships God; on weekdays God has little or no place in his thoughts."[1] If our heart is divided, our worship will be divided. If we are less than whole-hearted in our worship of God, the parts of our heart that are not worshiping God will be worshiping the god of this world. There is no middle ground.

The grace and mercy of God is very great, and it extends deep into our rebellious hearts. But when our actions betray the heart's intentions, we lose the covering of God. We have to dwell in the shelter of the Most High if we want to know the protection that comes from His being our fortress and refuge (see Psalm 91:1–2).

Thankful Hearts

True worship also flows out of thankful and grateful hearts. If we do not know what we have to be thankful for, our worship can become the singing of meaningless words.

At the English Football Association Cup Final there is a long-held tradition (since 1927) that the crowd sings the old hymn "Abide with Me" before the match kicks off. It is very moving to hear the familiar tune as thousands of voices sing the superb words of Henry Frances Lyte, one of England's greatest hymn writers.

"Abide with Me" was written in the author's dying days as he watched the setting sun over the sea at Torbay in Devon. The opening verse is a prayer for God to be with him as he prepared to cross the gulf that separated time from eternity:

> Abide with me: fast falls the eventide;
> The darkness deepens; Lord, with me abide!
> When other helpers fail and comforts flee,
> Help of the helpless, O abide with me.

The closing verse was his personal prayer of trust in God as he prepared to die:

> Hold thou thy cross before my closing eyes.
> Shine through the gloom, and point me to the skies.
> Heaven's morning breaks, and earth's vain shadows flee;
> In life, in death, O Lord, abide with me![2]

I wonder what those words mean to the thousands who have no knowledge of the Savior or what He has done for them. Each year, as I watch the scene unfolding on the television screen, I cannot help but pray that the spirits of some will be touched by the presence of God as they sing Lyte's words. But, in reality, the vast majority of the people who are singing those words have no understanding of God's love and mercy or what the cross was all about. How can they truly worship with thanksgiving if they have no idea for what they are thanking God?

It is easy to look at such a vast crowd and weep at this huge number of people who have no knowledge of the Scriptures, the plan of salvation, the wonder of the cross, the miracle of the resurrection, the way of salvation, the fact that Jesus is coming again, the Day of Judgment when the books are opened or that they all will have to stand before the throne of the living God.

One could draw similar parallels from the National Anthem of the United States. The "Star-Spangled Banner" gives triumphant acknowledgement to God, even with the majority of those singing the words not understanding that fact. The "Star-Spangled Banner" includes these words:

> Oh thus be it ever when freemen shall stand
> Between their lov'd home and the war's desolation!
> Blest with vict'ry and peace, may the heav'n-rescued land
> Praise the power that hath made and preserv'd us a nation!
> Then conquer we must, when our cause it is just,
> And this be our motto—"In God is our trust,"
> And the star-spangled banner in triumph shall wave
> O'er the land of the free and the home of the brave.[3]

How many of us who are worshiping the Lord in our congregations are as familiar as we should be with the amazing eternal truths that are the bedrock of our faith? These truths should give us endless cause for rejoicing and worshiping.

Oh, What a God We Serve!

As we draw this stage of the book to a close, I want to encourage you by sharing from Scripture why you need to be worshiping the Lord with everything you are and with understanding.

The following Scripture verses are what we believe. We do not read them like a mantra hoping they might be true, we read them with the certainty of knowing that these words are the unadulterated and eternal truth upon which our lives depend.

As you read them, worship God. Dwell on the words and their meaning. Apply each one to your own life with thanksgiving in your heart. Recognize that without the Savior the love of God could never permeate your heart with the saving truth. It is this truth we have believed, and it is this truth through which we have been born again to eternal life.

I Believe That . . .

- "God is love" (1 John 4:8).

- "This is love: not that we loved God, but that he loved us and sent his Son as an atoning sacrifice for our sins" (1 John 4:10).

- "God so loved the world that he gave his one and only Son, that whoever believes in him shall not perish but have eternal life" (John 3:16).

- "God was reconciling the world to himself in Christ, not counting people's sins against them" (2 Corinthians 5:19).

- "He [Jesus] is the atoning sacrifice for our sins, and not only for ours but also for the sins of the whole world" (1 John 2:2).

- Christ "took up our pain and bore our suffering . . . he was pierced for our transgressions, he was crushed for our iniquities; the punishment that brought us peace was on him, and by his wounds we are healed" (Isaiah 53:4–5).

- "While we were God's enemies, we were reconciled to him through the death of his Son" (Romans 5:10).

- God "reconciled us to himself through Christ" (2 Corinthians 5:18).

- "Through Jesus the forgiveness of sins is proclaimed to you" (Acts 13:38).

- "Through him everyone who believes is set free from every sin, a justification you were not able to obtain under the law of Moses" (Acts 13:39).

- "In Christ Jesus you who once were far away have been brought near by the blood of Christ" (Ephesians 2:13).

- "Christ redeemed us from the curse of the law by becoming a curse for us" (Galatians 3:13).

- "We have redemption, the forgiveness of sins" (Colossians 1:14).

- Christ entered the Most Holy place "thus obtaining eternal redemption" for us (Hebrews 9:12).

- The Son of God "loved me and gave himself for me" (Galatians 2:20).

- "The blood of Jesus, his Son, purifies us from all sin" (1 John 1:7).

- "There is now no condemnation for those who are in Christ Jesus" (Romans 8:1).

- "Because he himself suffered when he was tempted, he is able to help those who are being tempted" (Hebrews 2:18).

- "Whoever believes in the Son has eternal life" (John 3:36).

- "Christ was sacrificed once to take away the sins of many; and he will appear a second time, not to bear sin, but to bring salvation to those who are waiting for him" (Hebrews 9:28).

- "If the earthly tent we live in is destroyed, we have a building from God, an eternal house in heaven, not built by human hands" (2 Corinthians 5:1).

- God makes "known to me the path of life; you will fill me with joy in your presence, with eternal pleasures at your right hand" (Psalm 16:11).

I first read these Scriptures in this format as a child. They were printed this way in an old Victorian compendium of devotional snippets and evangelistic stories called *The Traveller's Guide from Death to Life*. My copy is a presentation edition given as a Sunday school prize to a member of my family back in 1897. As a child, I would pick this book off the shelf and read the stories. They had a deep impact on me at a tender age.

Let us never underestimate the impact of the Word of God even on the lives of children. The minds of young children have not yet been distorted by all the filth of spiritual pollution that today's generations have to contend with, and their spirits are more sensitive to the impact of truth.

Eternity within their hearts recognizes and leaps at the sound of eternal truth. Many great missionaries and warriors for God were touched by Scripture as a child. From a tender age, the zeal of the Lord was upon them, and when they were old they did not depart from His ways (see Proverbs 22:6).

I encourage you to start teaching Scripture to the children around you. You are not just giving them information to learn by heart, but you are giving them Holy Spirit–inspired words. The Spirit of God within the child affirms that these words are true. When Bible passages and truths are learned, the inner witness of the Spirit of God anchors truth deep in the heart and mind of the child.

Scripture hidden in the hearts of children will be there as a straight edge of truth as they grow into adults (see Psalm 119:9–16). If you are concerned for the destiny of the children around you, help them acquire a library of truth from the Word of God by learning Scripture with them. I thank God for the Scripture passages I learned as a child.

Worship in Song

We began this chapter by reminding ourselves that obedience to God is at the heart of true worship. Our daily lives should be a constant expression of the thankfulness, love and praise that comes from knowing and submitting to God. Worship can be exhibited in every area and in every second of our lives—in our behavior, in our relationships, through our words, through meditation, through our creativity and through music, drama or dance. The expression of our worship through praise and thanksgiving is a vital part of our relationship with God. We are made to worship, and through worship we are blessed.

God has given us a voice to use, both in speech and in song. Words and music were made by God to go together, and when the words fit the music, the truths of the words become memorable. The psalms of David are wonderful examples of words that were meant to be sung.

John and Charles Wesley knew the value of music and worship as a means of anchoring the truths of God in the hearts of converts. John would preach the Word, and Charles would convert John's messages into some of the most wonderful hymns that have been written in the English language. Charles Wesley made sure they could be sung to good tunes with strong and memorable melody lines so that people would take the truths away with them. He wanted the words not only residing in their minds, but also being sung on their lips. His hymn "Love Divine, All Loves Excelling" is still one of the most sung pieces of Christian music—even two centuries later. It is a fact that the things we sing or speak out are the things we remember most easily.

Through the preaching of John and the worship-leading skills of Charles, God transformed Great Britain. The eighteenth-century revival was an extraordinary time of power as the Gospel was preached throughout the land. It is questionable as to whether the preaching of John would have been as effective if his brother had not ensured that the teaching was not forgotten.

In a later generation, it was the songs of worship led by Ira D. Sankey that transformed the preaching of evangelist D. L. Moody into world-shaking messages. In more recent times, the song-leading skills of Cliff Barrows together with the singing of George Beverley Shea prepared crowds to hear the Gospel message from Billy Graham.

Today there are scores of Christian singers and worship groups producing anointed music. Their songs prepare our hearts to hear the truths of the Word of God. Worship really does open hearts to hear the truth. We all have different musical tastes, but I would urge you to listen to scripturally sound worship as you prepare to meditate on the Word of truth. Join in with everything you are, and let your heart and your body come together in unity as you sing your praises to the living God. He is worthy of all praise. Heaven will be filled with praise and worship—let us get ready now for the experience.

SUMMARY

Worship opens up our hearts to hear the voice of God. Worship is not just singing, but wholehearted commitment to the God who made and loves us. As we obey and worship Him, He fills us with His Spirit. We have so much to thank God for as we turn Scripture into a catalog of praise.

PRAYER

Lord, I choose to worship You with everything I am and everything I have. I want to worship You wholeheartedly and not give the enemy any access to the center of my being. Help me to give You first place in every area of my life as day by day I breathe in truth from Your Word and seek to live my life with and for You. In Jesus' name, Amen.

THE **NATURE** OF **MAN**

The word creation *is anathema to those who do not believe in a Creator. The word* atheist *is anathema to the God who created us!*

THE **SPIRIT** OF MAN

One of the fundamental cries of every human being is "Who am I?" It is a question of profound importance, especially to the many, many people who have not been given a deep sense of spiritual security from their parents. It is God's intention that all children receive this security from their earliest days.

Answering this question and establishing our identity is one of the most significant healing steps that any of us can take. The inner security this brings is life-transforming. People feel a divine inner contentment in being the person God intended them to be.

We can only answer the question "Who am I?" by looking first to our Creator God and asking Him for understanding of what it is that He has placed at the core of our being—our human spirit. That is where we will begin this stage of our journey to freedom.

You were created by God with a spirit, a soul and a body (see 1 Thessalonians 5:23). It is your spirit that is at the very core of your being. It is with your spirit that you fellowship with God, who is Spirit. It is in your spirit that your true identity is found. To know who you are, you need to understand how God intended your spirit to operate within you.

The Driving Force of Life

The spirit that God gave to each man and woman is the source of life and the driving force of every human being. God exercises His will as a spiritual being, and because we are made in the image and likeness of God, our spirit has the capacity to exercise will. When Jesus asked the disciples to stay awake and pray with Him but instead they fell asleep, His response was, "The spirit is willing, but the flesh [body] is weak" (Matthew 26:41).

When the will of the spirit is in line with the will of God, the soul and the body take their rightful places. In that order and under the leadership of the spirit, godly order is established in people's lives. Peace reigns, and the power and authority of God are established. This releases people into the fullness of all that God intended them to be. This is how it must have been for Adam before the Fall.

But the soul of man, which was given to us by God at our conception, also has a will of its own. The soul is the driver of the machine we call the body, and it is the controller of the flesh-life. When the soul is pulling in a different direction from the spirit, problems will occur. This is what happened at the Fall when the desires of the flesh took Adam into rebellion and away from doing the will of God. As a result, the enemy was given access to the whole human race.

The relationship between man and God was broken, and man received death as his inheritance (see Romans 6:23). This was the punishment that had already been prepared for Satan (see Matthew 25:41). Although man was now separated from God by a curtain of death, his spirit, soul and body still existed.

The soul is the primary controller of life in unredeemed people. Decisions are made without reference to God, and the spirit is, as it were, laid to one side with its influence ignored. In redeemed people, the spiritual relationship with God has been restored, and it is now possible for man to choose to submit to the headship of the spirit. It has to be a choice, because the Fall has given each of us a carnal nature that wants to submit to the god of this world.

This is the source of the battleground we refer to later in this stage of our journey when we look at Romans 7. It is here that Paul tells how there was often a battle within himself. The good things he wanted to do he found he could not do, and the bad things he did not want to do he was prone to doing (see verses 14–25). He was describing the battle between the will of his spirit and the will of his soul. And if we are really honest, we have to admit that this is a battle that we have to fight on a regular basis.

The Nature of the Spirit

We did not receive our human spirit fully mature and adult. It was, like every other area of our being, a baby and immature. God intended the conception of this baby spirit to have been through an act of love. It was then to be nurtured by God-loving, Spirit-filled parents beginning with its development in the womb and continuing after birth. When a baby is nurtured spiritually in this way, being fed daily with wonderful assurances of love and adoration and enjoying the sound of worship, praise and his or her parents praying, the child's spirit will grow into adulthood. At this point, it is functioning as God intended (see Ephesians 6:4; Proverbs 22:6).

But if all of this God-intended nurturing is missing, the spirit can be crushed or broken and unable to be the source of energy for life's purposes. Proverbs 18:14 contrasts these two extremes: "The human spirit can endure in sickness, but a crushed spirit who can bear?"

In the previous chapter we read, "A cheerful heart is good medicine, but a crushed spirit dries up the bones" (Proverbs 17:22). When the spirit is in good shape, it will carry us through all sorts of difficult times. But when the spirit is depressed, everything seems wrong.

It is interesting that all of our blood is manufactured by the body inside of our bones, and Scripture tells us that life is in the blood (see Leviticus 17:11). Have you ever wondered why some people just do not have any spark in their personality or seem so lifeless? The answer may well be that they have a crushed spirit that is in need of healing. Because of this, their bones are dried up spiritually and are not producing the dynamic life that should be flowing out to the body through the blood.

It is difficult for someone with a crushed spirit to fulfill his or her destiny in God because of all the lies and wounds that are affecting his or her ability to hear and know God. Our purposes and callings under God are tied up with our spirit. Paul's words on this subject are very important when he says, "For who knows a person's thoughts except their own spirit within them? In the same way no one knows the thoughts of God except the Spirit of God" (1 Corinthians 2:11). It is only the spirit within us that can discern rightfully what are the thoughts of God for us and what our destiny is.

Our Gender

Genesis 1:27 expresses the fact that both male and female members of the human race are made in the image of God. This must mean not only that our sexuality is a physical or an emotional expression, but also that our sexual identity is also contained within our spirit.

The logic of this is obvious but little appreciated. How could it be that God would not relate the core nature and future destiny of a woman to her feminine characteristics and her female body? God is a God of unity, and for Him to create a being whose spirit is at odds with his or her flesh would be inconsistent with the nature of God. God intended a female to have feminine characteristics in her spirit, soul and body. In just the same way, He intended men to have masculine characteristics in every part of their beings also.

Tragically, fallen man has gone so far from understanding sexuality as intended by God that many men and women have lost sight of what He planned them to be. The confusion of sexuality has resulted in unbelievable consequences, with millions of men and women trapped by the consequences of either their own sin, the sins of others against them or the sins of their ancestors. They have been deceived into believing that the distortion they have come to live with is what they were meant to be in the first place. The enemy has deceived the world into believing that the sexual distortions he has produced are normal. We will come back to this later in our journey.

The Conscience

Because eternity (the presence of God) is in the heart of every human being (see Ecclesiastes 3:11), no one will have an excuse on the Day of Judgement (see Romans 1:20). Paul talked about Gentiles, "who do not have the law, do by nature things required by the law . . . They show that the requirements of the law are written on their hearts, their consciences also bearing witness" (Romans 2:14–15).

The conscience is part of our human spirit. It is like an alarm bell that goes off whenever we do anything that would lead to the breaking of God's eternal laws. It is as if in the life of every human being there is a direct link between the conscience in the spirit and the decisions of the flesh.

The soul has the capacity to say yes or no to anything that is being contemplated, but it needs direction. God designed the conscience to do just that—to be an internal witness to what is right and wrong so that even without the written Law we would still have the opportunity to make godly choices and walk in God's ways.

The more times the soul stands against what the conscience is saying and does what it wants to do, the more damaged the conscience becomes. Ultimately, we say the conscience has become seared (see 1 Timothy 4:2)— quite like a nerve that has been so damaged by fire that it is now insensitive and is no longer functioning.

A seared conscience is dangerous. Once a person has arrived at that level of rebellion against God, there is little to stand in the way of the most horrendous crimes being committed without the person having any sense that what they are doing is wrong. If a man resists consistently the voice of the Lord in certain areas of his life, then his conscience can be partially seared.

An important prayer is to ask the Lord to resensitize your conscience. Ask Him if there are any areas of your life where you have been blinded by the god of this world and can no longer see things in godly perspective. The writer of the book of Hebrews made this point very clearly when he said, "Solid food is for the mature, who by constant use have trained themselves to distinguish good from evil" (Hebrews 5:14).

The training he mentions is taking in everything that is in the Word of God (solid food) and applying the scriptural truths to our lives. Even if we have not had good spiritual training, we will be able to have our discernment restored as we retrain ourselves under the hand of God.

Creativity

A few years ago, God gave my wife and me fresh understanding of the human spirit when we began to see tremendous breakthroughs in the healing journeys of people who had been very crushed and damaged when they were young. The breakthroughs came through giving them the opportunity to be creative and to do creative things.

Almost all of them had commented that they were not creative. In many cases they had been told when they were young that they were useless or no good, and they had grown up believing this lie to be the truth. The fact is that every single human being is creative, for we are all made in the image and likeness of a Creator. We reflect His nature.

When these people began to believe and put in practice the truth about themselves, they were amazed at the transformations that happened in their lives. This experience developed into a regular Healing through Creativity course. In these courses, the ministry team began to see real miracles taking place in people's lives as they painted, made models, danced, learned to swim, made pots, did woodwork, designed greetings cards and many other things.

This was not just a craft workshop. In fact, it was not about producing an amazing work of art in any shape or form—although for some people who did not have the confidence to exercise creativity, it did build up their personal worth and value when they found that they could produce something they were pleased with.

If we focus our attention constantly on the end product of becoming a healed and whole person, we will miss out on the real joy God intends for us. That joy comes from the relationship with Him that He is forging with us along the way. It is the same with creativity. God is a creator, and when we enjoy creating, we are being what God made us to be—creative beings made in His image and likeness. Through creativity, God bypasses our intellect and connects with us in the very core of our being.[1]

In this creativity course, we laugh together, we learn to play and we bond with one another. We are God's children together and experience family as God intended. This is something many people have never known. Through creativity God is building some of this back into His children's lives, and the participants learn that it is okay to just be rather than feeling compelled to complete tasks or to be doing something constantly.

People learn that they are important and special. It is not what they do or make that matters, but rather who they are. These are times when deeper relationships are forged with God. He rebuilds their lives, often without them knowing it is happening.

The spirit is the source of life for the whole being; therefore, if an individual's spirit has been crushed, broken, defiled or the natural giftings have been rejected, then such a person is going to suffer the consequences. In our workshops, these same people began to believe that they were special to God and that they were loved by Him. When they trusted Him to help them rediscover their identities through using their God-given creative gifts, miracles began to take place.

A lady came into the messy painting room and asked for a large piece of paper. Hour after hour and day after day, she painted this huge piece of paper black. Nothing else, just black. Sometimes she would step aside look at it and then add more black onto the picture.

On the final day when no one was around, she went back to her painting and wrote in huge letters *I choose life!* across the black paint. It was an enormous turning point in her life from suicidal despair to hope. She had never told anyone what the issues were, had never cried or asked for prayer. She just painted what she could not speak. Once the expression was out, she found freedom from her desperate desire to die. She began to move forward with living her life.

An elderly man who had suffered depressive illnesses all of his life was restored. People who had been crushed through abuse began to believe in both God and themselves. As each one tried something new, he or she emerged from the darkness as a butterfly coming out of its chrysalis.

God restores human spirits through the Healing through Creativity courses. Life flows back into people and joy overflows. In the final session of these courses, everyone always celebrates with great thanksgiving. The scene is extraordinary, especially when you compare the participants with how they had been three days previously. Our God is a life-transforming God.

If you are someone who has never thought of yourself as being creative, take a fresh look at yourself. Think of something you might enjoy doing. Get someone to join you in it if that helps. Do not listen to the voice of the enemy, but take encouragement from Exodus 31:6 where the Lord says, "I have given ability to all the skilled workers to make everything I have commanded you."

God has done that for His people, and God has not changed. Ask Him to show you what would be good for you to do now, and then ask Him what creative gifting He has sown in you that has yet to be discovered. Listen to your inner heart cry—it may be faint, but deep down there will be a hidden desire to create in a way that is wholly consistent with who God made you to be.

As you give voice to that inner desire and begin to allow yourself to be creative, you will begin to find the answer to that profound and important question, *Who am I?*

Inspiration and Vision

Finally, the spirit is the place where God gives inspiration and vision. The word *inspiration* simply means "what is breathed in." Receiving inspiration from God is breathing in encouragement from Him to lift up your eyes beyond your limited horizon. You can ask Him to show you what lies over the edge.

For some people that can sound quite frightening, because they only feel secure when everything ahead is known. But if you place your hand in God's hand and trust Him, you have no reason to feel insecure. He can see ahead of where you are now, and He is not going to take you to places that are not safe.

Little by little as you learn to trust Him with small things and discover that He is trustworthy, He will prepare you to receive fresh vision for your life. Scripture tells us that "Where there is no vision, the people perish" (Proverbs 29:18 KJV). We all need things to look forward to. When we are looking forward to those things that God has put into our heart, we will never be short of the energy of God to do them.

You need to test those things that you believe are visions from God. You should weigh them against His Word and present them to those in the Body of Christ whom you know, love and trust. You need encouragement with those things that are of God, and you need gentle restraint if something does not seem quite right. If that happens, it is not a disaster—it is part of the process of discovering your own identity in God and learning how to weigh and test things.

When you are convinced that something that God has shared with you really is of Him, you can move forward in the vision. You can trust Him to open the way forward as you bring every part of your being into line with the plans of God for your life. There are exciting days ahead as He redeems your past and heals your present. You can learn to trust Him more for the future (see Joel 2:25; Jeremiah 29:11).

And Finally

In 1 Corinthians 2:14, Paul tells us that spiritual things can only be discerned spiritually. When we are born again and filled with the Holy Spirit, our spirit allows us to enter into all of the spiritual blessings that God has prepared for us through reading the Word of God, prayer, teaching, worship and fellowship. God has given us a spirit so that we can discern these things, and the whole of our being will be blessed as a result of what flows from the life-spring of the spirit.

SUMMARY

The human spirit is the driving force of life. It is in the spirit that God gives us His energy for life and inspires us to do the things of God. The conscience is a vital part of the spirit, helping us to hear the voice of God day by day to make right decisions. The spirit is also the source of creative energy and vision. When the spirit is whole, God's energy inspires us.

PRAYER

Thank You, Lord, that You have placed a spirit within me. I want my spirit to be functioning in close fellowship with You, hearing Your voice and leading me into all the things You have planned and prepared for the rest of my life. Help me, Lord, to never grow tired of walking hand in hand with You and trusting You with everything I am. In Jesus' name, Amen.

THE **SOUL** OF **MAN**

We have now seen how God intended that your spirit would be the driving force of your whole being. Your soul and body—your flesh—should be the agents of your spirit working together in harmony one with another. The will of your soul should be in unity with the will of your spirit. This was the condition of humanity before the Fall.

At the Fall, Satan was given rights over humankind. As a result of Adam's choice, man's flesh became carnal in nature. Through succumbing to temptation, the soul took charge of the body, and together they acquired their own fallen identity as the flesh.

The Eternal Nature of the Soul

Your spirit and your soul were created by God, and together they were given your body in which to live. Because you are made in the image and likeness of God, your soul is eternal by nature—meaning that it cannot be destroyed by any process through the passage of time. When Scripture refers to death by saying "the soul who sins shall die" (Ezekiel 18:4 NKJV) it does not mean annihilation—the total destruction to nothingness. When the body dies it is not annihilated either. I believe every single atom and molecule of every human being who has ever walked on the earth (other than Jesus) still exists, having returned "to the ground it came from" (Ecclesiastes 12:7). Neither the soul nor the body are annihilated.

At death, life as we know it ceases to exist, and the soul departs to either paradise (the waiting room for heaven) or hades (the waiting room for hell). Not until after the final judgement at the end of time will the eternal consequences of the decisions we make on earth be actioned fully.

The parable Jesus told about the rich man and Lazarus makes it clear that paradise and hades are different places, that a gulf separates them and that there is no transference possible between the two destinations (see Luke 16:19–31). Lazarus, who was formerly a beggar at the gate of the rich man, was not allowed either to go and help the rich man in hell or to go back to earth and warn the rich man's family.

This is to remind us of how important it is that we know the Savior, that we recognize we have been redeemed out of the hands of the enemy, that we know our feet are now firmly on the eternal Rock who is Christ, and that we rest in the fact that our soul is secure in Him for time and eternity. I love Peter's description of what happens when a believer comes to God, "For 'you were like sheep going astray,' but now you have returned to the Shepherd and Overseer of your souls" (1 Peter 2:25). Peter sees clearly that outside of God your soul is in the care of a different overseer, and that to find Jesus as Savior is like the soul coming home. That is where we need to be if we are going to know God and experience His healing and restoration.

What Is the Soul?

The soul reveals your personality and gives expression to the person you are (the God-created core identity that is contained in your spirit). It is the living expression of your humanity that defines your existence in time and eternity. Jesus valued the soul greatly saying, "What good is it for someone to gain the whole world, yet forfeit their soul" (Mark 8:36). Your soul came into existence as an independent "living being" at your conception (Genesis 2:7). During your lifetime, the soul is tied to your bodily existence; however, its eternal existence does not depend on the continued existence of the body. After death, its life is independent of the body.

The soul was designed by God to work in balanced harmony with the spirit and the body. The soul links the life in the spirit to our physical selves. The soul does not have visible organs as such, but it does have departments that have specific functions. There are well over 700 references to the word *soul* in the Old and New Testaments. In some places there appears to be an overlap of meaning between the words used for the spirit and the soul. But at the very least, we can deduce from these references that the primary motivating influences within the soul are the mind with which we think, the emotions with which we react and the will with which we make decisions. We will look first at the mind and the emotions.

The Mind

The mind and the brain are not the same thing. The brain is the physical organ in which we store information. It is a bit like the hard drive of your computer. Just as computers can have hard drives of varying size and capacity, every human being is different. Their brain capacities can vary enormously.

The processes of education and training have two primary functions: equipping the brain with knowledge and understanding that can then be drawn on by the mind for use at a later stage, and training the mind in how to think creatively to use the available information for maximum potential benefit.

Before the days of satellite navigation devices, I would study a map and try to store in my brain a knowledge of the places I would be passing through on my journey. I would try to memorize how to reach my final destination. By the time I began the journey, I had stored in my brain as much information as I thought I would need.

There are two types of memory: the information we have stored consciously in our brains, and the memory that is the record of life's events—everything that has happened to us.

The second kind of memory is not related to any information we have stored in our physical brains. We must be able to take this memory with us into eternity, otherwise the parable referred to above about the rich man and Lazarus would have no meaning. According to Jesus, there was clear memory in both paradise and hades about what had happened on earth. There will be a day when the Book of Life is opened (see Revelation 20:12), and if we have no memory of our time on earth, the whole scenario recounted in Revelation would not have any relevance.

The primary purpose of the mind is to think. There is nothing that you and I choose to do that does not begin as a thought. Thoughts are the ultimate sources of all actions, good and bad. Thinking is done primarily with the mind—not the brain. The mind uses everything that is stored in the brain, but, obviously, it cannot use things that are not there. When I first began to restore old cars and repair car engines, I studied books. I got as much information into my head as possible; however, I had to refer back constantly to the workshop manual because I kept coming across things that I did not remember. I needed more information. As a result, the workshop manual was soon covered with greasy fingerprints.

In many ways the Bible is the workshop manual of life for God's people. It is vital that we read it, store up the information, remember what is in it and remind ourselves continually of the key principles by which we should live. I often say that if we get it in, the Holy Spirit will get it out when needed. But if we never get it into our brains, not even the Holy Spirit can get it out. I thank God often for the Scripture that I learned as a child. Those verses have become God's landmarks through my journey of life. Just as my workshop manuals were covered with greasy fingerprints, I pray that your Bible will be covered with the fingerprints of Christian service. I hope that like the Bereans described by Paul in Acts, day by day you will study the Word of God (see Acts 17:10–11).

While the mind can only use information that it has available, it can search out new information and then use that information to create new ideas. It can store these new ideas in the brain for future use.

When God gave me the vision for JOURNEY TO FREEDOM, it was a deeply spiritual moment. I believe God injected into my spirit the whole concept of what JOURNEY TO FREEDOM would become. I wrote it down during a time of prayer and then began to think about what it would look like. There was a lot of thinking to be done with my mind, using all of the knowledge and information that I had acquired throughout life. But there were lots of things I did not know, so I had to do research about what was possible to obtain new information to help me. The original concept came from God, but I developed the idea in my mind.

As a child, I remember seeing a poster that I did not understand. It said: *You are not what you think you are but what you think you are.* The poster had omitted deliberately the punctuation so as to draw attention to what it was saying. It should have read, *You are not what you think you are, but what you think, you are.* It was based on Proverbs 23:7: "For as he thinketh in his heart, so is he" (KJV).

And this is the crux of this whole discussion—what do we think about in the secret places of our minds? Paul gave some wise advice to his readers as he shared his own testimony of trying to live a godly life. "We take captive every thought to make it obedient to Christ" (2 Corinthians 10:5). If our thinking is in line with what Christ would think and do, then we will never go off track on our pilgrimage. A number of years ago the WWJD (What Would Jesus Do) bracelets became popular as people sought to bring godly order into their lives by being reminded of this foundational Christian principle. We may not need a bracelet to remind us, but the concept is a good one by which we should live our lives.

The things that excite us are the things that we will eventually do. Let us consider what Jesus said about sinful thoughts: "But I tell you that anyone who looks at a woman lustfully has already committed adultery with her in his heart" (Matthew 5:28). We may not take any action regarding these thoughts, but if the desire of our heart is to act upon them, then according to Jesus the thoughts are sinful. His words about adultery have always been a challenge. But perhaps in today's society where images of a sexual nature cannot be avoided (they are on display in every bookshop or newsstand), they are even more of a challenge.

As we think about the soul and the part that our mind plays in directing our will, let's be determined to ask Him to help us think on those things that are right and godly. Let's ask Him to help us avoid dwelling on the ungodly and sinful. That way we will not give the enemy any foothold in our mind. Paul's advice to the Philippians sums it up so well: "Whatever is true, whatever is noble, whatever is right, whatever is pure, whatever is lovely, whatever is admirable—if anything is excellent or praiseworthy— think about such things" (Philippians 4:8).

The Emotions

The emotions are a powerful motivating force that operates from within the soul. Emotions are the feelings we have about all sorts of things. They put color into our lives and give us pleasure or pain. When I sit among the crowd of supporters at my hometown football club, there is a mighty amount of emotion expressed. It gets all the louder as the game swings backward and forward as goals are scored or missed. It would be not as much fun going to such a match if we had no emotions.

What we do with our emotions can be good and healthy or manipulative and sinful. Emotions are a response to circumstances, but they can be used to influence and control others. God intended that we would be able to express the full range of emotions and to express feelings that are appropriate for the circumstances. We feel good when good things happen, and we feel sad when bad things happen. From a position of wholeness, we can weep with those who weep, mourn with those who mourn and laugh with those who are happy (see Romans 12:15).

But not all people are able to have appropriate emotional responses. This happens when there are unhealed areas of inner wounding. I will never forget the lady who, with a smile on her face, told our ministry team about all the terrible abuses she had suffered during her childhood. She was completely out of touch with the real feelings that were locked away inside of her broken heart. Her inability to express the appropriate feelings for what she was describing was a clear signal that something was terribly wrong.

There may be people you have to tiptoe around. You know that anything that annoys them will produce such a terribly angry reaction that you do everything you can to avoid the problem. It is just not worth the risk. Any inappropriate emotional response tells us that a person has unhealed areas that are in desperate need of healing.

Why not take a look at yourself in the emotional mirror? Ask yourself if you are able to express the full range of appropriate emotions for all sorts of different situations. If so, praise God. If not, ask the Lord to show you where there are unhealed events from your past that have left behind a trail of emotional pain. Also, take a look at all of your emotional reactions to people and circumstances. Are some of them excessive and hurtful to other people? You may even pray for the courage to ask someone you know quite well to tell you how they see you. An honest friend is a precious treasure.

I have seen that where people are not able to express fully their emotions—those that are pleasant as well as those that are not—depression or physical illness can result. As God brings healing to the underlying problems, it is amazing to see how He heals our emotional responses.

We still have one major component of the soul to look at later in this stage—the will. This is what determines our actions.

SUMMARY

The soul gives expression to the person you are (the God-created core identity contained in your spirit). It is your personality that is expressed through your soul. The mind, emotions and will are key parts of the soul that influence our behavior. If our thinking is right, then our conduct will be right. If our thinking is sinful, then it will not be long before we are doing sinful things. If our emotions are whole, our emotional reactions will be healthy. If they are not, we need to ask God to show us where in our lives there is damage that needs healing.

PRAYER

Thank You, Lord, that You know me better than I know myself. I invite You to be Lord of all my thinking, my emotions and my reactions. Please show me any areas of my life that are out of balance with what is right and what is best for me so that I can then look to You to reveal the underlying reasons and receive Your healing. In Jesus' name, Amen.

THE **BODY** OF MAN

28

We have already recognized that the body that God gave us is the most incredible, amazing and fantastic machine that has ever existed on the face of planet earth. Its brilliance will never be superseded. Being made in the image and likeness of God, man has taken what God has made and used it intelligently to develop his potential. The way it functions is stunning. One generation after another has exceeded in understanding and achievement far beyond anything that happened before.

We can look at the body with the eye of the biologist and discover that the human body contains 216 bones and 600 muscles. Its lungs contain 3 million tiny air sacs. There are nearly 100,000 kilometers of arteries and capillaries that transport 6 liters of blood around the body over 1,000 times a day. And 95 percent of the body's weight consists of oxygen, nitrogen, carbon, hydrogen, phosphorus and calcium—six of the most common elements.

While the biologist's assessment may be accurate, most scientists miss the point of what God has created and reproduced in countless millions of human beings generation after generation.

The Achievements of Man

My grandfather was born in 1880. The motorcar still lay over a distant horizon, flying was limited to the birds and no one dreamed of using anything other than a letter to communicate over any distance. Telephones, computers, radio, television, smartphones and tablets, satellites, space travel, the internet and over 99 percent of today's medical treatments were unheard of.

Have humans evolved since then? No. Humans have been using the God-given creativity and intelligence that resides within the spirit of every person to discover, research and develop knowledge. Have we used that knowledge to advance the physical condition of humankind? Yes, a million times and more. The more we know about the body and how it works, the more we are able to develop the potential of this amazing machine.

I remember the international excitement in 1954 when Roger Bannister was the first to run a four-minute mile. When I visited the track at Iffley Road, Oxford, eight years later, it seemed like hallowed ground. By the end of the century, just 46 years later, over 1,000 people had run the mile in less than four minutes. In fact, 17 seconds had been knocked off the record time.

I expect that in the world of athletics, we will continue to see records being broken for a long time to come as one generation after another benefits from the accumulated knowledge and understanding of our forefathers. This has nothing to do with evolution of species. It is human development being led by an intelligent soul that was inspired by a creative spirit who was made in the image and likeness of an intelligent Creator. The separateness and eternal existence of the soul is one of the primary distinguishing features that sets humans apart from the whole of the animal kingdom.

Human intelligence is not just a function of the body or the power of the brain. It is how the soul interacts with and uses the body to achieve its objectives. All other creatures are controlled only by instinct. Humans also have instinctive abilities and responses, but the activities of our bodies are controlled by our souls.

Animals operate only within the limitations of their God-given instinctive reactions. They do not have desires or needs for anything other than their comfortable survival. As long as they feel safe and well-fed, they are content. They have no built-in desire to better themselves in any way. Instinct provides those limitations.

Elephants, for example, have been and always will be limited to what elephants do—how they move, what they eat, how they breed, how they care for their young and everything else that is elephantine. We do not see elephants improving their lot in life one generation after another through the application of intelligent design and planning. Similar comments can be made about every other species on the planet.

The Body and Ill-Health

Having established again the uniqueness of man, let's return to a closer look at what happens when the body gets sick.

When our bodily machine is operating properly, we say that we are in good health. People do not consult a doctor unless they are ill. The primary training of a doctor is not initially how to recognize sickness, but rather to understand how the healthy body operates. Unless they know how it should work when everything is running normally, they have no way of telling what the problem is when a person presents with physical symptoms that indicate something is wrong.

The body can be physically ill because of a variety of causes, including injury caused by accidents, diseases that affect one or more bodily organs causing them to malfunction, sickness that is related directly to an ungodly lifestyle or behavior (sin), consequences of poor diet or malnutrition, sickness in the soul that causes a responsive malaise in the body, or the one item that featured regularly in Jesus' healing ministry, sickness caused by the influence of an evil spirit of infirmity.

I once cut my thumb rather badly when I tried to cut the head off of a fish I had caught. I closed up the wound as tightly as I could, covered the gap with surgical tape and kept the thumb well bandaged. My first course of action was not getting down on my knees and praying for Jesus to heal the thumb. Yes, I did pray that the thumb would heal quickly (which it did), but first I applied the obvious practical treatment. The medical profession is no different from this. Obvious physical issues are treated with various procedures and medicines so that the best possible environment is created in which the body can heal.

But what happens if healing does not take place? The fact is, doctors can only treat the symptoms that are presented to them. If the physical condition is related to something else that is happening in a person's life, medicine may be given to treat the presenting symptoms. But unless all of the underlying conditions are also resolved, the treatment will become long-term control of symptoms rather than actually healing the body.

In reality, probably as many as 75 percent of the symptoms that a patient complains about are caused by things a doctor can do nothing about. A woman, for example, may need long-term medical care for physical, emotional, psychological or psychiatric conditions as a result of sexual abuse she received as a child. The doctor can do nothing about the sexual abuse, but he has to continue treating the lady for all the consequences. It is unlikely that her need for some form of medical treatment will cease until she has been healed of the consequences of the sexual abuse.

Another person may be treated for a sexually transmitted disease. While the doctor may give advice, in reality the doctor has no authority or even influence over the sexual lifestyle of the patient. Yet another person may be prescribed antidepressants because he is experiencing a sense of worthlessness; however, his doctor can do nothing about the fact that her patient was fired, is unemployed and feels hopeless.

But there is something that can be done about many of these root issues that are problems of the soul. Things like forgiveness, dealing with the spiritual consequences of ungodly relationships, deliverance, emotional healing and healing for the human spirit are all foundational healing principles. Once the real issues have been addressed, one can then move on to be prayed over for physical healing. As mentioned earlier, sometimes healing happens even without specific prayer when these internal issues are addressed.

If we deal with all of the inner issues that are a result of things that have happened to us or things we have done, then we are removing the restraints that may have limited healing in the past (see James 5:16). This will then create a healing environment in which the person may be restored physically. None of this precludes the possibility of God doing a spontaneous miracle of healing, but instantaneous miracles, especially where the re-creation of cells takes place, are rare. The miracle of healing, however, is normal.

Our teams have seen many such miracles take place in people's lives by dealing with the underlying nonphysical issues that have stood in the way of physical healing. It is vital that we cover all of the nonphysical issues when praying for someone who is sick as a preparation for praying for their physical healing.

Caring for the Body

Each person's body is a true gift from God. It has been given to us for a season, and the length of time we have to live on earth can be related closely to how we treat and look after our bodies. God has a purpose for our lives, and it is only by using our bodies to the best of our ability and to the fullest extent that we will be able to realize the potential that God has stored up for our future.

Sadly, however, we are living in an age when almost a third of the world's population is overweight. Obesity is rampant. Childhood obesity has now become a major medical crisis in many countries. Perhaps the largest single reason why we are living through such an obesity crisis is that we are living in a society where hurting people have learned to use eating as a source of comfort. Food has become a way of repressing inner pain. People do not know how to cope with trauma caused by sexual abuse, pain from families breaking down or the deep loneliness of rejection. Comfort food provides an easy escape from the inner pain.

An overweight body is, however, a personal health hazard. Regular exercise is an essential part of looking after one's body, and the heavier a person becomes, the less exercise they feel like doing. The less exercise they do, the more they put on weight. It is not difficult to see how an out-of-control cycle soon dominates a person's life.

Without God's healing for the inner being and an ongoing relationship with Him, humankind will always look for a substitute to fill the aching void in their hearts. Distractions such as food, sex, television, cigarettes, drugs, music, work, religiosity or any of a hundred and one other things become artificial substitutes for real healing.

Scripture tells us that your body is the temple of God (see 1 Corinthians 3:16–17). In those two verses, Paul speaks very strongly about preserving and not destroying your temple. If we destroy our own body, it goes without saying that we will never be able to fulfill our destiny before God. One day we will have to give an account to God for what we have done with what we were given (see 1 Corinthians 3:13–15).

We can destroy our body in many different ways. It is a sad fact that for a whole host of reasons the life expectancy of obese people is shorter than those who are a normal weight. And almost every week, I read in the newspaper about young people who have lost their lives due to drug or sex related activities or from diseases contracted through smoking or other addictions. You do not have to commit suicide to destroy the temple God has given you. There are many other ways in which you can abuse your body and consequently either reduce your ability to achieve your potential or seriously shorten your life.

It may be that we have become weak-willed when facing all of the exciting foods we like so much and that are easily available. Greed can be very dangerous, and there is so much temptation for us. There are fast-food outlets, doughnut shops and restaurants with enormous portions on every corner. I believe that disciples of Jesus have a serious responsibility to look after their bodies so that all the investment God has made over their lifetimes is not wasted by their years being cut short as a result of their own negligence.

The Body Beautiful

God has created us to be in relationship with one another, and how we look (and even smell) not only matters to us but also to others—especially those with whom we are in close relationship. In fact, the whole of the fashion and beauty industry depends on the simple equation that exists between looks and relationships.

It is right and proper that we not only look after our bodies from a health point of view, but that we also keep our bodies clean and presentable. A cared-for body blesses the Creator who made it. Unfortunately, however, it is easy for that which God intended to be a Holy Spirit–inspired blessing to become a source of cursing under the influence of the spirit of the world.

As soon as the Fall took place, humankind acquired a carnal nature. The carnal nature is vulnerable to the temptation of using the blessings that God provided for ungodly purposes. The body that God created to be beautiful could then become an all-consuming idol and an object of worship—either of one's own body in pride and self-glorification, or of someone else's body in an attitude of lust. The created being would then take the place of the Creator. Self-idolatry is one of the primary temptations and sins of humankind. Receiving praise as if he was a god was the sin that resulted in King Herod being struck dead by an angel (see Acts 12:21–23).

Because of the dangers of lust and bodily temptations, many religious people down the centuries have despised the body. Yes, Paul did tell us to crucify the flesh (see Galatians 5:24), but that does not mean we must treat the amazing beauty and wonder of God's greatest achievement as if it were rubbish.

We must not allow the unclean desires of the carnal nature that focuses so much on the bodily lusts to control our behavior. These desires must be crucified (see 1 John 2:16; Romans 8:5–14). But that does not mean that the body itself is unclean or bad. A. W. Tozer stressed this point when he said, "That monkish hatred of the body, which figures so prominently in the works of certain early devotional writers, is wholly without support in the Word of God."[1]

After the Fall, Adam and Eve became aware of their nakedness. The potential for lust had entered into their now-carnal natures. As a result, shame and guilt came over them. They attempted to cover themselves with leaves, but God took the leaves away and gave them clothing made from the skin of animals (see Genesis 3:7, 21–23). This act of God required the sacrifice of an animal. It was a prophetic act that indicated that one day the sin of man would be covered by another sacrifice—the ultimate sacrifice of the Son of God for the sins of the world.

The Resurrected Body

One day our body will die—maybe in old age at the end of a long and fruitful life or possibly at an earlier time. Not everyone is blessed with the privilege of having a long life. Every day, we hear of people whose lives have been taken long before their time. I heard recently on the news that hundreds of people in Samoa had died because of a tsunami that was caused by an earthquake under the sea. I also heard of a young girl who had been hit tragically by a parcel dropped from an airplane. Our bodies have limited life-spans, and none of us knows the time or day when we will be packing our spiritual bags and leaving planet earth for a new destination.

While there is sadness and grief for the family and friends of those who pass, for all who know and love the Lord, our home-call is not bad news.

As Paul said, to be absent from the body is to be present with the Lord (see 2 Corinthians 5:8). There is a seamless transition into the eternal presence of our wonderful Savior. And, wonder of wonders, one day—only the Father knows when—Jesus is coming again. Then there will be a mighty resurrection when, like Jesus, we will be given an imperishable spiritual body (see 1 Corinthians 15:42). That body will have no capacity to be sick. All sickness has its ultimate origin in sin. The one thing that we will be glad is missing from heaven's realms is sin and all of its consequences.

Jesus' resurrection was the firstfruits (see 1 Corinthians 15:20), but at the end of time the full harvest for eternity will be gathered in. As we enter into the glory of heaven, we will become part of the great victory procession of the redeemed. There are exciting days ahead for the faithful who persevere to the end.

SUMMARY

Our body is an amazing, wonderful and beautiful machine that has enormous potential to be a great blessing. The enemy, however, can also use it for his purposes. It is incumbent upon us to look after it and use it for God's glory. We must avoid the temptation of making our body an object of self-worship, or of allowing it to be used as an object for lustful purposes. One day we will have a new resurrected body that will not have any of the imperfections caused by sin and its consequences.

PRAYER

Thank You, Lord, for the wonderful body You gave me. Forgive me, I ask, for all that I have done to limit its potential through sin. I choose to forgive all those who have damaged me and my body through what they have done to me. Help me now, Lord, to walk in Your healing for me so that I will fulfill Your destiny for the rest of my life. In Jesus' name, Amen.

MAN'S FREE WILL

29

We are now returning to look at the will, the third of the three elements of our soul. We first saw how thinking is critical to all of our decision-making processes. Then we recognized the influence of our emotions—our feelings—for it is not only what we think but also how we feel that influences our final choices. Sometimes our emotions can be so strong that we are unable to make rational decisions, and our feelings end up having more influence on the choices we make than our thinking. When that happens, we say that our hearts rule our heads.

It is the third motivating aspect of the soul, the will, that determines our actions, however. The will acts like a magistrate who hears the evidence in the court. Having heard all of the evidence, the magistrate then makes a decision on the basis of the information that has been presented. In a similar way, the will makes decisions and uses the agency of the flesh—the soul and the body—to create actions.

In the above decision-making process, however, there is one vital thing missing—the will of the spirit of man. The spirit of man has a will of its own. If the soul makes decisions without reference to the spirit, it is then vulnerable to making wrong choices, as we will see later.

This is exactly what happened at the Fall. Adam's soul made the decision to disobey God, and in so doing, the will of the spirit was overruled by the will of the soul. As a result, humankind's soul became carnal in nature, being then prone to acting under the authority of the god of this world rather than the authority of the living God. It does not mean that all the choices of the soul are always wrong, for there are many things we choose to do that are neither right nor wrong. God rejoices in our exercise of choice. But there are many things we can choose to do that would be wrong. The natural inclination of the soul is to make choices that suit the god of this world rather than choices that are in response to the love of God.

In Scripture there are many references to the word *heart*, many that imply that the heart is the place from which the core of a human being makes its choices. I understand the heart to mean the spirit and the soul together.

It is hard to understand. Even the Bible acknowledges that fact when it asks the question "Who can understand it?" (Jeremiah 17:9). But one thing is very clear from the earlier part of this verse, "The heart is deceitful above all things and beyond cure."

This is why all our decisions must be tested against the Spirit of God and the Word of God. Otherwise, the carnal nature we inherited from the Fall will lead us constantly into deception.

God's Risky Decision

How did this situation arise? It came about as a result of the riskiest thing that God ever did: He gave free will to man. As we recognized in the previous stage of our journey, in order to have a real relationship with humankind, God had to give humans the ability to make choices. Without that ability, no relationship could ever be deemed to be free. Any relationship between God and humankind would be more like that between an inventor and his preprogrammed machine.

We all love having friends with whom we can relax and enjoy their company. We hate it, however, when someone forces their company upon us uninvited. We feel trapped by someone who just talks us into submission. This is true especially if they get closer and closer to us talking with a louder voice as they insist on telling us all sorts of details that we do not need and do not want to hear. We feel even more threatened if someone not only imposes their stories upon us, but then also touches us or even holds us physically against our will. Any form of pressure to be in relationship with someone is controlling and abusive.

When something like this happens to us, there is a deep response in our inner being. We want to pull away from the person and to escape from the pressure. That is a godly response, simply confirming the fact that God has given us a free will. Anything that goes against the free-will principle that is part of our human nature will make us want to rebel and retreat from being involved in relationships like that. It is only relationships where both parties want to be involved that give the joy of friendship to both parties—and those are the relationships that God rejoices in and wants to have with human beings.

If people do not want to be in relationship with God, then there is no capacity for fellowship and partnership together with Him. If they do, however, then there is potential for amazing fruitfulness. There is a telling description of the relationship that Abraham had with God in the book of James that sums up everything about the sort of relationship that brings joy to the heart of God. This is what James said: "And the scripture was fulfilled that says, 'Abraham believed God, and it was credited to him as righteousness,' and he was called God's friend" (James 2:23).

A friend is someone with whom you share things. Someone with whom there is lots of participation from both sides of the relationship. You choose to spend time together because you enjoy each other's company. Adventuring together gives you both such pleasure and fulfillment. Abraham and God were adventuring together as he and his family set out to walk to the land God had prepared for his descendants.

Through Abraham, God was able to set down the spiritual and physical boundaries of a new nation. It was from this nation the Messiah would come to open the door for all people from every race and tongue. No wonder Abraham became known as the friend of God. They were sharing together as partners in the joy of fulfilling destiny. That is real relationship, real fellowship and real love.

God had a similar relationship with Moses. "The LORD would speak to Moses face to face, as one speaks to a friend" (Exodus 33:11). And when Jesus was talking privately with His disciples, He came to a point when He started to call them friends. This is what He said: "I no longer call you servants, because a servant does not know his master's business. Instead, I have called you friends, for everything that I learned from my Father I have made known to you" (John 15:15).

245

This is not saying that disciples of Jesus are no longer servants of God—we are. That servanthood is embraced within a much wider and higher relationship of friendship. I find it almost incredible to think that the Almighty God rejoices to call His disciples, who are in a very real sense unworthy servants, His friends. Friends with whom He wants to participate in the affairs of His Kingdom. All this comes out of that amazing gift of free will. What a privilege to be a friend of God. This is the kind of relationship that the creator of the universe longs to have with humankind, the pinnacle of His creation. He longs to have that relationship with you and me.

At the Fall, however, humankind used free will in a wrong way and chose to be a friend of Satan instead of a friend of God. But God's love for His creation never faltered. At the cross, Jesus carried through the ultimate act of friendship—dying for each one of us (see John 15:13). Now, because of His extraordinary sacrificial love, we have the opportunity to exercise our free will and choose life.

It is those who see the reality of sin and its consequences and who run into the arms of the Savior, saying, "I love You. I am coming to You because I want to. Thank You for opening up the way for me to return to You. I choose to accept Your gift of eternal life and be in relationship with You once again," who have the capacity to become friends of God.

God knows that when we truly love Him, we want Him for who He is. That relationship with Him is the desire of our heart. He waits for us to respond to His love. If He did not wait, He would violate the gift of free will that He gave to us. He cannot force us into relationship with Him. It always has to be a free choice. But what joy it gives to the heart of God when even one sinner repents and turns back to Him (see Luke 15:7).

The Battle of Wills

If only it was easier! I wonder how often you have thought something like this when facing temptations, difficulties and problems. Why is it so hard to make the right choice, even when you know what the right choice is? And why is it that even when you want to make the right choice for all of the right reasons, it seems as though there is a major undercurrent in your life pulling you in the opposite direction?

If this is how you feel, do not worry. You are in good company. This is exactly what the apostle Paul was trying to say in his letter to the Romans. He said, "I am unspiritual, sold as a slave to sin" (Romans 7:14). How could such a godly and dynamic apostle and servant of Jesus Christ say such a thing and confess to being unspiritual? Surely he was not a slave to sin—or was he?

When slaves were sold on the markets of the ancient world, they had no say in the transaction. The deal was done by the seller with the buyer. The slave was not involved in the deal. The slave had to obey the instructions of whoever owned him at any particular time. A baby born to a slave woman would become a slave as an adult. Slavery was the child's only inheritance.

By calling himself a slave to sin, Paul draws attention to the fact that the whole of the human race is like a child born into slavery. We did not have any choice in Adam's decision to submit to Satan's authority; nonetheless, we inherited the consequences. Adam sold himself to Satan, and when he came under Satan's control, all of his generational descendants also became slaves of Satan and, therefore, slaves to sin.

As a result, humankind acquired a carnal nature. From that moment on, the flesh of man was at enmity with the will of God. The flesh comprises the soul and the body, and the soul has a will. The soul of man has within it a force that opposes the will of God, so much so that Paul expressed the fact that he was a slave to sin in this way:

> For I have the desire to do what is good, but I cannot carry it out. For I do not do the good I want to do, but the evil I do not want to do—this I keep on doing. Now if I do what I do not want to do, it is no longer I who do it, but it is sin living in me that does it.
>
> Romans 7:18–20

I am sure you have experienced the following sort of thing happen in your own life. You are watching TV, and something comes up that is attractive to your carnal nature. There is an immediate battle within. Your soul may encourage you to keep the TV on to gain a quick-fix of sinful satisfaction even as your spirit encourages you to change the channel or turn the TV off. The longer you linger on the decision the harder it becomes. The picture keeps moving, and the soulish satisfaction starts to set in.

I love Martin Luther's comment on the battle for the will:

The human will is . . . a beast of burden. If God rides it, it wills and goes where God wills . . . if Satan rides it, it wills and goes where Satan wills . . . but the riders themselves contend for the possession and control of it.[1]

Which rider do you want to be holding the reins of your will?

We Do Have a Problem

When we were born again of the Spirit of God, our spirit that was dead to God was made alive again—was born again (see Ephesians 2:4–5). We were redeemed out of the hand of the enemy, and as a result our souls have been saved for time and eternity (see John 3:16). That is the good news. The bad news is that we still have a sin principle at work within our souls that battles against the will of God. It is as if the will of the spirit is at enmity with the will of the soul and will be until the end of our days. This means that living the Christian life will never be easy. We will always have to swim upstream against the desires of our own flesh and the tide of the enemy.

Hence Paul's frustrated cry at the end of this passage when he says, "Who will rescue me from this body that is subject to death?" (Romans 7:24). His answer comes immediately as he expresses the solution by saying, "Thanks be to God, who delivers me through Jesus Christ our Lord!" (Romans 7:25). Even though there may be times when a believer loses the battle of the will and sins, Paul has a triumphant answer to that problem: "Therefore, there is now no condemnation for those who are in Christ Jesus, because through Christ Jesus the law of the Spirit who gives life has set you free from the law of sin and death" (Romans 8:1–2). Sin has been dealt with, and our sins are forgiven.

This does not mean we can sin as much as we like. We must not think that being forgiven and not suffering consequences for our sin is the same thing. Far from it. Believers are not exempt from the consequences of their sins even though they may be forgiven. As a result, much of Paul's teaching in his various epistles is designed to encourage believers not to give way to the enemy or give him a foothold in their lives (see Ephesians 4:27). If they do, even though sin can be forgiven, the law of sowing and reaping will still apply (see Galatians 6:7–9). Peter urges us to "abstain from sinful desires, which wage war against your soul" (1 Peter 2:11) and tells us to be self-controlled and alert and to resist the enemy (see 1 Peter 5:8–9).

Winning the Battle

There is only one way to win the battle for the born-again believer. That is to always submit the will of the soul to the will of the spirit and then to the Holy Spirit of God. This makes it clear why the healing of a crushed and broken spirit is very important. If we are still crushed on the inside, for example, then the filter of our human spirit will always reflect its own damage in the way we live and act.

If in our spirit we submit our choices to God and seek His best for our lives at all times, He will never disappoint us. We will soon discover that His plans are indeed the best, and little by little He will help us resist the temptations of the enemy. This makes it easier for us to bring the will of our soul into line with the will of the spirit, and in turn with the will of God.

If we only do what God wants, will that not take away our free will? Not at all. The more we understand the ways of God and choose to walk in them, the more freedom we have to do the things that will be a blessing—first to God, then to others and finally to ourselves. Just as any good earthly parent enjoys watching the pleasure of their children, I believe our heavenly Father gets enormous pleasure out of seeing us enjoy the things He has gifted us to do. We discover that God blesses us when we do His will and when we do the things that we want to do. If we give God our will, He will empower us to use our gifts and abilities to bless both Him and us.

The choices that would please the enemy will always disappoint us, load us with guilt and shame and leave us more under the enemy's control than we were before. The sooner we reach that conclusion for ourselves, the sooner we will be at peace with knowing that God's ways are always the best ways.

Let us give the prince of preachers, Charles Spurgeon, the final word on this issue:

> I cannot think why some people are so fond of free-will. I believe free-will is the delight of sinners, but that God's will is the glory of saints. There is

nothing I desire more to get rid of than my own will, and to be absorbed into the will and purpose of my Lord. To do according to the will of Him who is most good, most true, most wise, most mighty, seems to me to be heaven. Let others choose the dignity of independence, I crave the glory of being wholly dead in Christ, and only alive in Him![2]

SUMMARY

Both our soul and our spirit have the capacity to exercise their will to make choices. We will know the greatest blessing when we are born again and our spirit is sensitive to the will of God. At that point, our soul can come into line with the will of our spirit. Both are then in line with the will of God. When we give way to the enemy's temptations, we give him the opportunity to rob us of the blessings God would want to pour upon us. But thanks be to God who gives us the victory.

PRAYER

Help me, Lord, to be sensitive to those times when the enemy is trying to make me see things from his perspective and tempt my soul to make ungodly choices. I want to live my life in harmony with Your will for my life. I ask that the Holy Spirit would strengthen and help me to consider what is right before making important decisions for my life. In Jesus' name, Amen.

MAN'S POWER, AUTHORITY AND DOMINION

So far on this part of our journey, we have looked at the nature of man as created by God with spirit, soul and body. We have seen how God intended each part to work and function together so that each human being is able to operate as a whole person who is created for relationship with Him. We have also seen what happened to humankind as a result of the Fall.

The final piece of this particular jigsaw puzzle will slip into place as we review the power and authority God intended humans to have. We will ask the all-important question, What can we still do on planet earth? Or to be more specific, What power and authority do we still have?

Power and Authority

Power and authority are different. A boxer has power in his muscles to fight an opponent, but he only has authority to use his power in this way in the boxing ring. An Olympic boxer without any strength in his muscles would be a disaster. Authority without power is meaningless. Conversely, if the boxer went outside the ring and started beating up people in the street, he would soon be in prison. The use of power without authority is rebellion.

While power and authority are clearly different, the right use of power can only be in submission to a rightful authority.

Power and authority were unique hallmarks of Jesus' life. They separated Him from every other teacher who had ever walked the land of Israel. It was His authority that was noted by His hearers. Luke told us that "they were amazed at his teaching, because his words had authority" (Luke 4:32). Later in the passage that describes the healing of the demonized man in the synagogue in Capernaum, the people asked, "What words these are! With authority and power he gives orders to impure spirits and they come out!" (Luke 4:36). The emphasis here is on the word *and*—He did not just speak to demons, as many other people had done in the past, but He spoke to them and they came out. They were not used to seeing this happen before their very eyes and "the news about him spread throughout the surrounding area" (Luke 4:37).

When Jesus was ready to send out His disciples to do the works of the Kingdom of God, He knew that on their own they would not be able to do the things He had been doing. While humankind at one time had God-given power and authority on planet earth, humans had limited power after the Fall. This was because they were now in an environment that was ruled by the god of this world. There is no way that the god of this world would have let the disciples set people free from the control of demons who were operating under Satan's authority.

We have already seen that Jesus had the power and authority to set people free. He had never come under Satan's authority, and He still had His own absolute authority. He had, therefore, all the power of the Godhead to set the captives free in fulfillment of Isaiah's prophecy (see Isaiah 61:1–2). The one who has authority can also delegate that authority to others.

When the disciples were sent out by Jesus, they had His delegated authority (which was higher than Satan's), and they had Jesus' power (see Luke 9:1–2). They were, therefore, equipped for the task. They found that they could do the same things that Jesus had been doing. "They set out and went from village to village, proclaiming the good news and healing people everywhere" (Luke 9:6). Luke records the fact that they came back rejoicing because "even the demons submit to us in your name" (Luke 10:17). It was the rightful use of the name of Jesus that gave the disciples authority.

When my British government sends me a tax demand, it is never signed by the queen or the prime minister. It is signed by some unknown (to me) individual who may have only just graduated from school. The fact that this person might be many years younger than me is quite irrelevant. Even though the letter may be signed by this employee, it is sent out in the name of the government. If I refuse to pay the taxes, I will end up in prison. The delegated authority of the person who signed the letter has all the weight of the government of the United Kingdom behind it.

But we must not think that using the name of Jesus to cast out demons always works automatically. For if we are using the name of Jesus but we do not know the Jesus whose name we are using, then we do not have His authority. In that case, the demons could have authority over us, and we could end up like the sons of Sceva. They tried to use the name of Jesus without having Jesus' authority. They ended up running down the street naked (see Acts 19:13–16).

Jesus also warned the disciples—at the very moment when they were so thrilled at the fact that the demons obeyed them—that it was more important for them to know that their names were written in heaven (see Luke 10:20). This emphasized the point that knowing Jesus was critical to being able to exercise authority safely over the works of the enemy.

Just before His ascension to heaven, Jesus spoke to His disciples and told them that all authority in heaven and on earth was His (see Matthew 28:18). He then commissioned the Body of Christ, the Church, to carry on the work of making disciples and doing the works of the Kingdom. In the book of Acts, we see the disciples who were empowered following their Pentecostal baptism in the Holy Spirit using both their authority and their power to proclaim the Kingdom of God in the same way that Jesus had done. There is an unbroken chain of command down the centuries that affirms the same foundational truths to one generation of believers after another, and it releases them to use the same power and authority that Jesus first gave to the disciples.

When the work of Ellel Ministries began in 1986, we did not have any experience in deliverance ministry. But God had filled our hearts with compassion for the hurting. As we began to minister to some very damaged people who walked through the doors and asked for help, we began to discover just how much harm the enemy had done in their lives. As we came face-to-face with some of the demonic powers that lay behind their conditions, we were shocked by what we saw. We were, however, also amazed and thrilled to discover that the power and authority God had given to the first disciples was still available for twentieth-century disciples.

We had so much to learn and made lots of mistakes. We found out, however, that when you make mistakes with a good heart, God blesses people in spite of the mistakes. God was gracious to heal His people even as we learned more about what the process of healing looked like. Little by little we put what we learned into training courses so that others could be blessed, too. It was clear that Jesus was still delegating His power and His authority to disciples who were willing to walk in His ways and do what He had asked them to do.

What Can We Do with Jesus' Power and Authority?

We must remember that Jesus only used His power and His authority to bless others as part of His Kingdom mandate. He healed the sick and cast out demons almost on a daily basis. On two occasions He used His power to multiply food for the crowd. He blessed the five loaves and two fishes (see Mark 6:30–44) and then seven loaves (see Mark 8:1–10) as He fed crowds of 5,000 and 4,000 people.

John tells us that "Jesus performed many other signs in the presence of his disciples, which are not recorded in this book" (John 20:30). But Jesus condemned those who just wanted to be impressed by seeing Him do a miraculous sign. He called them "a wicked and adulterous generation" (Matthew 12:38–40).

Doing supernatural signs to create an impressive performance was not allowed—either for Jesus or His followers. When you hear of supernatural things happening, even if they occur within a Christian environment, do not be deceived into thinking that they must be from God. Do not forget that the devil also has lots of power, and he is thinking constantly of new ways to deceive people (see 1 Timothy 4:1). Sadly, many people are deceived easily. They do not realize that God has given us the gifts of the Spirit so that we can discern which spirit lies behind such things. We are commanded to test all things (see 1 Thessalonians 5:21).

Jesus will never withdraw the power and the authority to cast out demons from His Church. He wants us to bring hope and healing to His people. Setting the captives free has to be part of God's standing orders for the Body of Christ. We will learn more about deliverance later in JOURNEY TO FREEDOM. In order for our ministry to others to be safe and effective, it is important that we operate under the godly authority of mature leaders within the fellowship of the Body of Christ.

How Else Can We Use God's Power and Authority?

Satan is a legalist, and wherever he has been given legal rights, he will exercise them. He does not give up his rights easily. But we have legal rights also, and wherever these exist we can use the power and authority God has given us through Jesus to overcome the works of the enemy. This will happen in areas where we have been given specific rights and authority.

God gave us free will. Even though we are living in a fallen world, we have absolute rights and authority over our own spirit, soul and body. If a person chooses to accept Jesus as Savior, there is absolutely nothing that Satan can do about it.

He may do everything he can to oppose such a move, but Jesus has a higher authority than Satan. We can come to Jesus without fear of the enemy. God's love is more powerful than all the works of darkness put together (see 1 John 4:4), and He has promised to redeem us out of the hands of the enemy (see Luke 1:68–74; Jeremiah 15:21). We can ask Him to cleanse, heal and deliver us as He prepares us to serve Him in the Body of Christ.

We can also have authority over the lives of our children. They are a gift from God's hands into ours (see Psalm 127:3). Parents were set in place as the spiritual covering for children, so parents can pray for their children with power and authority to cleanse them from every ungodly influence that has come down generational lines.

In fact, praying for generational cleansing was the normal routine in the early Church when they dedicated and baptized babies to God. The parents would use their parental authority to bring their child to the minister for prayer at this special time of dedication. Some of the older churches have retained such prayers for deliverance.

Jesus did not do magic tricks, even though this is what Satan tempted Him to do when he suggested that Jesus could jump off the pinnacle of the temple to demonstrate how the angels would protect Him (see Luke 4:9–12). He did not do signs to impress people. Neither should we attempt to do such things. Whenever we go outside our area of authority, we are in danger of losing our spiritual protection and suffering a backlash from the enemy.

I know of a number of people who tried to deal unwisely with the enemy's influence in places where they did not have any right or spiritual authority. As a result, they suffered serious backlash attacks. They entered a territory where Satan had a right over them. The backlash came in different ways including physical illnesses, various threats and damage to their lives and ministry.

Our Homes and Our Churches

We have spiritual authority over the places we live and worship (provided that we have a legal right to be using those places). We can spiritually cleanse the land and buildings we own or rent by taking our godly authority over every spiritual power that has been given influence in the past.

I heard recently of a man who bought a house that had been owned previously by people who practiced forms of witchcraft. He found the house to be a very frightening place in which to live. He sought the help of the local church minister who came and spoke a prayer of deliverance in his home. From that moment on the house was transformed, and he had no more problems. He saw the power of the name of Jesus at work. The whole of his future life was transformed as a result of understanding the power and authority we have in Jesus' name.

At most of our Ellel Centers, we conduct special courses teaching believers how the enemy can gain a foothold over land, buildings and the organizations that use them. More importantly, however, we teach people how to use authority to set them free. I could tell you dozens of stories of how God has transformed the lives of families, church fellowships and organizations. We do have a miracle-working God.

Let's thank God for His amazing provision, and let's rejoice in all Jesus has done so that we can use His power and His authority to know the victory of the cross and to triumph over the works of the enemy!

SUMMARY

Power and authority are different and need to be used wisely. Jesus not only exercised power and authority in His ministry, but He also delegated it to His disciples. He then sent them out to do the works of the Kingdom. He is still sending disciples out to continue the work through the Body of Christ.

PRAYER

Thank You, Lord, for showing me how to use Your power under Your authority in the Body of Christ. Help me, Lord, to be diligent to keep my own life and home environment cleansed from the works of the enemy. Help me not to make myself vulnerable to the enemy's influence by going outside the areas of authority You have given me. In Jesus' name, Amen.

WHAT HAPPENED WHEN MAN FELL

*Adam may have been the first to sin,
but he was not the last. We cannot
blame Adam for doing what we would
also have done. We are all guilty.*

SATAN'S STRATEGY WITH FALLEN MAN

There are some encouraging verses in the Word of God. In my own reading this morning I read these words:

> Praise be to the God and Father of our Lord Jesus Christ! In his great mercy he has given us new birth into a living hope through the resurrection of Jesus Christ from the dead, and into an inheritance that can never perish, spoil or fade. This inheritance is kept in heaven for you.
>
> 1 Peter 1:3–4

What a fantastic message with which to embark on this next stage of our journey to freedom. Regardless of the circumstances you may be in or of what is happening in this fallen world, God has given us a living hope. He has reserved an amazing inheritance that is being kept in heaven for you. I pray that each step of our journey will be an encouragement to you as you grow in the knowledge and love of God and as you prepare to one day receive your inheritance in heaven.

We are returning to look at Satan's strategy for undermining our lives. We need to learn how he tries to rob us of the inheritance God has reserved for us. We have already looked at how Satan operates, and in our last stage, we looked at the nature of man in more detail. You may already be wondering why it is that we are looking once again at Satan's strategy for fallen man.

Is that not focusing too much attention on the enemy? Good question. For it is true that if we do not take our eyes off the work of the enemy, we will not establish our life in the reality of Jesus' victory over the enemy or our destiny in God.

But it is equally true that if we do not understand how the enemy operates, we will be tripped up constantly by things we could have avoided. Perhaps Satan's most effective weapon against us is our ignorance of what he is doing and how he does it. That is how we become vulnerable to his secret weapons. That is one of the main reasons why we find that people need to come on Ellel's Healing Retreats later in life—in their younger days they were ignorant and fell into Satan's traps.

Satan's Strategy

Satan's strategy and weapons are a bit like those of the weaver fish. This fish buries itself in the sand but leaves a nasty little spine sticking up into the water of the sea. You can be walking happily along the beach or paddling in the sea when suddenly you feel a sharp pain where the spine of the weaver fish has punctured your skin and injected its poison. Its sting can be extremely painful. If you knew it was there, you would definitely not put your foot down on that particular spot.

Much more dangerous is one of the most vicious and horrible weapons of modern warfare—the antipersonnel land mine. These mines are hidden deliberately by the enemy just beneath the surface of the ground. You do not know they are there until you have stepped on one—and then it is too late. The sting of the weaver fish is only a very painful irritant, but the explosion of a land mine can maim or kill you.

Satan will use every type of spiritual weapon against you, ranging from those that are like the weaver fish to those that are the spiritual equivalent of lethal land mines. We need to understand where our weaknesses and Satan's strengths are so that we can be equipped for victory. We need to know what the hidden weapons of the enemy are so that we avoid treading on them.

Paul, too, was adamant on this topic. He said clearly that he did not want the believers he was writing to in Corinth to be ignorant of the ways of the enemy (see 2 Corinthians 2:10–11). He taught that if we do not forgive others, we are in danger of coming under Satan's influence and control. And in other places he gave considerable detail about how to resist and overcome the powers of darkness in our personal walk with the Lord (see Ephesians 4:25–5:14; 6:10–18). If Paul thought this was important, so must we.

Having understood that, we need to learn more about how Satan operates, so let's get on with the business of discovering what happened when man fell from his position of unrestricted grace and blessing. If that particular strategy was so effective with Adam that it trapped the whole human race, Satan will try to use it again in our lives.

In Ephesians 5:15–17, Paul says, "Be very careful, then, how you live—not as unwise but as wise, making the most of every opportunity, because the days are evil. Therefore do not be foolish, but understand what the Lord's will is." If Paul described the days in which he was living as evil, I wonder how he would describe the present day with its rampant and blatant evils?

Man's Vulnerability—Satan's Opportunity

Man became both very blessed and very vulnerable when God chose to give free will to humankind. God's decision to make man and woman in His own image and likeness with the capacity to make choices gave man the privilege of extraordinary blessing. But it also gave Satan his opportunity to manipulate man into serving him rather than God.

Let's summarize what we have learned about this so far:

Satan had been thrown out of the heavenly realms because of his rebellious pride of wanting to be like or above the Almighty. He wanted to receive the worship that was due to God. A third of the angels joined in his rebellion, and they were all thrown down to earth by the archangel Michael (see Revelation 12:7–9; Luke 10:18).

God created humankind to be in relationship with Him and to worship Him (see 1 Corinthians 1:9; Colossians 1:16). Satan craved the worship that man could give (see Ezekiel 28:17). If he could gain control over Adam and Eve, he knew he would both gain control over the whole human race and receive humankind's worship.

The spirit of man was made by God to be in close relationship with the Spirit of God, so there was little chance of Satan succeeding with any temptations that focused on man's spiritual life. He chose instead to use the vulnerability of man's flesh as the focal point of this first attack. His objective was to try to persuade man to use his precious gift of free will to make a choice that was contrary to the plans and purposes of God.

God's Boundary and Satan's Tactics

God only placed one limitation on man when He gave control of the whole planet to Adam: "You must not eat from the tree of the knowledge of good and evil, for when you eat from it you will certainly die" (Genesis 2:17). The problem was that the fruit of this particular tree probably looked like the most luscious in the garden. At least, that is what Eve must have thought and felt (see Genesis 3:6). We will look in more detail at the consequences of this critical event later.

I am sure that neither Adam nor Eve had any understanding of the meaning of death, for up until that point nobody had died. Death was not something Adam had seen or experienced. Satan, however, had already discovered that spiritual death meant being forever banished from the presence of God.

When Adam and Eve contemplated the temptation, the fear of death did not mean as much to them as it would after they had discovered the consequences of their disobedience. Satan had no intention of telling them what those consequences would be.

In most countries, cigarette packages are printed with warnings about the dangers of smoking. No one buying cigarettes can be ignorant of the potential damage to his or her health. It is there for all to see in bold, large print. The message is unmistakable. With such a clear and prominent warning of the dangers, it is hard to understand why there is any market for cigarettes.

Satan, however, does not give us warning signs about the dangers of his temptations. In fact, he does the reverse. If Satan sold cigarettes, his packages would be labeled "Smoking Gives Life!" He is such an effective deceiver that people believe his lies (see John 8:44; 2 Corinthians 11:3; Revelation 12:9; Revelation 20:3).

Sadly, millions of people either do not believe the warnings on the packets of cigarettes or they have convinced themselves that in spite of the statistics, they will be in the group that does not get cancer. They carry on smoking, thinking it will not do them any harm—until one day the telltale symptoms of something being seriously wrong stop them in their tracks, and they begin to regret their years of stupidity.

That is exactly how Satan works. He convinces people that either God's warnings are not true, or that even if the warnings are true for some people, they will not be true for them. He causes them to doubt God. That is his primary tactic when seeking to lead humankind into sin.

False Wisdom

Ultimately, the temptations of Satan are designed to target our opinion that we know better than God. Even though God does give us warnings, we believe that those warnings are really only for other people. At that point you are already doubting God and His Word and believe that God cannot be trusted. Ultimately, that leads to the belief that God must be a liar. That is the unavoidable conclusion of thinking that God's warnings cannot possibly apply to you.

When you have swallowed the lie that what God says may not be true or that you are an exception and it may not be true for you, the barriers to all manner of possible sins have been removed. You have only opened up a small gap in the secure boundary wall of God's love, but once you have gone through this particular gap, anything can happen. You have committed a serious sin, and the consequences can be enormous. You have broken a command of God that says, "Do not be wise in your own eyes; fear the LORD and shun evil" (Proverbs 3:7).

At that point, you have taken God off the throne of your life and put yourself on it. You are no longer trusting in the God who made you for relationship with Him. You have cast yourself adrift on the sea of life without an anchor to hold you steady or a rudder by which you can steer.

All ships that are cast adrift on the oceans of the world will be washed up eventually on some distant beach, broken up by the waves as they beat the ship against the rocks. Tragedy is inevitable. What a lie Satan puts in the minds of those who choose not to trust in the truth of God's Word.

How Temptation Works

Smoking is a good illustration of how Satan's temptations to the flesh actually work. In the days when cigarette advertisements were everywhere, the message that the advertisers tried to get across was the pleasure and contentment that smoking gives. The manufacturers were trying to tell people that they were buying a pleasurable experience that could be shared with other smokers.

They wanted to distract people from all of the long-term consequences of smoking—just as Satan wants to distract us from the long-term consequences of sin. The cigarette advertisements focused on the short-term pleasure of the smoking experience. In reality, however, they were selling an addictive nicotine fix with some dubious, pleasurable, short-term side-effects and serious long-term health problems.

The advertisements told the truth about a pleasurable experience (for those who were already addicted to smoking) but did not tell the whole truth—that the pleasurable experience customers were buying could also dramatically shorten their lives.

God, on the other hand, has always gone to great lengths to warn humankind of the ongoing dangers of all forms of sin. The Bible is His lesson book for the human race.

The first few chapters of Proverbs, for example, give plenty of warnings about the dangers of ungodly, adulterous relationships. In Proverbs 7:26–27, we read about the consequences of a man getting involved with an adulteress, presumably a prostitute: "Many are the victims she has brought down; her slain are a mighty throng. Her house is a highway to the grave, leading down to the chambers of death."

Verses 22–23 of chapter 5 are just as explicit: "The evil deeds of the wicked ensnare them; the cords of their sins hold them fast. For lack of discipline they will die, led astray by their own great folly." Satan, of course, does not refer people to these or other verses at the time of tempting them into wrong relationships. All he focuses on is the short-term pleasure that the sexual activity is supposed to bring them. He convinces people that the enjoyment they are contemplating can be justified, and there will not be any long-term consequences. At no time does he tell them the whole truth.

Because I have had the experience of ministering to many people in many different parts of the world, I can tell you without any hesitation whatsoever that the pleasures of sexual sin are short-lived. The dreadful mess brought into people's lives as a result can cause a lifetime of suffering for themselves and others.

Motivational writer and speaker Zig Ziglar said, "The chief cause of failure and unhappiness is trading what you want most for what you want now."[1] When people pour out their hearts in the privacy of the counseling room, they often say that what they most wanted was to be at peace with God and to be able to look forward to the joys of heaven. But they traded it all for something they wanted just for a moment.

Often the reason people have entered into such a bad bargain with the enemy is their ignorance of the Word of God. If someone does not know what is in the Word of God, how will they ever know they should not do the thing that they are anticipating? Yes, they do have a conscience they should be listening to, but for many people their personal conscience has been seared by the accepted norms of a society that is amoral but claims to be politically correct.

This illustrates how vital it is for children to be taught the Word of God. We should encourage them to memorize Scripture and set an example by the way we live. If the Word of God has gone into a child's heart, then in the face of the intense pressure there will be a piece of spiritual steel in his or her heart. This will provide both a reason to resist the enemy's influence and the strength to walk in obedience (see Proverbs 22:6; Ephesians 6:4).

It is when I think about the power and effectiveness of the Word of God to influence and direct the minds and hearts of humankind that I understand with fresh insight why the battle for the Word of God has been long, severe and costly.

I thank God for all of the men and women down the centuries who gave their lives translating the Bible into the languages of the world and making it available for people everywhere.

Why Temptation Works

Satan shows us something we would like to do, to have or to be. He focuses on the short-term pleasure at the expense of long-term joy and gain. He causes us to doubt what God has said and leads us to conclude that we know better than God. He never warns us of the consequences.

We will examine next how Satan operates by returning to the Garden of Eden to see what happened when Adam and Eve were tempted to eat the forbidden fruit.

SUMMARY

We need to understand how Satan works so that we will know how to avoid the traps he sets for humankind. His primary objective in all temptations is to encourage us to doubt God and His Word so that we do not have a reason to resist the temptation. Satan shows us short-term pleasures but never tells us of their long-term consequences.

PRAYER

Thank You, Lord, that Your Word is clear. Thank You that You have alerted us to what the dangers of sin are. Help me to understand clearly what You have written and to always listen to Your voice and not the voice of the enemy. In Jesus' name, Amen.

THE **FIRST** COMMANDMENT AND THE **FIRST SIN**

32

Boundaries make us feel safe, but they also stimulate our curiosity. We all love to look over a wall and see what is on the other side. It is part of the way God made humankind—we were built to be curious, to explore, to have adventure and to discover.

If we did not like the idea of exploring beyond the boundaries of our present existence, circumstances or technology, we would have discovered nothing—and I, for one, would not be typing JOURNEY TO FREEDOM on a laptop computer.

Undoubtedly, limitations pose questions for the creative mind, and they provide the potential for future opportunities and discoveries. Humans see obstacles and boundaries as things to be overcome. God has not only given us free will, but He has also made us creative. Humans have used their free will and creativity in a myriad of inventive ways.

A hundred years ago the ultimate boundary of human exploration was reaching the South Pole. The race was on to be the first man to stand on this remote destination—the very bottom of the world. In September 1909, Robert Scott announced in the London *Times* his intention to lead a Royal Geographical Society expedition to reach the South Pole.

Scott achieved his goal on January 16, 1912, but the Norwegian explorer, Amundsen, beat him to it. Amundsen got there on December 14, 1911, just one month before Scott. Tragically, Scott and his team never made it back to their ship. They all died on the journey home. Knowledge of their journey and achievement was found in a diary that was discovered in a tent with the frozen bodies of the team.

A hundred years from those extraordinary days, humans have now walked on the moon and are preparing to mount an expedition to Mars. Scott and Amundsen would have been astonished by the progress of where humanity's desire to explore has taken us in just one century.

God made humans unique in the whole of creation with an urge to explore, discover and to always be pushing beyond the boundaries of present limitations. And it is that godly desire to push beyond the boundaries of present limitations that Satan often uses to tempt us into exploring arenas that God did not intend for us. That is certainly what happened in the garden with Adam and Eve.

God's Only Limitation on Man

An adult can see dangers that a child cannot understand. For protection, a two-year-old will only be left to play on its own within the safety of a playpen. An older child will not be allowed to play out beside a road until he or she understands the dangers of traffic. These are wise limitations that are there until the child has outgrown the need for such boundaries.

But God, as the good Father that He is, put one boundary in place that was intended to be a permanent boundary for Adam and the whole human race. God did not want humankind to discover the nature of evil or participate in it. If they did that, then God and man could not be in fellowship and the whole objective of creating humanity for relationship with God would disintegrate (for man would become unholy and separated from God in His holiness).

We saw earlier in our journey that God is a God of covenant love. He made humans to be able to enjoy all His blessings and to share in the exercise of power and authority as the custodians of planet earth. God withheld nothing good from man, provided that man always used his free will to walk in the ways of God. If humankind followed God's ways, abundant blessings would be available for the human race for all of time.

This was the basis of the very first covenant—the expression of God's hesed love to mankind when He said that He wanted to share His blessings with us. This is the covenant that Hosea tells us Adam broke (see Hosea 6:7). He violated the condition for remaining in relationship with Father God and enjoying the blessings. Adam disobeyed God and obeyed Satan.

The Tree of Knowledge of Good and Evil and the First Commandment

In the beginning, man enjoyed the glorious freedom of the garden God had created for him. God only gave humankind one commandment: "You must not eat from the tree of the knowledge of good and evil" (Genesis 2:17). There is nothing in Scripture, however, that tells us that the fruit from this tree was poisonous or dangerous. Why should man not enjoy eating it?

The issue was not the physical nature of the fruit, but whether or not man was willing to trust and obey God. Would man listen to his God-given conscience and be obedient? If not, the spiritual consequences would be fatal. The fruit was attractive to the flesh. The soul and body were tempted, and the flesh wondered why God would create something apparently luscious but then deny man the opportunity of tasting it.

The spirit of man then remembered what God had said. When the serpent (Satan) came along and queried whether or not God had really told them not to eat of a certain tree, Eve said, "We may eat fruit from the trees in the garden, but God did say, 'You must not eat from the tree that is in the middle of the garden, and you must not touch it, or you will die'" (Genesis 3:2–3). Adam and Eve had not suffered from a memory lapse. If they were to eat the fruit, they would be doing so knowing that it was wrong. They would be without excuse.

At this point in the story, the arrowhead of Satan's temptation reached its target. He proposed that Eve, with Adam alongside her, should doubt what God had said. Satan's words were contrary to the words of God: "You will not certainly die. . . . For God knows that when you eat from it your eyes will be opened, and you will be like God, knowing good and evil" (Genesis 3:4–5). Adam and Eve knew what God had said, but by painting a picture of God as the deceiver, Satan was preparing the ground for man to be willing to disobey God.

First, Satan drew their attention to the fruit that God, so unfairly it seemed, had forbidden them to eat. Then he caused Adam and Eve to doubt what God had said. Finally, at the moment of temptation, Satan took their eyes very subtly off of the spiritual nature of the death God had warned them about and focused Adam and Eve's attention on the wonderful fruit that they were not allowed to sample. The flesh became the focus of attention and, in the end, it was the desire of the flesh that overruled their spirits.

The implication of Satan's temptation was that God could not be trusted and that He was keeping something very special from them. The serpent told them, "You will be like God," only if they ate this particular fruit (Genesis 3:5).

The First Sin

Eve looked again at the fruit and desired to eat it. It looked truly delicious. She thought about the benefits they would gain with this superior knowledge and wisdom that the serpent had talked about, and she decided to believe Satan and push aside the thoughts of what God had said. Instead of trusting God, she took the fruit and gave some of it to her husband. Satan had managed to tempt them to use their God-given capacities to explore and push boundaries to reach for something that God had prohibited for their own good. That is the essence of all sin.

Satan had said they would not die. They believed him, ate the fruit and discovered that in one way Satan was right—they did not physically die immediately. From that point of view, it might be said that Satan had spoken the truth—or at least a half-truth. The only bit of truth in what Satan had said, however, was that they did not die immediately after eating the fruit.

The short-term pleasure of taking the fruit was used by Satan to camouflage the long-term consequence. At the moment Adam sinned, his original covenant relationship with Father God was broken, and man was now spiritually dead.

Satan knew that the choice man made would separate all of humankind from God for eternity; however, he made sure Adam and Eve did not understand that fact when he tempted them to doubt God and take the fruit. As we saw at the beginning of this stage of the book, Satan never warns people of the consequences of obeying him.

At that moment, the eternal inheritance of the soul became death—eternal separation from God. Eventually, physical death would become the inheritance of the body. This meant that upon death man would enter the destination in eternity that had been determined by the choice made by the soul. The place that had been prepared for Satan had also become humanity's destination (see Matthew 25:41).

What Happened Next?

Man had failed his first big test. The issue was not that the fruit from the Tree of Knowledge of Good and Evil was poisonous but that disobedience to God was lethal. The test God put before humankind could have been anything that attracted the flesh of humanity if God had said no to it.

God had given Adam and Eve the whole universe to explore without limitation. He instructed them, however, that if they chose to disobey Him, they would be separated from Him forever. From the relationship that they had with Him, they already knew what good was. He told them that if they disobeyed Him, they would also discover what evil was. With the knowledge of good and evil came the reality that they would be separated from Him. For the rest of history, humans would have to struggle with the inner desire to do evil things alongside a desire to do the things of God.

So it was that humankind acquired a carnal nature, and throughout history every human being has had to contend with it in their inner being.

Uncovered

The knowledge of good and evil did not come because the fruit had acted like a powerful drug that affected Adam and Eve's souls and spirits. The knowledge had come because they had disobeyed God. They had crossed a forbidden boundary and had stepped into uncharted territory. Their eyes were opened, and they saw that humans had lost their protection and covering. Adam and Eve realized suddenly they were naked (see Genesis 3:7).

Their flesh experienced the sensation that was first experienced in their spirits. They were uncovered. While they were choosing to walk in the ways of God, they were protected and covered. Their spirits felt safe in the wonderful relationship they had with the Lord of the garden, and their nakedness was not an issue. But as soon as they sinned, their eyes were opened to the reality of what they had done. They were now uncovered by God.

What they were sensing in their spirits was soon transferred to their souls and their bodies. They knew they were naked. When a person realizes they are naked, they try to cover themselves. Man has been trying to cover his spiritual nakedness ever since. But we will have to wait a little before we understand the significance of this. For now, let's remember that Satan tries constantly to make us doubt God and to have us go our own way.

I imagine few people have stopped to look at the actual words of Frank Sinatra's famous song "My Way." Most people are enthralled by his wonderful voice and love the melody. Few realize that the song is all about someone who faces death and declares that he or she completed life in his or her own way.

One day we, too, will have to face the final curtain. I pray that as we walk together through our journey to freedom, we will find ourselves prepared for living God's way.

SUMMARY

The first commandment and the first sin set the scene for the history of the human race. When Adam chose not to trust God and to trust Satan's lies, he passed on to each one of us a carnal nature and an inheritance of death. Satan still uses the same tactics to deceive us today.

PRAYER

I confess, Lord, that if I had been Adam or Eve, I would have made the same mistake they did. Thank You that You had a rescue plan for the human race and that because I have a Savior, I need not fear passing through that final curtain. I choose to live my life Your way. In Jesus' name, Amen.

MAN DISCOVERS THE LAW

33

Earlier in our journey to freedom, we saw that when man breaks a commandment of God, there is a law that comes into play. We are now returning again to look in more detail at this vital principle.

From Commandment to Law

At first there was only one commandment—not ten. That very first commandment was a simple one: "You must not eat from the tree of the knowledge of good and evil" (Genesis 2:17).

God gives us commandments because He loves us; therefore, in giving humankind that first commandment, He was expressing the protection of love. We can assume that He also desired that humankind's response of love in return would be to obey gladly the commandment. God did not want humankind to discover evil and then have to live out history separated from Him or carrying the burden of sinfulness into eternity.

But as soon as the commandment put a boundary in place, Satan saw his opportunity. He capitalized on humanity's curiosity and desire to explore new things, and he deceived Adam and Eve into breaking the commandment. The whole of history has paid the price of their choice. Man broke the commandment and discovered a law.

This spiritual law had profound consequences for humankind that could only be discovered when the commandment was broken. I wonder what the world would be like now if humans had stayed within the loving provisions of God, if they had respected the limitation that God had specified or if they had chosen to develop the world with unlimited access to all of the resources of heaven.

The sort of law we are talking about is not something that you can discover without committing sin—no wonder God did not want us to come under it. As gravity is an absolute and unchangeable law in the physical realm, so is the law of sin in the spiritual realm.

Beachy Head is a high cliff near Glyndley Manor and the Ellel Center in southeast England. It is a chalk cliff with a sheer drop of 162 meters (530 feet) onto the rocks and into the sea below. There is a sign that warns walkers of the danger ahead. It says, *DANGER: Do not proceed beyond this point.* Those words form a simple commandment that the local authority has put there to protect people.

You may see that commandment and take objection to being told what to do. You might complain that it goes against your free will. You may decide to break the commandment and continue walking toward the edge. The moment you step off the edge, something will begin to happen that you can do absolutely nothing about. You will begin to fall. When you break that commandment, you will discover very quickly the law of gravity.

Gravity is an unchangeable physical law that affects every single object in the whole universe. In fact, it is gravity that keeps our universe stable and makes life sustainable for human beings. It is gravity that holds the earth in constant orbit around the sun and holds the orbit of the moon around the earth. You cannot see gravity, but we all know it is there. It is a hidden law that God built into the physical universe.

Even though God is a spiritual being, He created the physical universe. Because He is spiritual, it is no surprise to discover that just as there are hidden physical laws that underpin and control the physical realms, there are also hidden spiritual laws that operate powerfully in the spiritual realms.

Humans are both spiritual beings and physical beings. We live at the interface of the spiritual and the physical. As physical beings, we are subject to the physical laws of the physical universe, and as spiritual beings, we are subject to the spiritual laws of God's spiritual universe.

The physical laws are a direct consequence of the nature of matter in the created realms. And the spiritual laws are a direct consequence of the nature of God in the spiritual realms. Because humans live at the interface of both realms, whatever happens to us in the spiritual realm has an effect on both the spiritual and the physical. Conversely, whatever happens in the physical realm will have an effect on both our physical and spiritual dimensions.

Satan Lays the Trap

The big mistake many people make in fighting the battles of life is to think it is all right to listen to Satan to find out what he is offering. They have no intention of committing whatever sin it is that Satan is putting before them. *But how can we resist something unless we know what it is?* they might think.

Many people have recounted to me how they were drawn into Satan's trap by listening to a temptation. After having contemplated the temptation, they discovered that it was too powerful for them to resist. The best time to resist temptation is the moment you are aware of who is trying to get your attention.

Satan never offers us anything that is worth listening to. If you give him the opportunity to tell you something, you can be guaranteed that the process of listening is lowering your defenses. This process often takes you to the point where resistance becomes impossible. And to make things even more difficult, he can pose as an angel of light and offer you things that look as though they could have come from God. In reality, those things are from Satan's reservoir of deception (see 2 Corinthians 11:14).

The huge mistake that Adam and Eve made was listening to Satan's voice. They did not use their spiritual discernment to identify the nature of the voice. When they discovered that it was not God, they did not reject it immediately. They listened to what Satan had to say, and at the end of the conversation, they were interested in his argument. They had become involved in the discussion—a dangerous thing to do.

Satan had created in them a sense of injustice—*Why should we not eat of this beautiful fruit?*—and had suggested to them how much better they would be with all the wisdom they would acquire from eating the fruit.

They were now ready to agree with Satan, and they became trapped by their free will to push the boundaries of exploration in a direction that God had not authorized.

It was Satan's idea, but it was their choice. None of us can ever say that Satan and his demons make us do anything. We may feel as though we are under compulsion, but it is always our choice that is the ultimate problem.

What Law Did Adam and Eve Discover?

Adam and Eve had no idea that by obeying Satan they would be giving him access to control the rest of their lives or that they would be putting him in place as the god of this world. But that was the consequence of the law they were activating. It seems such a huge consequence for what might be thought of as such a small sin. All they had done was decide to have a bite out of a very special fruit that God had put there in the first place. Not such a big sin, really.

Satan always minimizes the consequences of sin at the time of temptation but maximizes the consequences after we have sinned.

It was not the magnitude of the sin that mattered but whether or not they were willing to trust God in all things, regardless of whether the matter was small or large. If trust and obedience are not at the heart of your relationship with God, then the relationship itself is out of order. Sooner or later you will be heading for trouble.

The consequence was not related to the nature of the sin, but to whether or not what man did was right or wrong. Adam made an ungodly choice. He became wise in his own eyes and put himself on the throne of his life (see Isaiah 5:21; Proverbs 26:12; Proverbs 3:7). He trusted Satan rather than God and obeyed what Satan had planted in his heart. All at once, law came into play and fell on Adam and Eve and all of humankind like a ton of bricks. The sin seemed small, but the consequences were devastating.

You and I can have different degrees of authority in our life, but if we choose to obey someone else, we submit whatever authority we may have to the person we choose to obey. We are putting them in charge. Satan was quick to take up control over planet earth when man obeyed his temptation.

Authority over the planet had been given to man. Up until the point that Adam and Eve sinned, Satan had power but no authority. After they sinned, he acquired man's authority to go alongside his power. He assumed immediate control. No wonder Jesus referred to him as the prince (ruler) of this world (see John 14:30), and Paul described him as the god of this age (see 2 Corinthians 4:4).

This was not a job description that God had given him. This was a position that humankind had offered unwittingly and that Satan had happily taken. When Satan was tempting Jesus in the wilderness, he told Jesus that all the authority and splendor of the kingdoms of the world had been given into his hands and that he could now give them to whomever he wished (see Luke 4:5–7).

Jesus did not disagree with Satan's statement. It was a fact. Satan offered control of these kingdoms to Jesus in exchange for His worship. It would have put Satan above the Godhead—the very position he had always craved (see Isaiah 14:13–14). How I thank God that Jesus resisted every one of Satan's temptations and remained free of Satan's control.

The transaction through which Satan had gained control of all the kingdoms of the world took place in the garden. At the very moment that Adam and Eve ate the fruit of the Tree of Knowledge of Good and Evil, an exchange took place in the heavenly realms. Put simply, the law that Adam discovered was this: Whomever we obey in the spiritual realms has a right to assume control of all the realms for which we are responsible.

I saw this law played out dramatically before my eyes when ministering deliverance to a woman who had come out of Hinduism. The spiritual powers had been in control of her life because she had obeyed them and worshiped them. As the spirits manifested, each one distorted her flesh to the point that her body looked like the demon that was being cast out. When the monkey god was being cast out, for example, her face was contorted to look like a monkey.

Whenever we break God's commandments, we will discover that a law comes into force. It is never a law that God wanted us to discover, but nevertheless, it is a law that is there.

Later we will be looking at how this principle works in regard to the Ten Commandments that God gave to Moses. If we choose to disobey these or any of God's commandments, we will always discover that a law comes into force.

SUMMARY

When we break God's commandments, we discover that a law comes into force. When Adam doubted God and trusted Satan, Satan was able to assume control of all that humankind had been given by God.

PRAYER

Thank You, Lord, for teaching me from Your Word about the dangers of listening to Satan's voice. Forgive me for the times when I have not immediately rejected the voice of the tempter, and as a result I have been trapped in ungodly behavior. Open my eyes and ears to see and hear what Satan is trying to do in my life. I only want to live for You from this moment on. In Jesus' name, Amen.

GOD COVERS THEIR NAKEDNESS

You may think we are spending rather a lot of time in these first three chapters of Genesis, but the principles we are studying are so profound that they not only influence the whole of human history, they also explain the reason for the cross. They set in motion God's amazing plan of redemption. They are also critical to being able to understand some very key issues in the healing ministry.

If we do not understand the significance of these chapters, we will struggle with being able to understand much of what follows in the story of God's people. We will struggle with the challenge of seeking to live a godly life in the middle of a fallen and increasingly hostile, sinful world.

Earlier we saw that when Adam and Eve first sinned and ate the forbidden fruit, their eyes were opened just as Satan had said. But what they saw was not what they expected. They had not anticipated such a sudden change in their spiritual condition or, subsequently, their circumstances.

This is how the Bible describes their experience: "Then the eyes of both of them were opened, and they realized they were naked; so they sewed fig leaves together and made coverings for themselves" (Genesis 3:7). This verse contains three significant moments in the story that are of enormous significance for us today.

1. Their eyes were opened.
2. They realized they were naked.
3. They tried to cover themselves.

Their Eyes Were Opened

I wonder what they saw. The garden itself would not have changed. They still had the remains of the fruit they had been eating in their hands, and I suspect they let what was left fall to the ground. I am sure that they wished desperately that they had never listened to what Satan had said.

When the Scripture says their eyes were opened, I do not think that it was talking about their physical eyes. To understand what was going on, we have to appreciate that it seems as though we have three sets of eyes.

We have the physical eyes through which we see things in the physical realm, and we have the eyes of the soul that focus on the things of the flesh. When they are perverted for evil use, they will facilitate things like greed and lust. There are also the eyes of the spirit through which we see and understand things that are spiritual in nature. You might also say that we have the eyes of our understanding.

A person may say, "Oh, I see," in a conversation. They do not say that because they have seen something with their physical eyes, but because they have come to understand what the other person was talking about. We have many ways of seeing things, all of which are important.

What Adam and Eve saw on that fateful day was the realization that they had been deceived by the serpent and that they had been left with the consequences of their sin. This is the normal way in which Satan works when tempting people. He gets them to the point of sinning and then leaves them to sort out for themselves the consequences of what they have done. He leaves them in the mess that he instigated.

Up until that moment, Adam and Eve had felt totally secure, safe, protected and loved by God. They were in the place where their Creator had put them, and they were loving every minute of exploring the garden in the security of God's hesed love. Suddenly, things were different. The consequences of sin are always immediate, even if they are not appreciated or understood immediately.

It must have felt as though a very cold and hostile wind had blown suddenly across the garden. The intimate relationship they had experienced with God was now broken, and in its place was the cold, manipulative presence of the new god of this world. They were not covered by the hesed love of God.

Having responded to Satan's temptations, they now had a part of their souls (the carnal nature) listening to the voice of the enemy. They must have been very aware of Satan's evil influence in their hearts. They knew now what evil was and were already experiencing the consequences of their choice. They had knowledge of both good and evil. They also knew that their relationships with God could never be the same again. God cannot compromise with evil in any way.

They Realized They Were Naked

Having lost their spiritual coverings, they were aware immediately of their nakedness. I believe that this awareness was of their spiritual nakedness before they realized their physical nakedness. They were no longer under the covering of God's hesed love, and probably no longer under the intimate protection of the angelic beings. They had no protection and were uncovered completely.

They were experiencing the reverse of Psalm 91:1 that tells of the protection we have when we dwell in the shelter of the Most High God. They were no longer dwelling in that place of intimate shelter—not because God had withdrawn it, but because they had moved away from it. Their protection had vanished suddenly, and they knew what they had done. Their eyes were opened to the reality of their new situation.

Almost simultaneously with the awareness of what they were seeing would have come the awareness of what they were feeling. While we may think in terms of feelings being centered in our emotions, in this instance I believe the feelings of their spirits would have been the first to be alerted as to what had happened. The conscience is centered in the spirit, and it is the conscience that first detects and responds to sin being committed. Guilt and shame would have followed quickly behind the awareness of what they had done.

Guilt is what we feel as a result of sin. It is not something that we can control. It is an automatic response of a sensitive conscience that is offended by sinful behavior. Guilt can have immediate physical side effects, such as causing people to behave unnaturally or to blush, especially when they are confronted by the person they have sinned against. Our guilty behavioral responses often lead to exposure of whatever sin has been committed.

They Tried to Cover Themselves

There is no doubt that Adam and Eve felt guilty, because their next response was one of shame. Guilt and shame work together and motivate us to try to cover up what we have done. They wanted to cover up the nakedness they felt. Covering themselves up, however, did not make any sense. There was only Adam and Eve in the garden. No one was looking at them. They had no physical reason to cover up their bodies and hide them from each other. But spiritual things had changed radically.

When people have sinned and do not want anyone else to know what has happened, they will often go to extreme lengths to try to cover up the consequences of their spiritual sin. There is absolutely nothing that we can do to deal with the consequences of our sin, so we will try to hide it from everyone else.

Adam and Eve's reaction of making clothing out of fig leaves is a typical response of someone who is ashamed of what they have done (see Genesis 3:7). They were trying to hide themselves from the glare of God and to put things right in the only way they knew how. They could never put things right, and what they did was woefully inadequate.

Having covered themselves, they heard the sound of the Lord God walking in the garden (see Genesis 3:8–9). Their next act of defense was to hide themselves among the trees in the hope that God would not see them. God, however, already knew what had happened. The omniscient God was not ignorant of the change in spiritual authority over Adam and Eve's lives, and He was aware of the place that Satan now had as the spiritual authority over the world.

When God called out to them, "Where are you?" (Genesis 3:9), Adam's reply showed fear. Fear is one of the responses that follows the exposure of sin. For Adam, first there was guilt, then there was shame and finally there was fear. Adam and Eve were hiding because they were afraid of what the consequences were going to be (see Genesis 3:10). They knew their lives were in the hands of the omnipotent, all-powerful God.

They were now afraid of Him—not afraid of Him in the sense of awe and respect, but in the sense of panic and trepidation. What was God going to do? I remember standing at the front of the class when I was nine. I had been caught doing something wrong, and I stood there awaiting my eventual punishment. I knew in a tiny way something of the fear that Adam and Eve must have felt as they waited for God to respond to their sin.

When God asked them if they had eaten of the tree, Adam answered by moving immediately into the self-defense technique of blaming others. He blamed both Eve and God when he said, "The woman you put here with me—she gave me some fruit from the tree, and I ate it" (Genesis 3:12).

It is fascinating to see how Adam slid over the fact that he could have said no and that he had been told not to eat of this fruit even before Eve had been created. Adam did not take up his headship responsibility to stop her from taking the fruit. He and Eve sinned together. There was no escape.

Then God challenged Eve and she blamed Satan, saying, "The serpent deceived me, and I ate" (Genesis 3:13). Neither Adam nor Eve owned up to the fact that they had chosen to eat the fruit or that they were responsible for the choices they had made.

God Covers Their Nakedness

God must have been grieved deeply by what had happened. The moment Adam and Eve sinned, the whole relational project of the human race was put into jeopardy. There is no way that humankind, who had chosen to go under Satan's covering, could ever enter into heaven's glory in this condition.

Satan was already destined for the lake of fire (see Matthew 25:41). Now that humankind had chosen to be under Satan's covering, wherever Satan would spend eternity would be the place where humankind also would have to go. And that was definitely not heaven.

In the event of this happening, however, God's rescue plan had been formulated. Death was now humanity's inheritance, and unless death itself could be overcome, there would be no way back for Adam and his descendants. The great experiment in relationship and fellowship between God and man was over. Unless, that is, God intervened.

Death could only be overcome by someone who was not under the curse of death—and it could not happen without the shedding of innocent blood. God looked at the pathetic coverings of fig leaves that Adam and Eve had made for themselves and in a dramatic prophetic act, God clothed them in animal skins (see Genesis 3:21).

Animal skins could only be used from a dead animal through the taking of the animal's life. When God provided the skins, the first sacrifice had taken place. Blood had been shed to provide a prophetic covering for Adam and Eve—a covering that spoke of the fact that one day there would be a sacrifice that would cover completely their sin and the sins of all of those who would look to the Lamb of God.

There is so much amazing and wonderful truth in these extraordinary first few chapters of the Bible—truth that speaks of the life-transforming hesed love of a God who was already preparing for the time when the ultimate sacrifice would have to be made.

God saw the terrible sin of Adam and Eve and had mercy. God has seen your sin and my sin and equally has mercy. None of us deserve the mercy of God, but what a joy it is to be able to share in the good news that God planned for our salvation even before we had been born and before we chose to sin (see Ephesians 1:4–7).

SUMMARY

When Adam and Eve sinned, their eyes were opened to the difference between good and evil. They knew they were now uncovered. They were guilty and ashamed and tried to cover themselves. But God had a better plan. When He clothed them in animal skins, He was making a prophetic statement about the sacrifice that He would one day make for the sins of the whole world.

PRAYER

Thank You, Lord, that You still loved our first parents after they had sinned. Thank You, Lord, that You still love me even though I have sinned. Help me never to forget the depths of Your love for fallen humanity and Your willingness to be the answer to man's desperate need. In Jesus' name, Amen.

BROKEN BUT LOVED 35

Many years ago, I inherited an antique soup tureen from a favorite great aunt. It looks magnificent—at least from the front. The other side is a different story.

At some time in its history, the tureen suffered an accident. As a result, one of its handles was broken off. While the handle has been wired back into place to make the tureen look great from the front, it is practically worthless. If it had never been broken, it would be worth a lot of money. But it is broken, and it can never, ever pretend to be anything else but badly damaged. Nevertheless, I really love that tureen. It does not matter to me that it has been broken. It is a constant reminder of a little bit of family history and of the lady who gave it to me.

More about the Carnal Nature

We have seen how one of the consequences of the Fall of man was the acquisition of a carnal nature—a nature at the core of our soul that is predisposed toward responding to the desires of the flesh, especially the ungodly ones. Before the Fall we only had knowledge of good, but after the Fall we also acquired the knowledge and experience of evil.

Man discovered that the essence of evil was choosing not to trust God. The practice of evil first came through listening to the temptations of Satan and then by obeying the desires of the carnal nature. Having discovered evil, we now have a desire for it that has been planted deep in our flesh by the enemy. For the rest of history, the battle lines of war have been drawn up in the souls of humankind.

We can never again pretend that we are perfect. We can be forgiven and cleansed, but our carnal nature—like the wires on the soup tureen's handle—serves as a permanent testimony of what happened at the Fall. The truth of Scripture is evidenced in the hearts of humankind. In the garden, humankind's pure and perfect relationship with God was broken.

Before a person is born again, the carnal nature will oppose the Spirit of God's attempts to draw him or her to the Savior. It is full of a thousand excuses for why the claims of the Savior should be ignored or rejected. The soul has to overcome its own built-in resistance to salvation that comes from the knowledge of evil we acquired at the Fall. It must use its free will to choose life.

Without the conviction of sin that comes through the Spirit of God witnessing to the truth of the Word of God (see John 16:8) no one would ever choose life and turn to God in repentance. The preaching of the Word in written or spoken form is still one of the greatest needs of humankind and will remain so until the day Jesus comes again.

Even as I write these pages of JOURNEY TO FREEDOM, I am stirred in my spirit with an even greater urgency from the Lord to tell the world what Satan is trying to hide from humanity. To decide for Jesus is always a big decision, and it is ultimately the only decision we will make that really matters. Everything else is peripheral to this central issue—it is the only issue that bridges time and eternity.

After we are born again and our spiritual relationship with Father God has been restored through Jesus, the carnal nature continues to operate from within and oppose our newfound desire to love and serve the Lord. We can understand fully Paul's battle that we have already referred to on several occasions (see Romans 7:14–25). This battle is the difficulty he has in doing what is right because there is another law working within him that wants him to do what is wrong.

Even when we are redeemed, the carnal nature stands as a permanent witness to the day when man's wrong choice broke his relationship with a holy, covenant-keeping, loving God.

No matter how skillfully my soup tureen could be repaired, the repair could only camouflage the damage. It will never heal the damage to the point that the tureen is once again unbroken—the tureen is broken forever. And no human being can ever have a relationship with God based on the unbroken perfection of their prefallen condition—for as Scripture says so clearly, "All have sinned and fall short of the glory of God" (Romans 3:23).

When the relationship with Adam was broken, the relationship with all of Adam's seed was broken also. All humans carry in their hearts the evidence of that brokenness. Even though every human is still made in the image and likeness of God, we are all born in that broken condition—much-loved by God, but broken, nevertheless. Just like my soup tureen that is much loved, but broken, nevertheless.

Jeremiah described the carnal nature when he said the human heart is "deceitful above all things and beyond cure" (Jeremiah 17:9). Yes, we can be healed of the wounding we have sustained in our lives—whether it has come as a result of our own choices or other people's actions—but we cannot be healed of the carnal nature while we are on earth.

For now we still have to be on our guard against the enemy's temptations that try to take advantage of evil desires that arise from the carnal nature—which will always be lurking in our heart.

James put it this way: "Each person is tempted when they are dragged away by their own evil desire and enticed. Then, after desire has conceived, it gives birth to sin; and sin, when it is full-grown, gives birth to death" (James 1:14–15). This is why Paul was so keen that in our daily walk we should "take captive every thought to make it obedient to Christ" (2 Corinthians 10:5). Our actions always stem from our thoughts. If our thoughts are in submission to Christ, our actions will glorify Him.

The message that comes across loud and clear from both James and Paul, and from many other Scripture passages, is that as believers we will always live in a war zone. The battle being waged against us is by the enemy from without and through our carnal nature from within.

But do not let this news depress or disillusion you. Which is better: to be in the midst of a real battle with the peace of God in your heart and knowing that you are on the victorious side, or to be adrift on the ocean of eternity without hope and not even realizing that you are lost? The vessel of your life may at times seem as though it is in a storm, but rejoice, Christ is with you in the vessel (see Isaiah 43:2).

Questions We Need to Ask

As we draw toward the end of another stage of our journey to freedom, I would like to look back at the lessons we have learned and ask some important questions about their relevance to our lives today. The temptation is to think because events happened long ago that they are not applicable today. Surely there are many more important things we need to look at in our Christian walk. But are there any more important things than the very foundations of our humanity?

QUESTION 1

Are there areas of your life where you listen too much and too long to the voice of the enemy?

If Adam and Eve had not entered into their conversation with Satan, they would not have had any reason to doubt God. The best time to resist temptation is before it has been explored fully. Once having explored the possibilities, pulling back from the brink is very difficult. It is a bit like the feeling many people have if they look over the edge of a high building or cliff—they feel as though something is drawing them downward.

When we look over the edge of temptation and start to think of what we will be missing if we do not do it, we are already in a very vulnerable position. That is where Satan wants us, and it is exactly what many people do, especially when wrestling with a temptation to which they are vulnerable.

A man with a gambling problem should not spend time looking at what is being offered on various gambling websites. He may think he has no intention whatsoever of placing another bet, but the fact is that he probably will. The same can be said of those who have problems with pornography.

A person who has been hurt by others may continue to think about how they are going to take revenge. This type of thinking process is not only opposed to God's way, but it also burns up emotions and diverts us from whatever the Lord might want us to do with our lives. Even if we do not take the action, the enemy has already won a battle if he has diverted you from God's way and from your calling.

All the desires of the flesh have their origins in our carnal nature. Unless the temptations are stopped at the source, they have a habit of growing deep roots into our soul. Those roots then seem to have irresistible lives of their own. We cannot change the carnal nature, but we can stop growing things in its fertile soil. God can help you pull the roots out, but you must want to be free (see Galatians 5:16–26).

QUESTION 2

Adam and Eve tried to cover themselves with fig leaves. Are there things in your life that you are trying to hide from God, from yourself or from others? Do you ever use "fig leaves" to try to make yourself acceptable to God?

One of Satan's tactics is to draw our attention to the obvious ungodliness within our carnal nature and load guilt on us. We then try to cover ourselves with fig leaves of our own making. Instead of owning humbly the truth about ourselves and accepting the sacrificial covering that Jesus provided for us, we will often feel forced by guilt and shame to cover the unworthiness in our hearts. We may, for example, try to earn God's approval with good deeds, superspirituality or generous giving. We can be tempted to use religious activities to divert our attention from reality (see Isaiah 64:6; Galatians 2:21).

There may be specific sins that seem to have followed you throughout your life that you have never wanted to bring into the light. They may have a controlling influence on you. The longer you try to cover them, the deeper the root will go into your heart.

In cases when the door to the enemy has been opened up from the inside, there may also be a demonic dimension that needs to be dealt with. James showed us how to deal with such situations when he was giving instructions to the elders about how to pray for someone who is in trouble or who is sick. "Therefore confess your sins to each other and pray for each other so that you may be healed" (James 5:16). Confessing the problem deals with the pride and releases the power and presence of God to heal and deliver.

QUESTION 3

When you are feeling unloved, unwanted, insecure and uncovered, and your flesh is crying out for security, where do you go for covering and comfort?

Paul refers to God as "the God of all comfort" (2 Corinthians 1:3). A child may be crying in distress, but as soon as a parent picks up and cuddles the child in his or her arms, the tears subside, and peace generally comes. We need to take a lesson from the heart of a child who feels secure in the arms of his or her mom or dad. God is the perfect Father who knows everything there is to know about us, and He still wants to pick us up and hold us in the security of His arms (see Ephesians 1:3; Psalm 103:13). His covering is perfect.

The enemy tempts us not to trust in God's covering. He prompts us to look to a whole range of possible substitutes such as alcohol, pornography, overeating, wrong relationships, earning acceptance through good works, spending money on more possessions or striving for recognition through more achievements.

Manufacturing our own fig leaves may feel good for a season (often very short), but we are making the problem worse. Each time we do this, we distance ourselves a little bit more from the One who is the only answer to our spiritual nakedness.

As you review these very personal questions, I pray that you will look honestly at your life and ask God to show you the areas you are trying to cover over with your own fig leaves. These are challenging but very important issues for us to consider. When God draws our attention to problems, it is because He wants to be the solution.

Covenant Faithfulness

It is salutary to remind ourselves of the nature of sinful man, but it is glorious to remind ourselves that God is faithful in spite of who and what we are. We can trust in God to be our covering. He is a covenant-keeping God who always keeps His promises. He does not and cannot change. He is the "same yesterday and today and forever" (Hebrews 13:8).

Yes, He is a God of holiness and purity, and we as sinful human beings cannot be in any covenant relationship with Him on the strength of our own righteousness. But, mercifully, our sin and our carnal nature has not changed anything in respect to the Father's love for us.

As we walk through our journey to freedom, we will see more and more clearly how precious the love of Jesus is. He became sin for us so that we who are sinful may enter into the presence of God covered by His righteousness (see 2 Corinthians 5:21). What a transforming miracle it is to know that we are redeemed and that our sin is covered.

SUMMARY

The carnal nature is at the root of many of our problems. Recognizing that it is there and choosing not to give way to its demands will help us resist the temptations of the enemy and avoid being trapped by making ungodly choices. Even though we are broken as a result of the Fall, we are still much loved by God. He rejoices that through Jesus our relationship with Him has been restored.

PRAYER

Thank You, Lord, for showing me what the effects of the Fall have been in my life. I am so grateful that even though I have been broken, I am still much loved. Help me from now on not to try to cover my own issues but to accept the sacrificial covering that Jesus provided for me. Help me, also, to recognize the voice of the enemy when he speaks and to choose not to even listen to what he has to say! In Jesus' name, Amen.

A FINAL WORD OF ENCOURAGEMENT

Congratulations on completing book two of your personal journey to freedom. I pray that a deeper understanding of the nature of God and of who He made you to be will strengthen you in your daily Christian walk, and that knowing how the enemy operates will equip you to both recognize and resist temptation.

Life is a journey, and as you press on in your walk with God, you will find Him to be utterly faithful to the promises in His Word. I encourage you to read what Isaiah prophesied in chapter 61, verses 1–3, about what the Sovereign Lord would do when He came. These words became the mission statement of Jesus, and He declared into a desperately needy world that He would heal the brokenhearted and set the captives free. What Isaiah wrote and what Jesus did are together a huge encouragement to us to trust in the faithfulness of God. These promises are true—I have seen God do just that in countless people's lives.

And I can also testify to the truth that when you get the foundations of faith that I have shared in these two volumes of JOURNEY TO FREEDOM firmly in place, they will form a secure platform for the rest of your life, on which you can build your future with God and step into the destiny He has for you. I encourage you to persevere in your life and faith, recognizing that each one of us is "God's handiwork, created in Christ Jesus to do good works, which God prepared in advance for us to do" (Ephesians 2:10). Let us live in the reality of God's faithful promises, and I pray you will know God's richest blessings every step of the way.

NOTES

Chapter 2: God Is Creator

1. C. S. Lewis, *Miracles: A Preliminary Study* (New York: Harper Collins, 1947), 44.

Chapter 3: God Is Holy

1. Ezekiel Hopkins, *The Works of the Right Reverend and Learned Ezekiel Hopkins* (London: Harry G. Bohn, 1855), 87.

2. Billy Graham, "Wonders of Nature," Billy Graham Evangelistic Association, August 15, 2018, https://billygraham.org/devotion/wonders-of-nature.

3. Paul A. Schilpp, ed., *Living Philosophers*, vol. 7, *Albert Einstein: Philosopher-Scientist* (New York: MJF Books, 1949), 653.

4. For an account of the events, see Alex Last, "The German Officer Who Tried to Kill Hitler," BBC News, July 20, 2014, https://www.bbc.com/news/magazine-28330605.

5. Thomas à Kempis, *The Imitation of Christ* (Mineola, N.Y.: Dover Publications, 2012), 38.

Chapter 5: God Is Love

1. Charles H. Spurgeon, *The Complete Works of C. H. Spurgeon*, vol. 6, *Sermons 286–347* (Harrington, Del.: Delmarva Publications, 2013), 1009.

2. Glynn Harrison, *Ego Trip: Rediscovering Grace in a Culture of Self-Esteem* (Grand Rapids: Zondervan, 2013), 159.

Chapter 6: God's Love in Action

1. Isaac Watts, "When I Survey the Wonderous Cross," Godtube, 2019, https://www.godtube.com/popular-hymns/when-i-survey-the-wondrous-cross/.

Chapter 8: God Is All-Knowing (Omniscient)

1. "Watch Your Thoughts, They Become Words; Watch Your Words, They Become Actions," Quote Investigator, January 10, 2013, https://quoteinvestigator.com/2013/01/10/watch-your-thoughts.

Chapter 10: God of Covenant

1. Andy Langfor, ed., *The Book of United Methodist Worship* (Nashville: The United Methodist Publishing House, 1992), 1024.

Chapter 13: Lucifer—and His Fall from Heaven

1. Ronald Knox, "Ronald Knox Quotes," Quotes.net, April 4, 2019, https://www.quotes.net/quote/38173.
2. Charles Stanley, "Satan's Strategy," *Daily Devotions with Dr. Charles Stanley*, Crosswalk.com, September 25, 2018, https://www.crosswalk.com/devotionals/in-touch/in-touch-sept-24-2010-1638547.html.
3. Jordan Stone, "Three Books Every Pastor Should Read: On Spiritual Warfare," Ordinary Ministry, February 20, 2014, https://jordanmarkstone.com/2014/02/20/3-books-every-pastor-should-read-on-spiritual-warfare.

Chapter 14: From Lucifer to Satan

1. William Shakespeare, *Hamlet* (Overland Park, Kan.: Digireads Publishing, 2012), 69.
2. William Shakespeare, *The Merchant of Venice* (New York: Simon and Schuster, 2010), 88.
3. Alfred Kazin, "The Freudian Revolution Analyzed," *New York Times*, May 6, 1956, 218.
4. Saint John, *The Collected Works of St. John of the Cross*, ed. and trans. Kieran Kavanaugh, trans. Otilio Rodriguez (Washington: ICS Publications, 1979), 95.

Chapter 15: Satan's Power and Authority

1. Charles H. Spurgeon, *Spurgeon's Sermons*, vol. 11, *1865*, ed. Anthony Uyl (Woodstock, Ontario: Devoted Publishing, 2017), 36.

Chapter 18: Satan's Objectives

1. C. S. Lewis, *The Screwtape Letters*, annotated ed. (New York: HarperCollins, 2013), 93.

Chapter 20: Satan's Eternal Destiny—and Ours!

1. Charles H. Spurgeon, *Smooth Stones Taken from Ancient Brooks: Being a Collection [. . .] from the Works of the Renowned Puritan Thomas Brooks* (New York: Sheldon & Company, 1860), 93.
2. Charles Baudelaire, *Baudelaire: His Prose and Poetry*, ed. T. R. Smith (New York: Boni and Liveright, 1919), 82.
3. J. I. Packer, *God's Words* (Downers Grove, Ill.: InterVarsity, 1985), 83.

Chapter 23: Created for Love and Relationship, Part One

1. Ravi Zacharias, *Jesus among Other Gods: The Absolute Claims of the Christian Message* (Nashville: Thomas Nelson, 2000), 149.

2. Watchman Nee, *The Latent Power of the Soul* (New York: Christian Fellowship Publishers, 1972), 11–12.

Chapter 25: Created to Worship

1. D.L. Moody, *D.L. Moody on the 10 Commandments* (Chicago: Moody, 1977), 21.
2. Henry Francis Lyte, "Abide with Me," Hymnary.org, https://hymnary.org/text/abide
_with_me_fast_falls_the_eventide.
3. Francis Scott Key, "The Star-Spangled Banner," Smithsonian, https://amhistory.si.edu
/starspangledbanner/the-lyrics.aspx.

Chapter 26: The Spirit of Man

1. For more information on this topic, I recommend *Healing through Creativity* by Fiona Horrobin (Sovereign World, 2019).

Chapter 28: The Body of Man

1. A. W. Tozer, *The Pursuit of God*, updated ed. (Abbotsford, Wis.: Aneko Press, 2015), 97.

Chapter 29: Man's Free Will

1. Martin Luther, *Bondage of the Will 1525: The Annotated Luther Study Edition*, ed. Kirsi I. Stjerna (Minneapolis: Fortress Press, 2016), 181.
2. Charles H. Spurgeon, *Spurgeon's Sermons*, vol. 8., *1863*, ed. Anthony Uyl (Woodstock, Ontario: Devoted Publishing, 2017), 366–367.

Chapter 31: Satan's Strategy with Fallen Man

1. Don Meyer, "Remembering Zig Ziglar," HuffPost, January 9, 2013, https://www.huff
post.com/entry/remembering-zig-ziglar_b_2439457.

Peter Horrobin is the founder and international director of Ellel Ministries. Ellel Ministries was first established in 1986 as a ministry of healing in northwest England. Many lives were transformed through what God was doing, and the ministry could not be contained in one location. In the early nineties, the work quickly expanded to other parts of the country and into eastern Europe. Today the ministry is established in well over 50 operational centers in over 35 different countries.

Peter was born in 1943 in Bolton, Lancashire, and was brought up in Blackburn, also in northern England. His parents gave him a firm Christian foundation with a strong evangelical emphasis. His early grounding in the Scripture would equip him for future ministry.

After graduating from Oxford University with a degree in chemistry, he spent a number of years lecturing in colleges and universities. He transitioned from the academic environment to the world of business, where he founded a series of successful publishing and bookselling companies.

In his twenties, Peter started to restore a vintage sports car (an Alvis Speed 20) but discovered that its chassis was bent. As he looked at the wreck of his broken car, wondering if it could ever be repaired, he sensed God saying, *You can restore this broken car, but I can restore broken lives. Which is more important?* It was obvious that broken lives were more important than broken cars, so the vision for restoring the lives of people was birthed in Peter's heart.

A few years later, he was asked to help a person who had been sexually abused. Through this experience, God further opened up to him the vision of a healing ministry. He prayed daily into this vision until 1986 when God brought it into being. Ellel Grange, a country house just outside the city of Lancaster, provided the first home and the name of Ellel Ministries. Many Christian leaders affirmed the vision and gave it their support. Since then, a hallmark of Peter's ministry has been his willingness to step out in faith to see God move to fulfil His promises, often in remarkable ways.

Under Peter and his wife's leadership, the worldwide teaching and ministry team has seen God move dramatically in many people's lives to bring salvation, hope, healing and deliverance. Together Peter and Fiona teach and minister on many different aspects of healing and discipleship. Ellel Ministries operates by faith and depends on donations and income from training courses to maintain and expand the work.

Outside of Ellel Ministries, Peter was the originator and one of the compilers of the amazingly successful and popular *Mission Praise*, now in its thirtieth anniversary edition (HarperCollins, 2015). It was originally compiled for Billy Graham's Mission England in 1984.

The story of Peter's life and of how God built and extended the ministry is told in his book *Strands of Destiny* (Sovereign World, 2018). He describes many of the extraordinary and miraculous events through which God has sustained the ministry across the years. JOURNEY TO FREEDOM is a culmination of over thirty years of experience teaching the foundational principles of healing and discipleship and ministering to people all over the world.

For details about the current worldwide activities of Ellel Ministries International, please go to www.ellel.org.

More from Peter Horrobin

What is your heart crying out for? Is it healing from despair, anxiety, anger or chronic illness? In this fortifying book, Peter Horrobin teaches you the basis of faith and helps you learn to walk in deep healing, restoration and freedom. Your struggles will be reshaped into a beautiful story of life transformation by the God who cares zealously for you!

Building on the Rock
Journey to Freedom #1

There are countless moments in our lives when we need wisdom urgently. God has provided the book of Proverbs to give us the baseline we need for clarity. This 40-day devotional, built around key verses in Proverbs, provides a rich source of wisdom to feed the soul and encourage the spirit so you can be empowered to live in the light of heavenly counsel.

Wisdom from the Proverbs

This 40-day journey of faith explores key verses from the Psalms that David recorded during times of distress, joy and triumph. Within these pages, you will find meditations and prayers to anchor these truths into your own life, and spaces to journal what God is speaking to you. Watch His hand in your life on this journey of discovery and transformation!

Encouragement from the Psalms

✔Chosen

 Stay up to date on your favorite books and authors with our free e-newsletters. Sign up today at chosenbooks.com.

 facebook.com/chosenbooks   @chosen_books

 @Chosen_Books